99 WAYS TO MAKE MONEY USING TWITTER

from the editors of
GEEKPRENEUR

 NEW MEDIA ENTERTAINMENT LTD

Book design by DesignForBooks.com

ABOUT
THE EDITORS

Geekpreneur is a group of bloggers, social media experts, web designers and marketing writers who aim to help creative thinkers turn their ideas into cash.

Geekpreneur's blog, www.geekpreneur.com, has been online since 2007. It offers expert advice on productivity, social media, technology and entrepreneurship, and is responsible for one of the Internet's most downloaded ebooks on Twitter.

CONTENTS

Contents

Contents

GEEKPRENEUR

INTRODUCTION

Twitter's growth has been as rapid as it's been surprising. In one month alone it grew over 1,382 percent—and that was before Oprah (@oprah) sent her first tweet. For a service that only allows its users to send tiny and public messages of 140 characters, the rate at which people have been creating accounts and making connections has been tremendous.

But it's not just the numbers of people who are using Twitter that's particularly eye-catching. It's also the types of people who are using it and the claims that are being made of it.

Twitter can help entrepreneurs, businesses and the self-employed earn income.

Twitter's biggest growth rate has been among the over-40s. It's a service predominantly used by older folk with high incomes who see Twitter as a way not to keep in touch with old friends—Facebook does that more efficiently—but as a tool to promote their businesses and build their business networks.

Much of the benefits of using Twitter then are financial. Twitter can help entrepreneurs, businesses and the self-employed earn income.

Sometimes that income is earned indirectly. The biggest benefit that Twitter use can bring to a business is stronger branding. Just by talking to customers, answering questions and being personable, a business is able to create a new kind of relationship with its customer base. That's a benefit being picked up by a number of savvy large companics.

But the income can also be indirect. Individual twitterers too are earning money with direct sales. They're tweeting coupons, making special offers and promoting sales through their timelines, relying on Twitter's viral power to spread the word further and faster than they could do alone.

In this book, we've looked at 99 ways in which Twitter's users are generating income with their timelines. They range from the simple and the small to the complex and the kinds of income that allow Dell to declare that Twitter has earned them more than a million dollars in sales.

In each chapter, we've explained what the strategy is, how twitterers are using it, how you can do the same thing and where to make your first steps. We've also made sure that each chapter contains a real-life model so that you won't need to re-invent the wheel yourself. You'll be able to see how other twitterers are using the strategy to generate income for themselves or their businesses and build on their platform for yourself.

We've also included a key to illustrate each strategies difficulty and value:

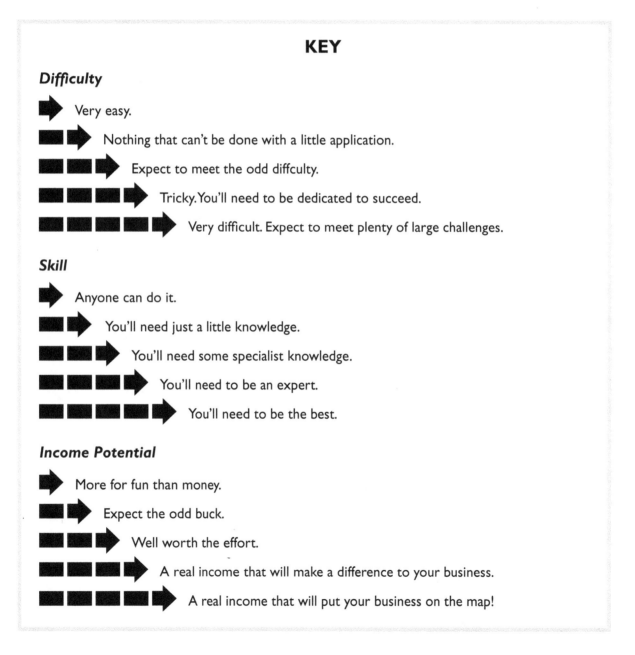

KEY

Difficulty

Very easy.

Nothing that can't be done with a little application.

Expect to meet the odd diffculty.

Tricky. You'll need to be dedicated to succeed.

Very difficult. Expect to meet plenty of large challenges.

Skill

Anyone can do it.

You'll need just a little knowledge.

You'll need some specialist knowledge.

You'll need to be an expert.

You'll need to be the best.

Income Potential

More for fun than money.

Expect the odd buck.

Well worth the effort.

A real income that will make a difference to your business.

A real income that will put your business on the map!

TURN YOUR TWITTER BACKGROUND INTO AN UNFORGETTABLE BRAND

What is a Twitter Background?

Open an account at Twitter and you'll be offered one of twelve different backgrounds and the option to upload a design of your own. Those backgrounds appear behind your timeline.

This is the first place that Twitter's commercial potential becomes clear—as well as the extent to which businesses are using it. While teenagers on MySpace tile their favorite pop stars to decorate their pages, and Facebook and LinkedIn don't even provide the opportunity, Twitter's commercial users are making the most of the background as a branding tool.

They place their image on the page, describe their products and tell readers where they can go to learn more about them.

It's not a perfect solution. Backgrounds are just pictures so URLs and email addresses placed on them aren't clickable. Users still have to type the address into the browser by hand. The timeline itself takes up most of the page leaving just a narrow strip visible on the left and sometimes on the right as well.

And perhaps most importantly of all, when someone follows you, they don't need to return to your timeline. They can read your tweets on their own page or an a Twitter client. Your background then will be at its most effective the first time someone sees it.

When you have thousands of followers though, and when you're adding plenty more each day, a well-designed background can be a very powerful way to drive followers to take action and build an image of your business.

DIFFICULTY

SKILLS REQUIRED

INCOME POTENTIAL

Twitter's commercial users are making the most of the background as a branding tool.

for Success

Skip the Free Stuff ... Unless You Plan to Build on It

A number of designers, including TwitterImage, offer free backgrounds. Although these are usually more attractive than those offered by Twitter, they aren't customized and they don't include text. You might be able to use them as the basis to build a branded image but alone, they're no replacement for a professional background image.

Break the Rules

A sidebar on the left of the page is a good place to start planning your background but the real fun comes when you start breaking the rules. TwitterImage's designs are particularly effective because they surprise.

(continued on next page)

How Twitterers Are Branding with Their Backgrounds

When Twitter started, few people did anything with their backgrounds. Most people were happy to use one of the images offered or simply place some image that was meaningful to them but meant little to anyone else behind their timeline. The background was treated a little like desktop wallpaper or the background picture on a mobile phone.

As Twitter's users became increasingly commercial however, so the value of that piece of Web real estate grew more apparent. In time, it became clear that there was enough space to provide both a marketing message and a memorable image.

There is now a standard Twitter background design. The image itself will be wide enough to stretch across even the largest monitors. The top left-hand corner will usually have a logo or the name of the twitterer. Beneath that will be a larger picture of the twitterer than the image that appears in the bio and will be followed by a vertical sidebar that may carry a descriptive sales message but will almost certainly carry a list of URLs such as the twitterer's blogs and the address of the commercial website. The bottom of the sidebar may also carry a second image of a product.

That layout has become the default starting position for Twitter timelines but there are plenty of variations. Marketer Carrie Wilkerson (@barefoot_exec), for example, keeps the information in the sidebar to a minimum, using the space in the top left-hand corner to create a pictorial image to match her brand, "The Barefoot Executive." At the top of the page, she also calls on followers to "Request your Free Audio and Transcript at The-Barefoot_Executive.com" and adds a second URL to TheBossMovie.com.

Even though that top line can clash with the navigation bar and Twitter's own logo, the result is a page that both brands her as a particular kind of marketer and tells readers where they can go for more information, helping to boost her customer base.

How to Do It

There are a number of different ways that you can create a commercial Twitter background. The easiest is to pay someone to do it for you. Most graphic designers—and you can find plenty of them at Elance. com—should be able to knock up a background for you in no time at all and at a reasonable rate.

Alternatively, TwitterImage.com (www.twitterimage.com) is a company that specializes in Twitter backgrounds. The firm charges $100 for the background but has been known to provide free backgrounds for twitterers with more than 5,000 followers. TwitterImage is responsible for the backgrounds used by professional blogger Darren Rowse (@problogger)and dot com mogul John Chow (@johnchow).

It is also possible to create your own background from scratch. The image can be no larger than 800kb, should be 1898 x 1593 (although stretching the size to 2048 x 1707 will make certain that it fits even the largest screens), and the sidebar on the left should be 80 x 587 and begin 14 pixels from the top of the page.

If you know something about graphic design, have an eye for images and time to spare, you can certainly have some creative—and very effective—fun designing your own Twitter background.

Getting Started

The design work itself though begins before you open a graphic program and even before you contact a graphic designer or TwitterImage to create your background.

You first have to decide what you want your background to do. What sort of image do you want it to portray, and which links would you like it to market?

Remember that you'll usually only have a small amount of space on the left so the image can't be huge and remember too that Twitter works best when it's personal. Top twitterers tend to use pictures of themselves even if, like actor Stephen Fry (@stephenfry) the picture is a stylized cartoon. Know what you want your background to do and your designer should be able to create the background that puts your marketing message across.

for Success

(continued)

Don't Include Too Many URLs

Twitter's bio only lets you include one URL so when you realize that you can include as many as you want in your own sidebar, the temptation is to toss in all your addresses. This is what William Nabaza (@Weblord) does, and the result is a mess with a long list of address at the top of the page. Readers don't know which address to type in first, so they ignore them all. Limit your list to three URLs, including your blog and your commercial site. That should be enough to create curiosity and start readers learning about you.

A Model to Follow

Joanna Penn's (@thecreativepenn) background was created by TwitterImage and is a great example of how to create an effective branding image. The background as a whole is an attractive red with swirls and floral patterns that are smooth and easy on the eyes.

The sidebar on the left contains a memorable logo, Joanna's name and title summarized in three words—"Author, Speaker and Coach"—and is followed by just two links: one to her website and blog, and the other to her free eworkbook. The sidebar also contains a pitch that explains why followers should visit her sites and includes a larger version of her profile picture.

The result is a background that's attractive, memorable tells us something about Joanna, and creates curiosity to learn more. It's simple, effective and easy to copy.

PUT A SALES MESSAGE IN YOUR BIO

2

What is the Twitter Bio?

While Twitter has developed into a useful marketing tool, it wasn't designed for promotions. In fact, Twitter was intended to do little more than enable its users to send public SMS messages. That sort of usage didn't require more than the very simplest of bios—and that's what Twitter offers: a single line consisting of no more than 160 characters.

Clearly, it's going to be difficult to squeeze an effective marketing message into 160 characters, which is one of the reasons that the background has become such an important branding tool. But it is still possible to make the most of that bio section, summarize your skills and services, and even deliver a call to action.

Alone, a carefully-written bio is unlikely to deliver revenues. At best, it will deliver clicks either on the link above or one placed in the bio itself. That may turn followers into customers or clients but a bio's most powerful use is as one important element that tells readers who you are and what you offer.

DIFFICULTY

SKILLS REQUIRED

INCOME POTENTIAL

How Twitterers Are Selling with Their Bios

Perhaps the most common way that people are writing their bios is to create a string of adjectives. Singer and motivator Lynn Rose (@LynnRose) for example, describes herself in her profile as "Voice of Transformation, Speaker, Singer, TV and Radio Host for people reaching their fullest self expression."

The pattern for bios like this is to have between two and four descriptions, then end with a short summary. Often that summary will be something personal, such as "and family man" or something humorous like "and bad fisherman."

Tips
for Success

Change Your Bio Regularly to Match Your Project

Tweets can do an excellent job of describing what you are doing at one particular moment, but the bio can be very helpful at providing broader context. One very effective strategy is to use it to theme your timeline.

If you're focusing on raising funds for your new business, for example, producing a book or preparing for an exhibition then writing a bio that says "Entrepreneur and inventor currently raising funds to build new jet technology" or "Photographer and digital artist currently preparing for a show at the Whitney" doesn't just tell people who you are and what you do. It also tells people what you're doing now so that they'll understand your tweets.

And as your project changes, you can change the bio to suit.

(continued on next page)

Elizabeth Grant (@TheQuantumCoach), a life coach, ends her bio with a smiley and an upbeat message. But her bio takes a slightly different approach. Instead of providing a string of adjectives, she creates two sentences that try to summarize her work: "Spiritual mentor and life coach specializing in quantum techniques. Basically, I teach people how to be happy and abundant from the inside out. :-) It's fun!"

It's difficult to say which of these two approaches is the most effective, or even how you'd measure that effectiveness. If the aim of the bio is to tempt people to follow then one option would be to create one of each kind of bio, test them for a week and see how they affect the follow rate.

If the primary aim of your bio though is not to pick up followers but to generate clicks to your website, then it might be a good idea to follow the approach taken by Danny Brown (@dannybrown). In addition to the link to his personal site placed above the bio, Danny also places a different website address in the bio itself: "Join me for the 12for12k Challenge—social media for good. Ask me for information or visit http://12for12k.org."

A bio like this doesn't just offer readers another way to learn about the twitterer. It can also supply information about that twitterer. That's an important difference. Tweets can tell followers what you're doing at one particular moment but often new readers lack the context. When Stephen Fry, who is one of Twitter's most popular users, was filming a nature show for the BBC, for example, he changed his bio frequently to let his followers know where he was and the name of the show he was creating.

At the very least, it saved him answering questions from followers asking him why he was in Mexico or Borneo and what exactly he was doing.

How to Do It

Adding your bio to your Twitter profile is very simple. Click the Settings tab at the top of the page and you'll be taken to your account page. The bio field is about halfway down. You won't need to do any more than type in your bio and hit the Save button.

Or rather, you won't have to do any more than paste in your bio because it's a good idea to create the text in Word first so that you

GEEKPRENEUR

can get the phrasing right. Just keep an eye on the character count—including spaces—so that you don't get any nasty surprises when you come to do the pasting.

Getting Started

The first step for creating an effective bio is to read before you write. Take a look at what other people in your field have written in their bios so that you can see what sort of approaches they took.

At the very least, you should be able to build up a good list of keywords that you can throw in if you decide to take that approach—as well as read the kind of approaches don't work too.

If a bio doesn't make you curious, build a desire to click on the link it contains or the one above it, or get you looking at least at the first tweet in the timeline . . . it didn't work.

A Model to Follow

Choosing a model to follow is a good way of making the bio-writing easier. But it's important to make sure that you choose the right model for your field. Browsing the timelines of other twitterers is one good approach but you can also take a look at the bios used by these twitterers:

Scott Monty's (@ScottMonty) bio combines his professional identity with a personal touch and link to a project-based website. It's a good example of how a corporate twitterer can still create an interesting, inviting bio: "Head of social media at Ford Motor Company, husband, dad, host of http://ihearofsherlock.com, and a generally nice guy. Formerly from Boston."

Harper's Magazine (@harpers) takes a slightly different approach to corporate tweeting but most importantly, it also explains who's actually writing the tweets. That's a good way to ensure that the timeline can be both corporate and personal: "An American general interest magazine published from 1850. Links to articles + misc tweets from Web Ed. Paul Ford and VP, PR Kathy Park. Tweet us, we listen!"

for Success

(continued)

Use a Different URL in Your Bio

If you are going to focus your bio on a particular project, it's a good idea to include a special URL too. The single URL that Twitter allows you can link to your website, but the address you include in your bio should lead to your special project.

That will give readers a place to go to learn about you, and a place to go to learn about what you're doing now.

Make it Personal

As always, Twitter's strength is its ability to personalize messages. That's true of bios too. Just as followers expect tweets to read like messages from real people so they expect bios to look like more than corporate summaries or resumes.

Once you've defined yourself professionally, adding a phrase or two that describes your likes or interests will help readers to realize there's a real person behind the timeline.

FIND FOLLOWERS WHO BRING REVENUE

What is Finding the Followers Who Bring Revenue?

Twitter is all about connections. While Facebook relationships are capped at 5,000 and tend to be made between friends and colleagues, Twitter allows people to forge as many connections as they want and to contact freely anyone they find interesting.

That makes it a hugely valuable tool.

Twitter's users include celebrities, CEOs and experts in a range of different fields. Any Twitter user can contact those personalities directly, simply by hitting the Reply icon in their tweet. Although there's no guarantee that the recipient will respond, in practice, people often do.

As a networking opportunity, few sites offer such easy access to such a wide range of helpful connections.

Although creating the connections themselves won't generate revenue, it will set up the sort of channels that just about every commercial Twitter user will need to make money with the site.

How Twitterers Are Finding the Right Followers

The benefits that can come from following—and being followed by— the right people on Twitter are almost endless. The most obvious way that twitterers are benefitting is simply by picking up information. Biz Stone (@biz) and Evan Williams (@ev), two of Twitter's founders, are often the first people to appear on someone's follow list not because their tweets are so insightful but because keeping track of their comments can make sure that you're the first to know about changes to the site.

DIFFICULTY

SKILLS REQUIRED

INCOME POTENTIAL

GEEKPRENEUR

Following the right people then can effortlessly bring in a stream of useful information.

But it also creates a bank of people to turn to for advice.

One of the most common—and effective—uses of Twitter is as a way of asking for help. Twitterers with large and well-selected lists of people they follow can ask even a technical question and receive the kind of expert help that would have cost a great deal of money had they needed to pay for a consultant. Pam Evans (@PamEvans), for example, only had to comment that she was trying to figure out an issue with QuickBooks for one of her followers to refer to Fiona Maclean (@fionamaclean), a Quickbooks consultant on Twitter.

And that viral power is something that can also be enhanced by choosing the right followers. While it's important to pick people who know a lot, following people who are followed by a lot of other people can be valuable too.

How to Do It

There are two ways to sort through the six million-odd people on Twitter to find the twitterers worth following. The first is to use Twitter's search engine to look for keywords related to your topic.

Unlike Google's search engine, Twitter's result page isn't static. As you view the results, a notice informs you of the number of new, relevant tweets posted since you made the search.

That will give you a list of people who are talking about the topics relevant to you but on Twitter, there's always a small number of people who dominate conversation points. Anyone interested in following technology news, for example, will add Robert Scoble (@scobleizer) to their follow list, if only because he's so influential.

So rather than simply following the people who turn up in the search results, the next stage is to look at who they're following. In particular, look for the people with lots of followers and who contribute the most to the discussions. Reply to some of their posts so they reply to you and your name will appear in their timeline.

That should bring you a pile of new, relevant followers and enough to give your timeline a firm foundation.

Tips

for Success

Look for Twitterers with Large Followings

One quick way to build up a long follower list is to persuade someone with a large following of their own to reply to one of your tweets. Point them in the direction of some useful information so that they'll thank you, answer a question that they've posed or even ask one and you'll stand a good chance of getting a reply. When Lisa Lynch (@alrighttit) told Stephen Fry about her breast cancer blog, for example, he recommended it to his then 50,000 followers and she saw a massive spike in her own followers, in the number of readers her blog received and in media interest too.

Just steer clear of random praise. That makes you look like a fan rather than an active participant and someone that other people should turn to.

(continued on next page)

for Success

(continued)

Know Your Keywords

The follower list starts with searching so you'll need to know what you're looking for. While some points of discussion should be fairly obvious, using Google's AdWords Keywords tool at http://adwords.google.com/select/KeywordToolExternal might throw up some interesting surprises.

Be Active

Creating the sort of valuable follower list that you can later tap for advice and sales is only the beginning. You have to maintain the list as well. That means continuing to tweet regularly, replying to your followers' questions and comments and answering their direct messages too.

Getting Started

Your list of powerful followers might begin by searching to see who's discussing your topic, but nothing really begins until you join that discussion. Twitter is a series of open conversations in which anyone can take part.

If you spot people you know on Twitter then those timelines can certainly be a good place to begin but don't be afraid to dive into other people's exchanges, especially with offers of help.

In fact, searching Twitter for questions on your topic that you can answer can also be a very useful way to make initial contact and show that people should be following you.

A Model to Follow

Tim Beyers is a tech writer for the Motley Fool and he tweets on Twitter at @milehighfool. His tweets though do more than discuss his writing and his personal life. They also contribute technology news, provide his own comments on the topics he writes about and they invite comments from others, a useful way to pull information and ideas out of his network of writers and technology experts.

More importantly, Tim Beyers is also a co-founder of #editorchat, a regular, open Twitter-based chat designed to help writers and editors work better together.

While that's a good idea in itself, it also places Tim at the center of a network of freelance writers on Twitter.

Any freelance writer using the service to chat with other writers and look for opportunities will eventually find their way to Tim's stream. And if they then want to connect with other writers, browsing the list of people who are following Tim will yield a rich source of potential friends and professional contacts.

TWEET YOUR BRAND MESSAGE

What Are Brands on Twitter?

Whenever a new marketing channel becomes popular, one of the first things anyone ever says of it is that it could be a useful means of building a brand.

That's usually because "branding" is such a vague term. It can mean anything from creating a corporate image that's so powerful it puts a company on the map to just making sure the business's name is still in the public domain.

A billboard by the side of the road is a useful branding tool when it carries an ad for Coca Cola.

But Twitter provides many more functions than a static billboard and the ways in which it can brand a product and a company are much more skillful and much more flexible.

They can be much more powerful too.

DIFFICULTY

SKILLS REQUIRED

INCOME POTENTIAL

What Twitterers Are Doing to Build Brands with Their Tweets

The advantages of building a brand on Twitter are tremendous. At the moment, Twitter is the coolest game in town. It's new enough for businesses who use the site to create the impression that they "get it," which means that they can win the custom of the kind of hip, geeky customers who like to tweet.

It can also be viral. Say something smart in your timeline, announce a competition or show up nice and high on other people's follow list and you should find yourself picking up plenty of new followers. Your tweets will get passed around and more people will get to know you, and helped by your recommendations.

Marketing doesn't get any more powerful than that.

Tips
for Success

Keep it Personal ... But Polite

You might be representing your company but Twitter's most powerful benefit is the way that it can personalize a corporation. That can only happen though if you let your own personality show through.

Do remember though that readers will see you as the firm so keep your tweets polite and friendly.

Use the Background

The Twitter background will be a valuable part of your branding power so make sure that you create visuals that are hard to forget. M&Ms famously created two Twitter timelines at @msgreen and @mmsracing to promote two different kinds of images for its products, appealing to women and men separately and summarizing that appeal in the timelines' background images.

(continued on next page)

And above all, when a business uses Twitter, it changes from a corporation into a human being. That's probably the most common goal that companies on Twitter are aiming for.

Simply by talking about their work with a human voice, taking the time to answer questions and join discussions, they appear approachable, friendly and on the customer's side.

As a way of becoming trusted and not just recognized, few tools are as powerful as Twitter.

How to Do It

Building a brand on Twitter doesn't require any more than delivering the same kind of tweets that individuals post . . . but with the awareness that you're representing a company.

That doesn't mean that you should only be tweeting company news or product announcements. That would suggest that you don't "get it," that you consider Twitter to be a loudhailer rather than a two-way communications device.

Twitter brands through conversation, direct contact and relationship-building.

Biz Stone, for example, does an excellent job of representing Twitter itself on his timeline by posting cool information about new twitterers and updates about the company. But he mingles that corporate information with personal anecdotes, often related to Twitter. So he'll point out that he just made a fresh pot of coffee after taking the last cup because that's how things work at Twitter HQ, or he'll describe a visit from a staff member's relative. But he'll also mention that he's going to the ballet that night or that his wife is cooking supper.

The impression is that Twitter isn't a company. It's a collection of individuals working together to create a product about which all of them feel passionate.

That's an impression that creates a real relationship between a company and its customer base.

Getting Started

You won't need to do anything too special to begin branding yourself or your company on Twitter.

Having created your account in the usual way, the biggest challenge will be finding the right sort of users to follow you.

That may be a little tricky, especially as you'll want to reach two different kinds of audience. You'll want pick up followers who already know your company so that you can deepen your relationship with them, and you'll also want pick up new followers who have never heard of your firm's name so that they become new customers.

The goal, after all, will be to turn all of your followers into loyal, repeat buyers.

So you can begin by searching for references to your company's name and following anyone who has mentioned you. Respond to some of their tweets but make sure that each reply you post is unique. One mistake that several companies have made is to use cut-and-pasted tweets to congratulate people on their purchases whenever they've mentioned them on Twitter. The result is to make their customers feel that the company is watching them instead of talking to them.

Follow other people who have tweeted about your company's industry then relax and tweet personally to ensure that your timeline is friendly . . . and makes your company look friendly too.

A Model to Follow

Perhaps the most successful example of a company branding itself with a Twitter timeline is Zappos.com (@zappos), an online footwear and clothing store. Faced with operating in a very competitive market, CEO Tony Hsieh has made his company famous by making himself accessible on Twitter. He tweets about what's happening at his company and also about the life of a successful Internet company boss.

It's the accessibility here that makes the difference. Customers buying from a website are used to feeling that they're purchasing from a catalog. Thanks to Tony Hsieh's tweets—and the company has a long list of tweeting employees at twitter.zappos.com—customers can feel that they're buying from real people who care about the product, the service and the customer.

for Success

(continued)

Answer Questions Sparingly

While answering questions can be a very useful way of keeping your timeline personal, there is a difference between a timeline that's used for branding and one that's used for customer service.

If you're being asked lots of questions, or if you can see that twitterers are raising lots of issues about your company that you think should be discussed, then create a separate timeline for those conversations. Successful branding is all about staying on message. That's hard to do when you're fielding questions.

5 FOLLOW YOUR WAY TO VALUABLE INSIDE INFORMATION

DIFFICULTY

SKILLS REQUIRED

INCOME POTENTIAL

What is Valuable Inside Information o n Twitter?

Twitter has done more than create another channel through which marketers can provide potential customers with information about their products.

It's also provided a channel through which marketers can hear what potential customers think about their products.

That's a huge difference and for marketers and public relations professionals, it marks a real revolution. For the first time, it's possible to gauge exactly what people think, say and are doing in relation to a company—information that in the past could only be gathered using an expensive survey whose own questions often altered the answers.

Through Twitter, it's possible to listen in on millions of conversations, and even intervene in those conversations, squashing criticism before it spreads and turning happy customers into active evangelists.

Although, like branding, this practice may not generate direct revenue itself, the value of knowing exactly how your product is being received in the market—and then being able to intervene in that market—could well make it the most valuable aspect of Twitter, when used carefully.

What Twitterers Are Doing to Find Valuable Inside Information

Companies that wish to use Twitter to keep track of what people are saying about them are faced with a bewildering range of tools to help them. None of them stands out. Simply reading tweets posted by followers limits the tracking to the follower list, and when you have thousands of followers becomes impossible. The list of mentions, located to the right of your timeline, only lists references to your username not the name of your product or your company.

Restrict yourself to those methods and it's inevitable that some tweets will always be missed.

Twitter's search function covers all conversations and is useful for looking historically at tweets that have already been posted. But results aren't updated automatically and you can only track one keyword at a time.

There are tools available that make listening easier but it's not how Twitter's users are picking up the information that's so important. It's what they do with the information they receive.

Best Buy, for example, used to have a Twitter account called "gina-community" which was used to send messages to people who had mentioned buying a product at one of its stores. The person running the account had a list of pre-written tweets in which they could simply paste in the name of the product.

The result was a timeline consisting of a series of tweets that said little more than "I hope you enjoy the ___ you bought at Best Buy." The tweets were dull to read and the effect on a twitterer receiving a message like that was more likely to have been a feeling that someone was watching them than a sense that they were enjoying a benefit from shopping at one of the company's stores.

Starbucks (@starbucks), on the other hand, uses its timeline not just to thank customers who say they've enjoyed their coffee but also to keep an eye on complaints. It even directs people to another account at @mystarbucksidea.com so that they can make improvements. The result is that the company picks up valuable information about which services its customers like and the customers feel that they're being listened to, not watched.

How to Do It

Ever since Twitter disabled the automatic Track function on the site, twitterers have been looking for a reliable tool to alert them to particular keywords. TwitScoop (www.twitscoop.com), for example, lists all of the recent mentions of a keyword and even includes a graph

Tips
for Success

Know How to React

Tracking keywords on Twitter is the easy bit. It's knowing how to react to the tweets you see and what to do with the information you gather that's the tricky part. As you read tweets related to your company, you will see both complaints and praise. In response to complaints, you need to have positive suggestions rather than explanations; in response to praise, you need to have courses of action rather than just expressions of gratitude. Asking those who liked your product to leave feedback on your sales page, for example, lets you thank them and alerts people reading your stream that you have another satisfied customer.

Choose Your Replies Carefully

If you're picking up lots of references, you won't be able to reply to everyone and you may not want to anyway. One good strategy is to prioritize those twitterers with lots of followers. Their

(continued on next page)

for Success

(continued)

complaints will have larger repercussions and if they reply to you then your company's name will win a second appearance in front of their large audience.

Use Your Replies to Keep Records

One of the challenges of tracking keywords on Twitter is that there's no way to record references. Monitter will only show you the last 25 or so tweets and searching for a term will require you to look through page after page of tweets to find the mention you're looking for. Faving tweets is one option but another is to use the Reply button. Reply to a tweet and you'll be able to look through the most important references to those keywords.

showing recent usage rate. TweetScan (www.tweetscan.com) functions like search, listing the latest references but automatically updating at regular intervals.

Perhaps the best tool though is Monitter.com (www.monitter.com), if only because it lets you track multiple terms simultaneously. Initially, the tweets appear in three distinct columns which refresh constantly as new, relevant tweets are posted. But by clicking the plus sign at the bottom of the page, it's possible to add extra columns and track more keywords.

You can track phrases as well as single words, not phrases and it's probably the best way to keep an eye on references to a range of different terms related to your business.

Getting Started

Placing your ear to the ground can be very enjoyable. You won't need to do any more than open Monitter and type in a bunch of keywords. Immediately, you'll begin to see the latest tweets that mention those terms. It can make for some fascinating reading.

That will get you started, but it won't tell you everything. You'll also need to create a list of the most important keywords to follow. Your business name could be one, but you might also want to track mentions of your competitors or terms related to your industry as a whole. Noting the rate at which new tweets are added will also give you an idea of which terms are the most important. You might well be surprised.

A Model to Follow

One good example to follow is Starbucks (@starbucks). A glance at this timeline, one of a number operated by the company, shows a large number of replies interspersed with occasional personal comments—a good mix that allows the company to maintain a human feel.

Some of those replies are in response to questions posed directly by twitterers—again, a good sign that customers feel that the timeline is responsive enough to approach—but others are made in response to discussions held between twitterers. When John Boghos (@jgboghos), for example, urged people to write to the timeline and encourage Starbucks to bring back all day bold coffee, Starbucks was able to respond by explaining that the company was discussing exactly that idea with its customer and invited him—and his readers —to join the debate.

6 BOOST YOUR CUSTOMER SERVICE

What is Twitter-Based Customer Service?

You can track keywords on Twitter for all sort of reasons. You can discover what people are saying about your company, identify suggestions to improve your products and services, and you can gauge just how much of an impact you're making on your market.

You can see just what people are saying about you.

It's inevitable though that one of the things you're going to see are complaints.

Twitter lets you deal with them. See someone complaining about a product you supplied and your customer service rep can weigh in with an explanation . . . before everyone sees their moan.

But customer service has to be done carefully. It's bad enough to find that a product you bought doesn't work; it's even worse to find that the company's representatives are uncaring or unhelpful. Twitter's advantage as a customer service tool is its immediacy: you can respond right away to a complaint. But you still need to have a solution.

Like keyword tracking, using Twitter as a customer service tool isn't something that will bring direct income. But as you hold discussions with customers, it will spread your name across the site and by squashing complaints as they arise, you'll prevent dissatisfied customers from putting off other buyers.

GEEKPRENEUR

What Twitterers Are Doing to Boost Their Customer Service

Few firms on Twitter are using the site as their sole channel for delivering customer service. Twitter always has to be used in conjunction with other channels such as email and telephone. Twitter's advantage though is that it allows twitterers to approach a customer service rep directly and receive a response right away instead of going through a series of phone menus.

Often, in fact, they can receive a reply without even asking for one. Frank Eliason (@comcastcares), probably Twitter's most famous customer service rep, is known for tweeting the phrase "Can I help?" whenever he spots someone complaining about the service Comcast provides. He doesn't always get a reply but the fact that someone is available all the time makes everyone feel that they're just a short tweet away from assistance.

How to Do It

Finding the complaints is simple enough. Responding with an initial expression of concern is straightforward too. The challenge of supplying customer service on Twitter is being able to supply the kind of responses that will turn an unhappy customer into an evangelist ready to tell everyone what a friendly, helpful service yours is.

It's a good idea then before you start offering help to spend a little time just reading the tweets to see what sort of complaints and requests people are making. That's valuable information anyway. You can create a series of responses and answers so that you're ready with the appropriate help right away.

That's always going to be easier for larger companies than smaller ones. Comcast, for example, is able to pass on some requests to technicians. Often though, Frank Eliason will send a direct message to a complainant asking for a telephone number, and call them directly. Not all issues can be dealt with in a 140-character tweet.

Perhaps the biggest difficulty for small firms considering using Twitter as a low-cost, easily accessible form of customer service is that someone has to monitor the tweets constantly. Outsourcing to a country with relatively low salaries won't help either as the customer service

for Success

Put Your Picture Up

When Frank Eliason first started using Twitter for Comcast's digital service, he placed the company's logo on his timeline instead of his own picture. Customers though kept asking where his picture was. So he swapped the logo for his own photograph. Other Comcast timelines (such as @ComcastBill and @ComcastGeorge) now do the same thing.

Just Ask to Help

Often, just asking how you can help is all you need to do to make a good impression and show customers that someone cares. That's particularly important when the criticism isn't about the product itself but the company's service as a whole. A sympathetic—and public—conversation with someone who actually listens can go a long way towards negating a negative experience and prevent one bad employee from harming the entire company's image.

(continued on next page)

Tips

for Success

(continued)

Remember that Twitter Isn't Everything

Customer service on Twitter is immediate, effective and public. Complainants can get a response immediately, without waiting for hours on the phone, while they're working . . . and everyone watching can benefit from your advice too.

But Twitter can't be the only way to deliver customer service. Even for the most effective users of the site, Twitter is often a jumping off point to a phone call or even a visit from a technician.

rep needs to create a personal feel in his or her timeline. Twitterers want to sense that they're chatting with a real person who cares about their problem, not a faceless company.

If you can't afford to employ a full-time customer service person, then you'll need to use your own timeline, interspersing your tweets with as much troubleshooting as you can.

Getting Started

Begin by tracking references to your company name so that you know what to expect. Don't offer to help immediately though. Just take a couple of days to see what kind of complaints are cropping up, and give yourself time to prepare solutions for them.

Using Twitter can be fairly intensive so you might also want to set aside particular hours of the day when you monitor tweets while also leaving yourself time to search the archives for the tweets you missed.

You might not be able to respond to all of the complaints posted when you weren't monitoring the site, but you should respond to complainants with lots of followers, or issues that are particularly important.

A Model to Follow

Frank Eliason, Director of Digital Care at Comcast, has set the standard for Twitter-based customer care with his timeline at @comcastcares. For a company whose customer service had long been a source of derision, Frank has gone a long way towards showing that the company is interested in its customers and that any poor service was the result of a few employees rather than representative of the company as a whole.

Not only does Frank include his own image in his profile but his background introduces himself, explains his role in the company and perhaps most importantly of all, also includes the URLs of his personal blog and his family website. Although that's a big step for an employee, it is entirely in keeping with Twitter's style. Readers don't feel that their space is being infringed upon by a large company. Rather they see Frank as a fellow twitterer trying to help other twitterers.

Note too that Frank's tweets contain both practical advice such as "reboot the router" and requests from people to direct message him with their telephone number. Where possible, Frank tries to provide help through Twitter so that the solution is immediate but when more information is needed, he's not averse to picking up the telephone.

And finally, even though Frank adds a personal touch to his tweets, very few of his tweets are personal. You rarely find a tweet that isn't directed to a customer. That's the advantage of employing a full-time customer service person on Twitter: while the image is personal, the service remains professional.

7 FIND TIPS THAT MEAN BUCKS

What Are Valuable Tips on Twitter?

MySpace now has a reputation of being made up primarily of teenage girls. For a long time Facebook was the preserve of college students. Twitter though remains largely a forum populated by well-educated professional types. According to a survey conducted by *Hitwise* in the summer of 2008, Twitter's largest age grouping is 35-44 year olds and 12 percent of twitterers have household incomes of over $250,000 per year.

Those figures may have changed a little now. Twitter is growing prolifically and as more people join the site so the average income and percentage of high-earners is likely to fall. But it remains true that Twitter is filled with people whose heads are filled with valuable information. Sports stars, CEOs, doctors, marketers, designers and many more are all on the site and posting tweets.

And they're all sharing their advice and their expertise for nothing.

For other members of Twitter, that makes the site a rich resource. It's a place where they can get the kind of guidance that could have cost them hundreds of dollars an hour in consulting fees. They can ask questions, hold discussions and turn an expensive problem into an opportunity that opens new doors.

What Twitterers Are Doing to Find Valuable Tips

While Twitter might be filled with helpful people, it does take a little technique to extract the kind of information that could be of highest value.

GEEKPRENEUR

Fortunately though, it doesn't usually take a great deal of effort. One of the great advantages of Twitter is that the site's members are generally a helpful, friendly bunch willing to lend a hand.

To find the help they need though, twitterers are doing a number of things.

The first thing they're doing is following the right people. We've already seen that can take a little bit of searching. With several million people on the site and no groups to gravitate naturally towards, twitterers are left to search for keywords, pore over follower lists, track discussions and browse Twellow (www.twellow.com), a Twitter directory.

That all takes time, but it does bring results and should lead to a follower list filled with potentially valuable people.

The next thing they tend do is ask direct questions. That could be a question aimed specifically at one particular expert, or it could be a query fired out to the twitterer's followers as a whole, often with a request for a re-tweet. Response rates can vary depending on who the tweet is aimed at, and the size of follower lists.

Ask an expert with 20,000 followers a question and there's a good chance that it will get lost in his or her stream. Ask your own 20,000 followers a question and there's a great chance that someone will have the answer. Throwboy (@throwboy), a manufacturer of throw pillows for a geek audience, for example, only had to mention that he was having trouble installing his new Mac hard drive for some of his 476 followers to start weighing in with expert help and suggestions.

How to Do It

Making the most of the valuable information held by members of Twitter is remarkably easy. Twitter is such a friendly platform that once connections are made, everyone is usually very willing to help whenever asked.

But those connections do have to be created and nurtured before the assistance starts flowing.

There are few places that demonstrate more clearly than Twitter that you can only ever take out what you put in. Create a timeline, follow lots of people but don't tweet and it's unlikely that your calls for help will be answered. Any followers you have will be the sort of people who follow anyone who follows them.

Tips
for Success

Join the Conversation First

Usually, when you need help, you need it right away. But your question is always more likely to be answered if people feel that you've already been helping them and others. If you're planning to use Twitter as an information source, it's a good idea to pay for that information in advance.

Search for the Answer

There's a good chance that your question has already been asked—and answered—on Twitter. Before you post your question, use the search facility to see if anyone else has asked it. Even if you don't find exactly the answer you need, you might well find a bunch of people to ask.

(continued on next page)

Tips
for Success

(continued)

**Keep the
Question Specific**

Twitter might be filled with clever, knowledgeable people but they can only reply in 140 characters. Looking for someone to explain the reason behind Hamlet's hesitation might not yield too many answers. Asking something simple and specific such as how to filter the news feed on Facebook is more likely to produce results.

Because they don't feel they have a relationship with you, they won't feel that your general call for help is addressed to them. The same is even true of a question aimed at an expert on the site. They're far more likely to answer queries posed to them by people who take part in the discussions they raise on their timeline, whose own timelines include plenty of replies and tweets, and who have plenty of interested followers.

But if creating the kind of active timeline that's most likely to pick up expert replies takes some dedication, asking the questions doesn't. If your timeline is active, just posting your query should be enough to get a reply. If you don't get an answer within a day or two try asking again . . . but add "please RT!" to prompt your followers to spread the request further.

One good strategy is also to begin your question with the phrase "Does anyone know . . . ." That will make sure that it's picked up by Ask Tweeters (@asktweeters) a service that posts general questions posed on Twitter and invites anyone to answer.

Getting Started

Picking up valuable advice begins by finding and following the right people to ask. Twellow is a good place to look for specialized people to follow but WeFollow (www.wefollow.com), a Twitter directory created by Kevin Rose, founder of Digg, is also a useful place to track down solid information nodes. The site claims to list over two million technology twitterers alone.

Once you've identified people worth following, it's just a matter of shooting out your question. In general, technology questions that can deliver practical advice are most likely to yield responses but general questions can work too.

A Model to Follow

Few people use Twitter specifically to mine experts for knowledge. But there are some good examples of questions that were well-phrased—and perhaps more importantly, well-targeted—to produce answers.

Ann Etchison (@ann1622), for example, is an educator who asked this question on her timeline: "How do you create an environment where students can have access to the relevant web 2.0 tools? Policies? Web 2.0 presentation #ASCD09." The question wasn't aimed at anyone specifically, but the use of the hashtag (referring to a conference) meant that it was spotted by other experts in her field and retweeted.

Raul Pacheco (@hummingbird604) however, carefully selected the target of his question ("@bluefur But how do I know which part of my style.css blocks the ordered lists?"). He asked it directly of Gary Jones (twitter/com/bluefur), a twitterer for a Web hosting company. Both strategies yielded useful answers.

8 REACH NEW CUSTOMERS WITH A TWITTER DIRECTORY BUSINESS LISTING

DIFFICULTY

SKILLS REQUIRED

INCOME POTENTIAL

What are Twitter Directories?

One of the biggest challenges for any business hoping to use Twitter for marketing purposes is getting seen. Winning followers usually requires a combination of careful following and active tweeting but that's just one way of putting the name of your business in front of potential customers using Twitter.

Another is to make sure that your business is listed on one of the directories that serve Twitter.

These aren't resources that are officially related to the website—although it's possible that some might want to be—and they tend to rely on twitterers submitting themselves. That means they're more likely to be filled with self-promoters than function as a comprehensive resource for corporate searchers on Twitter. You can think of them as functioning a little like Yahoo's old directory rather than as a kind of Google for Twitter that covers everything and delivers the results in the most relevant way possible.

But that still means directories are valuable. They provide useful starting points for people looking for experts to follow in their field. They make it much easier to bring people into your timeline. And they're free.

While submitting your name to a Twitter directory shouldn't be the only way you market yourself on the site, it should certainly be one of them.

    (g) GEEKPRENEUR

What Twitterers Are Doing to Make the Most of Twitter Directories

There are currently three different directories listing twitterers in a variety of categories:

Twibs (www.twibs.com)

Twibs is the smallest of the three Twitter directories and although registration is easy, usability for searchers isn't particularly friendly. Advertisers are listed under alphabetical tabs and then ranked either by number of followers, or again, alphabetically.

To find a twitterer that you might want to follow then, you'll need to search for keywords that match the tags entered when the business registered. Because search terms and tags don't always match, there's always a chance that you'll miss some useful candidates—and that people looking for services like yours will miss you. Most people are also likely to search the directory by followers, which gives established twitterers an advantage.

Where Twibs may be useful though is that it also allows businesses to add promotions to their listings. For retailers that may be particularly useful.

WeFollow (www.wefollow.com)

WeFollow was created by Kevin Rose, founder of Digg, and uses a unique, viral system to bring in new listings. Instead of registering on the site itself, twitterers can simply reply to @wefollow with up to three hashtagged keywords. The result isn't just that registering is very simple, but WeFollow's name is spread across Twitter's timelines, making more twitterers aware of the service—and making itself more useful. While Twib has only a few thousand registrants, WeFollow quickly gathered several million.

It's also easier to browse. Twitterers are categorized by keywords so users can easily find celebrities, social media experts, musicians and more. That does mean it's less business-oriented than Twib and that popular twitterers in popular categories will stand out, but it's useful and easy to join.

Tips
for Success

On WeFollow, Look at the Biggest Keywords First

Signing up to WeFollow is deceptively simple: type three keywords into a reply to WeFollow's timeline and you're in. And that's why it's so easy to get things wrong. Choose unpopular keywords and no one will ever find you. Before you register on WeFollow, take the time to browse the site and see which keywords other people in your field have used.

On Twellow, Use the Extra Categories

Twellow might add twitterers automatically but leave it to the site to advertise your stream and you're missing a giant opportunity. In addition to the categories to which Twellow places you automatically, you can also place yourself in up to ten others ... and create an extended bio. Those are powerful advantages.

Twellow (www.twellow.com)

Twellow was the first Twitter directory and is operated by WebProNews, an online business news service. Twitterers are added automatically, so it's possible that you're already listed. You'll then be able to "claim" your profile by entering your Twitter password, after which you'll be able to edit your profile, adding more links and further information.

Searchers on the site are able to browse a huge range of categories and sub-categories. North American users can look on a map for regional followers and it's even possible to use the site as a kind of Twitter client, keeping track of your followers' latest tweets.

Twellow's real strength though lies in the detail of its directory. While Twib seems to be aimed at small retailers and WeFollow at fun people to follow—the first category on its homepage is "celebrity"— Twellow feels like a Yellow Pages for Twitter.

How to Do It

Registration on each of these directories is free, so there's no reason not sign up for all of them. Each though has its own registration process. Twib requires members to register on the site; WeFollow requests a hashtagged reply; and Twellow may demand nothing at all but allows you to provide more information if you claim your profile.

Getting Started

While the registration process is simple enough, placing your Twitter details on a directory should actually begin long before you reach the directory site to sign up. Each of the directory services uses the Twitter bio as its summary, so you'll need to make sure that the information you provide in that field is helpful, accurate and effective.

As always with Twitter, you have very little space here, so you'll need to keep the bio brief. Robert Clay (@marketingwizdom), for example, describes himself as "Author, speaker & designer of world-class low-risk/high-return marketing strategies for entrepreneurs and aspiring market leaders"—a single sentence that says exactly who he is and what he does.

Twellow also allows you to edit your bio separately. Debbas (@debbas) describes himself on Twellow as "Founder of promotional items and printing. Professor of Marketing. Social Media Expert. JV contact me. Writer for a magazine and writing books. Enjoy Wineries." His Twitter profile also invites readers to be interviewed. On a site that contains a page of similar bio summaries, brevity and keywording are crucial if you want to stand out.

A Model to Follow

Kevin Rose (@kevinrose) probably doesn't need to list himself anywhere. Familiar to millions of Digg users, most of the people who want to follow him probably know exactly where to find him on Twitter. But Kevin not only lists himself on his own directory, WeFollow, he also lists himself on Twellow and Twibs.

His bio contains a Twitter-friendly combination of professional detail and personal likes, and on Twellow, he has made the effort to list himself in eleven categories—including "tea."

While listing your business on a Twitter directory takes very little skill, Kevin's willingness to place himself on more than one site, and the detail in his bio are great examples of the importance making the most of the free marketing resources available.

HOW TWIBES CAN BRING YOU BUYERS

DIFFICULTY

SKILLS REQUIRED

INCOME POTENTIAL

What Are Twibes?

Social media and social networking usually revolve around online social clubs. Facebook might allow its members to keep in touch with friends and acquaintances but to make new contacts, you'll need to identify a group or a network.

Members of Flickr, a photo-sharing site, also use groups to coalesce around specific photography topics and even LinkedIn relies on former workplaces to provide networking forums.

Twitter though has no groups. Twitterers post their tweets and rely on recommendations, replies in other members' timelines and the site's search function to find other members—and for members to find them.

Some twitterers though have found a way to group together. They've created "twibes," interest-based groups that make it easy for like-minded members to find each other and swap tweets. The activity happens off Twitter at www.twibes.com, but members do need Twitter accounts to take part in the group's activities. Having joined, all of your tweets that contain set hashtags will be listed on the group's page at Twibes.com, and you can post tweets directly to the twibe's page. Everyone is free to browse the tweets posted on the page and relevant to the twibe's topic.

How Twitterers are Selling with Twibes

Twibes are one more way of finding interesting people to network with on Twitter. In theory then, they should be a good way too of finding buyers for services or products.

In practice, that's rarely the case.

Producers are much more likely to define themselves by what they create more than buyers will define themselves by what they consume. So the Writers Twibe has around 500 members but there is no twibe for literary agents, even though there are plenty of them on the site. Similarly the Handmade Twibe has almost 1,000 members but few of the tweets posted on the group's page appear to be from buyers looking for items to purchase.

Instead, we see plenty of tweets like this one from "Sandy" (@designsbysandy): "I offer FREE SHIPPING on all my handmade jewelry items http://tinyurl.com/dl7ssc".

Tweets like these might have some effect in a timeline that also provides interesting news and craft tips, plenty of exchanges with other twitterers, and most importantly, followers who are also customers, but it's unlikely to generate many sales on a twibe page used mainly by other producers.

Turning membership of a twibe into revenue then will require a more careful strategy. It needs a group that's broad enough to include both buyers and sellers, and it needs the kinds of targeted tweets that will keep both sides interested enough to continue using the page.

The Wedding Twibe, for example, is used by both wedding professionals such as photographers and planners, and also by brides looking for advice about buying a dress or choosing a menu. The professionals are able to provide valuable information that clients will find helpful, while those buyers are able to review all of that information from lots of different professionals in one place.

Links, in particular, can be a useful tool on these pages. Wedding planner Patricia Ann (@plannerpatricia) placed this simple tweet on the Wedding twibes page: "Need help on what to wear to a wedding? http://bit.ly/naBMc". Potential clients browsing the page would then have a reason to click away from Patricia's competitors in the group, read her advice and review the services she's offering.

for Success

Create a Twibe

Most of the twibes at Twibe.com function as ways for professionals and members of interest groups to network with each other. That's fun and can be beneficial but ideally, you also want to be talking directly to buyers. If you can't find a group that contains both buyers and sellers, then create one. You'll need to work hard to bring in members—many of the twibes at Twibe.com have just a handful of members—but if you *can* get the twibe running not only will you have a forum to show off your products and services to clients, as the founder of the group, you'll also have a higher status than your competitors.

(continued on next page)

Tips

for Success

(continued)

Use Links

When you do find buyers on Twibe, you want to get them off the site and into your store as quickly as possible. Links are an invaluable way to do this. They'll give buyers a reason to leave Twibe.com and visit your website, where you can also explain your offer and make the conversion.

Post on Twitter and in the Twibe

Twibe allows its members to post tweets from the twibe page, and it also allows them to restrict those tweets to Twibe itself, effectively turning the site into a rival to Twitter. But for a marketer the benefit of Twibe is the ability to reach more prospects. You'll want your tweets to be visible both to your twibe's members and your timeline's followers. You'll also want the twibe members who see your tweets to become followers and followers to see that you're a twibe member.

How to Do It

Joining a twibe requires little more than browsing the groups at Twibes.com and clicking the "Join" button. You will then be sent to your Twitter page, where you'll find a pre-written tweet waiting to be posted, announcing that you've just joined the twibe. Twitter will ask for your permission to link your tweets to the twibe, and Twibes.com will ask how you want to receive updates. You can choose between direct message, email or checking the Twibes website. (Unless you don't mind very full inboxes, you'll probably be best off checking the twibes page yourself).

Finally, you'll be ready start tweeting from the twibe page itself. And here, you'll have two options. You'll be able to write a tweet that will only appear on the twibe page or you can also allow the tweet to posted to your own timeline.

Unless your timeline is particularly personal—in which case it might be best to create a professional timeline and link that to the twibe—there's no reason not to double the reach of your twibe tweets and post them on both pages.

Getting Started

The first step to selling with a twibe is find and join one. That's simple enough. Even when there are lots of different twibes available covering the same topic, because there are no limits to the number of twibes you can join, it's possible to pick all of the most popular. You could then make sure that your tweets appear on several of those twibe pages at once by including a number of different hashtags.

But joining a twibe is the easy bit. Making money from one will be much harder. When you're picking your twibe then, read the tweets on the page to see if they're likely to appeal to other producers or whether they also have information that could help buyers. Check at least some of the twibe's members too to see how varied they are. While professional networking can be valuable, you'll need to be tweeting to twibe members who buy if you're going to generate direct sales.

A Model to Follow

Rather than look at the way a twitterer uses a twibe, look instead at a model twibe to join. The Wedding Twibe (www .twibes.com/group/Wedding) is relatively large and its timeline has a good range of different kinds of tweets. Some tweets have been written by people who have just got married while plenty of others have been posted by wedding professionals from photographers to designers.

Even if clients only make up a small proportion of the group's membership, the range of different kinds of professionals using the twibe can also create opportunities for partnerships and joint ventures.

10 FIND RISING OPPORTUNITY IN TWITTER'S TRENDS

DIFFICULTY

SKILLS REQUIRED

INCOME POTENTIAL

What Are Twitter's Trends?

Twitter has been described as the Web's watercooler. In practice, it's even more than that. It's a giant open forum in which everyone is discussing every topic imaginable from the latest technology to plate tectonics. Anyone can join those discussions, and no less importantly, anyone can listen in on those discussions too.

While savvy twitterers use a number of techniques to turn lurkers into participants—Darren Rowse, for example, says that he asks at least one question a day to prompt a discussion—the number of people reading a popular timeline's tweets always vastly outnumber the people who respond to them. On a good day, Darren's tweets can generate over 200 replies but that's still only a fraction of the roughly 50,000 people who have chosen to follow him.

While writing tweets is valuable, reading them counts too, especially for companies who want to know what people are saying about them. But it's also very useful for businesses that want to stay in tune with what's on people's minds, understand the topics that are being discussed and know which subjects are currently in vogue.

There are a number of tools that allow Twitter's readers to follow not just conversations and tweets, but track the popularity of the topics that people are tweeting about too.

Of course, what you do with that information is a whole different challenge.

     (g) GEEKPRENEUR

How Twitterers Are Tracking Trends

Twitter makes trend tracking available to various depths and levels of detail. Open Twitter's search page, for example, and directly beneath the search box is a list of ten popular terms currently being discussed on the site. It's even possible to follow these trends as they're updated in a timeline at @TrendUpdates.

As a general overview of the topics being mentioned on Twitter, that has some limited use, but mostly the updates show little more than the broadness of the site's discussions.

TweetStats (www.tweetstats.com) provides information that's a little more useful. The service is mainly intended to allow twitterers to keep track of the number and frequency of the tweets they post and the percentage of replies to tweets in their timeline. (Interestingly, it reports that top marketers tend to have timelines that are around 50 percent tweets and 50 percent replies to other people's tweets). But the site also offers trending reports in the form of graphs and tag clouds that reveal the most popular terms being discussed at any one time on Twitter.

A second tag cloud also shows the 50 most popular trends of all time. ("iPhone" and "Obama" seem to do particularly well; "Gaza" and "Christmas" are frequently discussed on Twitter too.) Again, that might reveal which television shows are the most popular or how quickly minds are turning to the holidays or the change of seasons, but for companies outside of the entertainment industry, none of that information is going to be particularly useful.

Far more valuable is Flaptor's Twist (twist.flaptor.com). This doesn't just allow users to see which keywords are currently the most popular. It also lets users compare the frequency and usage of particular keywords.

The detail is far greater than that provided by other trending services; you can see the number of tweets containing the search term on any particular day. And you can also compare more than two terms at a time.

So a photography blogger wondering whether to review a Canon, Nikon or Olympus camera could search for all terms to see which is currently the most popular on the site—and note the appearance of spikes on certain days when the companies made product announcements. A developer considering developing an iPhone app but unsure

Tips *for Success*

Poll Your Results

Trend tracking on Twist provides a graphic view of the discussions taking place on Twitter. But it's only part of the information you can squeeze out of the site. Once you've discovered which subjects twitterers are more likely to discuss, you can search to see who's been talking about them—and quiz them directly—and you can create polls that bring up more detailed information.

Discover that Nikon is the most frequently-mentioned camera-maker on Twitter, for example, and you could reply to some of the people who mentioned the company and ask them what they like about it. You could also put up a poll that asked which Nikon camera model twitterers own. All of those results could yield information useful to anyone blogging about photography or selling camera products.

(continued on next page)

Tips
for Success

(continued)

Target Your Keywords

Playing with Twist can be very addictive but if you want the results to be meaningful, you'll need to know which keywords to look for. Use AdWords keyword tool at adwords. google.com/select/ KeywordToolExternal to find phrases you might not have considered.

Keep Records

And it's very easy to lose track of the results you find. Printing your results won't allow you to see details that relate to each day on Twitter but they will let you see which terms were the most popular and save you repeating the search.

whether to create a game or a text editing tool could check the number of discussions taking place about each subject. A retailer wondering whether it's too early to start promoting their summer collection could compare the number of times "summer" is mentioned to the rate at which people are discussing "spring."

As a method of market research, comparing keywords on Twitter may be fairly crude. It's unlikely to be as accurate as focus groups and market testing. But it's non-intrusive, completely subjective, can be combined with polling to provide a more detailed picture and, best of all, it's free and easy to do.

How to Do It

Part of Twist's beauty is its simplicity, and the fact that it delivers such pretty results. You can have plenty of fun tossing in different keywords to see how they're trending on Twitter.

In fact, perhaps the biggest difficulty of using Twist is not spending too much time on it—and recording and making sense of the results.

Those last two challenges are harder than they look. It is important to stay focused when using Twist. Know which terms you're searching for and print the results as they turn up so that you don't have to redo searches you've already conducted. And remember that while knowledge is valuable, it's not worth anything until you act on it.

Getting Started

The best way to begin tracking trends on Twitter is to give Twist some time. Play with terms and run your cursor along the graphs to see how spikes relate to events outside the site.

Once you've got a feel for the site, draw up a short list of terms to compare, pull up the results and print them out.

A Model to Follow

Trend tracking isn't something that's done publicly so you can't see how other twitterers are using Twist and making the most of the information available. Broadcasters ABC were said to have used the service to track the reactions to President Obama's first State of the Union address, but perhaps the best model to follow is the results you get when comparing any two company names on the site.

How you use that information though will be a model you'll have to create yourself.

SHOW YOUR PRODUCTS BY ADDING PICTURES TO YOUR TWEETS

What Are Pictures on Twitter?

DIFFICULTY

SKILLS REQUIRED

INCOME POTENTIAL

Twitter doesn't actually provide a means of adding images to posts. It doesn't even provide a way of adding 141 characters. But a number of developers have come to the rescue by creating systems that allow users to upload images and link to them directly from their tweets.

Those systems tend to be very user-friendly. The key though is to make the most of them: to pick the right pictures to upload, show them to the people who would find them interesting and useful, and create an effect that can generate revenue.

None of those things is as simple as creating the image itself. But they can be done and twitterers are doing it.

How Twitterers Are Adding Pictures that Show Their Products

Twitterers are generally using two tools to illustrate the posts. Some are using MobyPicture (www.mobypicture.com), a service that allows users to post images shot on their mobile phones. The service is integrated with Tweetie, a popular iPhone app (http://www.atebits .com/tweetie-iphone/) making posting both pictures and tweets simultaneously a breeze.

Most people though are using TwitPic (www.twitpic.com). Created by Noah Everett (@noaheverett) and still solely run by him, TwitPic has the advantage of being very easy to use. All you have to do is upload the picture, add a message, and unless you tick the box, your text will be added to your timeline with a link to the image page. Viewers can then see the image and add their own comments.

That's all very straightforward. More interesting is the sort of pictures twitterers are adding and how they're using the images to illustrate their posts—and sometimes to make money too.

Most twitterers, of course, are simply adding images for fun.

When über-twitterer Stephen Fry was traveling around the world shooting a nature series for the BBC, his pictures—taken usually on his iPhone—of places as far apart as Mexico and Borneo made for fascinating viewing. Others photograph what they're eating, the game they're watching or just something interesting that they spotted on the way to work that day.

All of those images help to make a timeline more interesting and give people a reason to read the tweets.

Other twitterers though are able to make more creative use of the service. Photographers in particular are able to use their timelines to talk about the shoots they're currently conducting and upload images to show at least some of the results. If their followers include editors and potential clients then those images allow them to demonstrate samples of their work and put themselves in the running for new jobs.

Perhaps the simplest and most effective option use of images on Twitter though is to show items that the twitterer is selling. @zoerenee-ashley, for example, posted this tweet in her timeline to display a picture of earrings that she was selling: "http://twitpic.com/2wmlw—CHLOE [Earrings] For Sale $15.00 Created 04/06/2009." Lance Bowers (@slick37075) tweeted this when he was looking to sell his bike: "http://twitpic.com/2wff7—2007 KUWAHARA LAZERLITE—for sale" and designer "Little Gonzales" (@littlegonzales) used TwitPic to offer a preview of a t-shirt design that he was about to launch—a good way to help build interest in his product: "http://twitpic.com/2wk4b—New tshirt design, to be available for sale v.soon!"

Each of those methods allows the twitterer to use Twitter to post ads on their timeline and market them to followers, while showing pictures of their products to potential buyers.

How to Do It

Placing your images on Twitter can be very simple. TweetDeck (www .tweetdeck.com), for example, now allows users to add images together with their tweets. Just hit the TwitPic button, choose the picture and

for Success

Follow the Image Comments

Like other image-sharing sites such as Flickr, TwitPic allows viewers to leave comments underneath your pictures. Don't ignore those comments. They give you extra space to engage your readers and answer questions.

If you're selling a product, for example, invite people to ask questions and use that space to make your pitch and overcome objections.

Use TwitPic

Although TwitPic has had server problems—a result of its rocketing growth—it does remain the easiest image service to use. The fact that it's incorporated into TweetDeck can be a big help and the ability to see other thumbnails on the same page can keep people looking at your pictures.

It might not be the most technically reliable but it is the most effective—and recognized—service.

(continued on next page)

Tips

for Success

(continued)

Take Good Pictures

So many of the pictures posted alongside tweets are poor. It's as though writing shorthand in the text box excuses shortcuts in the viewfinder. It doesn't. A good picture won't take up any more space than a poorly shot one.

Images can give a timeline much more depth—and quality images can give it a much higher standard.

the image is uploaded. The URL is then added automatically to the beginning of the tweet.

That's painless but a little deceptive. The URL is short, so the first thing the reader sees in the tweet is a meaningless jumble of words and letters—not the most enticing opening for a tweet. If you are going to use TweetDeck to upload your images, be sure to move the cursor back to the beginning of the post so that the link appears at the end.

That will allow you to pull the reader in and let him or her understand what the image will be about!

Getting Started

Begin by signing into TwitPic. You won't need to do any more than enter your Twitter username and password. You can then hit the Public Timeline link at the top of the page to see the images other twitterers are uploading.

TwitPic does allow you to look through all of the images uploaded by a particular user. What you'll find though is that many of the images are pretty poor. Either shot on mobile phones or snapped on the move, they look like snapshots rather than quality images.

Upload good pictures then, and not only will you have better images to illustrate your posts and tempt buyers of your products, you'll also give people more reason to look through your images and continue clicking those image links.

A Model to Follow

Although there's no shortage of people uploading images to TwitPic, the best model to follow is probably Stephen Fry. Although his pictures aren't always great, and he has the advantage of shooting from exotic places about exciting things, he does use his images to add interest to his timeline.

If you're going to say something interesting on Twitter, it really can help to show it too.

GEEKPRENEUR

CREATE VALUABLE JOINT VENTURES

What Are Joint Ventures?

There are few more powerful marketing tools than a partnership with someone that brings real benefits to both sides. When an artist teams up with a framer, for example, both sides get to show their work at their best and attract new buyers.

When an author delivers a reading in a bookstore, the store gets to bring in more readers, and both get to make more sales.

And when a software maker persuades a computer company to install its programs on their machines, the programmers get new users and the computer manufacturer gets a more useful product.

But finding joint venture partners has never been easy. The two partners need to have complementary markets, be able to deliver something that the other partner could not have produced alone and each side has to trust the other.

That's always been the trickiest bit. Joint ventures take work and sometimes expense. When you're promoting a partner, you want to be confident that they're pushing you in return. That's why partnerships like these have tended to be formed in person rather than online, and it's also why conferences and seminars have always been such valuable networking opportunities.

But Twitter also provides an opportunity for potential partners to find each other, get to know each other—and start working together too.

How Twitterers Are Creating Joint Ventures

As is often the case when someone needs something on Twitter, the easiest option is to put out a general call and see if anyone bites.

DIFFICULTY

SKILLS REQUIRED

INCOME POTENTIAL

Tips

for Success

Go Local

The firmest joint ventures tend to be those that can be sealed in person. Because Twitter lets you search within a limited geographic region, try looking for joint venture partners who live or work locally.

The Internet might be a big place but if you can find someone near you, you should find that you're able to build trust faster and make your relationship deeper.

Work on the Relationship First

Joint ventures might be profitable but they're also often quite demanding. You'll certainly have to invest time and it's possible that you'll have to invest valuable resources too into creating the sorts of products that neither of you could have created alone. As in any partnership, each side has to trust and believe in the other.

And as in any partnership too, that trust comes through knowledge and time. Connect on Twitter. Talk fi rst. Then de al.

(continued on next page)

Mary Allen (@LifeCoachMary), for example, placed this tweet in her timeline: "Curious who has lots of coaches in their database?? @coacheva and I are looking for a few more JV partners. DM one of us."

Richard Jones (@twitme10) took a similar approach with this tweet: "Looking for 10 JV partners with lista for Experiencial Business Training launch in AUS only serious people respond. DM me with ur interest."

And it's possible, of course, for someone looking for a joint venture to actively seek out opportunities like this. Twook4It (www.twook4it. com) provides a list of tweets that indicate the twitterer is "looking for" or "searching for" something. Many of the tweets listed have been posted by businesses looking for "JV"s.

But a true joint venture is often fairly complex and requires much more detail than can be supplied in a 140-character tweet. A better solution then is to use Twitter to find potential joint venture partners, form a relationship with them but bring that relationship to a partnership away from Twitter.

New Jersey wedding photographer Bob LoRusso (@LoRusso Studios), for example, found local invitation designer Maria Elena (@designedbyme) on Twitter. They met and agreed to cross-market each other's services. Bob placed copies of her invitations in his studio and Maria supplied him with "Thank You" cards that he sent to clients following a booking.

The connection was made on Twitter but the partnership was formed in person.

How to Do It

Rather than simply asking if anyone is interested in forming a joint venture, you can take two other approaches.

You could go through your follower list, check out your followers' websites and try to see how you might be able to help each other. That's a strategy that will take time, especially if you have a lot of followers. Only a small number of those followers are likely to be good potential joint venture partners so you'll be looking at a lot of websites and wondering a lot about how a partnership could work.

A better option then might be to think about the sort of joint venture that you might like to form and look specifically for someone who might be able to supply it. For Bob LoRusso, someone who designs wedding invitations was always going to be a good bet. They both have the same clients, they're non-competing and they're in the same neighborhood.

Having found someone though, avoid launching into the joint venture with your very first tweet. Join their discussion first. Point out things you have in common. Build the trust that will form the foundation of the relationship.

Then suggest a way of working together.

Getting Started

There are two possible ways then of starting a joint venture on Twitter, and either could work.

The first is to try to spot an opportunity with your most loyal followers—the twitterers who communicate with you most often and with whom you already have some sort of relationship. Because you have a connection, moving it into a partnership should be relatively simple.

The other option is to develop an idea for a joint venture, search the site for someone who might be able to supply it, then start working on the relationship. You shouldn't suggest the joint venture though, until you already have that connection.

Tips

for Success

(continued)

Work the Network

One way to shorten the time needed to create the relationship is to ask for references. Few of your followers are likely to be joint venture partners but some of them will know people who could be. If those followers can give you a referral, you'll already be well on your way to building the trust that leads to deals.

A Model to Follow

Bob LoRusso's joint venture with Maria Elena might not have been formed on Twitter but it was where the connection was formed. And the fact that it moved quickly off the site and into local meeting places is what really makes it a great model.

Bob and Maria found each other on Twitter, were local enough to meet in person and work in industries that are complementary enough to form a partnership. The two also maintain their relationship by tweeting to each other.

That's exactly how Twitter can help form—and maintain—a joint venture.

---

13 BUILD A TIMELINE THAT PROMOTES YOUR PRODUCT

DIFFICULTY

SKILLS REQUIRED

INCOME POTENTIAL

What is a Timeline that Promotes a Product?

Most timelines on Twitter are about people. They describe what individuals are doing and allow those individuals to make new connections and build relationships.

Some timelines are corporate. They allow business to form similarly strong relationships, respond to customers and reinforce their brand.

A few timelines though have been created specifically to promote a particular product. M&Ms, for example, created two timelines, @msgreen and @mmsracing, to market the same product to two different audiences.

The principles remain the same as those used for successful corporate marketing on Twitter: timelines have to be personable, interactive, and contain plenty of useful and interesting information.

Done correctly, product timelines can be very effective at generating curiosity, creating viral marketing and building a loyal following even before the item has launched.

How Twitterers Are Using Product Timelines

The M&Ms timelines were notable for their sophistication. They were the work of professional marketers who were using different colored sweets to target directly different market segments with the same product.

So one background was feminine while the other was masculine, and the writing styles were different too.

GEEKPRENEUR

Few product timelines are as complex as these. Most, in fact, are like @throwboy, the manufacturer of a range of geeky pillows. The background has been optimized to show image of the product; the bio ("Throwboy™ makes speciality throw pillows that cater to a geek audience") explains exactly what the product is all about; and the link above the bio takes followers directly to the website where they can browse the catalog, learn more and place orders.

It's the tweets that provide such good examples. Most of the posts are directed at individual followers, allowing new followers to feel that they're walking into a party and making veteran followers feel that they're part of a small community of friends. Interspersed between those conversational tweets are updates about new designs, announcements of new pictures on the Facebook group, and even requests by the writer for suggestions for buying a new computer.

That's a very basic timeline that doesn't depart too far from a typical Twitter presence but which creates strong loyalty towards a product.

Electronic Arts' timeline, created to promote The Sims 3 (@TheSims3), is much more sophisticated. Created even before the product was launched, the timeline generates curiosity about the new product and engage followers to bring them close to the new game.

So like @throwboy, many of the tweets are conversational (and some are words of thanks to twitterers who have posted fan pics, suggesting that the timeline already has close followers). Some of the tweets offer tempting hints ("Expect to see some familiar faces in The Sims 3—including Mortimer and Bella!").

And some are powerful motivators, driving followers to the product's website: "We've hidden a fun Sims 3 Easter egg. See if you can find it! http://tinyurl.com/d8kusu".

Again, the timeline helps to create a strong relationship between potential customers and the product based on close interaction and plenty of curiosity.

How to Do It

Product timelines require little more than the sort of posts that you can find on personal timelines too.

The background should be formatted so that the nature of the product is clear. The bio should describe what the product does and the

for Success

Keep it Personal

A product timeline might be commercial but Twitter's basic rule still applies: you have to make the timeline personal. You want users following your timeline not just because they think they're going to pick up the occasional coupon or stumble upon a discount. You want them following you because they're becoming raving fans for your product. You want them to feel for your product what Apple fanboys feel for anything that Steve Jobs produces. That means talking to them, answering their questions and making them feel part of your product's community.

(continued on next page)

for Success

(continued)

Reward Your Followers

But that doesn't mean you shouldn't reward them as well. Those rewards don't have to take the form of discounts and coupons—although that is one option. Sneak previews can also be a form of rewards, as well as canvassing for opinions of design options and feature ideas. Making your followers feel a part of the creation process will both deepen your community and give you valuable information.

link should lead to your home page so that customers can gain a much clearer idea of what you're selling.

You'll need to build up followers, talk to them directly and be available to answer questions, especially about availability, format and ordering.

But you'll also need to provide news about the product and reward followers—who will be your most loyal customers—by giving them previews, discounts and rewards.

The hardest part of creating a product timeline is likely to be finding the followers. That will need to be your first step.

Getting Started

Writing tweets that create a community around your product should be both simple and enjoyable. You'll be interacting with people who love what you've created and can't wait to talk to you about it—and tell their friends about it too.

It should be very satisfying. The challenge is finding the followers in the first place.

In time the quality of your tweets and your followers' responses to them should help word of your product spread virally across Twitter. Initially though, you won't be able to search for product buyers. The best you'll be able to do is monitor Twitter for mentions of your product and follow anyone who referred to it in a tweet.

So you'll have to rely on your off-Twitter resources. @throwboy, for example, also uses Facebook to keep his followers engaged and expand the range of his social media marketing. Those Facebook friends are one source of Twitter followers. Customer lists are another and so, of course, would urging website visitors to follow you.

A Model to Follow

Twitter is filled with timelines created by marketers hoping to sell products. Many of them are successful. They have long follower lists and include the kinds of tweets that build communities and lead those followers to take action.

Product timelines though are slightly different. They have to balance their obviously commercial nature with the need for the kind of personal communication that works best on Twitter.

Electronic Arts timeline @TheSims3 is a great example of how to overcome that challenge. It's sophisticated, interactive, responsive and includes plenty of bonuses to keep followers interested. Created before the launch of the product, it creates curiosity while the previews and Easter eggs keep followers engaged and rewarded.

⑭ BECOME A PROFESSIONAL TWITTERER

DIFFICULTY

SKILLS REQUIRED

INCOME POTENTIAL

What is a Professional Twitterer?

Tweets might be only 140 characters in length but tweeting effectively takes time. To stay on the radar of other twitterers and to be seen as an active partner in the site's discussions, twitterers have to look for people to follow, engage in the conversations and update regularly.

The tweets themselves might take only a few minutes to write but managing a Twitter account for a business demands commitment.

Just as writers have spotted an opportunity to help companies keep their corporate blogs up to date effortlessly, so some wordsmiths have begun offering their services to companies looking to cash in on Twitter's marketing and public relations opportunities.

The fees themselves can vary tremendously depending on the number of tweets per day and the sort of posts you'll be expected to produce. Tweets created on behalf of a celebrity, for example, are likely to demand little more than the ability to build relationships, focus on the star's main area of interest and maintain an image. Tweeting for a company however, is more likely to be oriented toward customer service and promotional work, and would require a greater integration with the firm.

Landing clients might be difficult until Twitter becomes accepted as a mainstream form of corporate communications but if you can find buyers willing to pay, you'll be getting paid to tweet!

ⓖ GEEKPRENEUR

What Professional Twitterers Do

Professional twitterers might be asked to perform a range of different functions depending on the client. In general though, you'll be taking over or building a client's Twitter account. You'll have to send out regular tweets, build followers and engage in conversations.

While that may sound similar to the sort of functions anyone with a Twitter account is likely to perform anyway, there are some important differences that do raise unique challenges.

Twitter was created with the idea of telling people what you are doing right now. When you're tweeting on someone else's behalf, that's not going to be so easy. Companies aren't individuals and projects move slowly, so for corporations you'll be tweeting opinions rather than actions, looking for and reacting to complaints on the Twitter-sphere and perhaps issuing discount coupons, announcing product releases or managing competitions. You'll need to stay in close contact with the firm's marketing and customer services' departments, establish regular goals and report on how you're meeting them.

And tweeting on behalf of an individual such as a celebrity or a CEO is harder still. Tweets work best when they're personal. Britney Spears (@britneyspears) was criticized after advertising for an online networking expert on the Harvard job board and now makes clear when her staff are tweeting for her. Shaquille O'Neal (@THE_REAL_SHAQ), Lance Armstrong (@lancearmstrong) and Demi Moore (@mrskutcher) have amassed huge followings by doing what other twitterers do: they let their followers into their daily lives. A ghost-twitterer won't have such close access and it's likely that the client will want to retain a level of privacy. Maintaining a balance between a timeline that's personal and revealing enough to be interesting but general enough for someone else to write will require a good understanding of both the client and the areas on which he or she wants to focus.

How to Do It

Professional twitterers need to overcome three challenges. They need to find clients. They need to understand—and help clients to understand—exactly what the Twitter account can do for the client. And they need to build and maintain the account.

for Success

Offer Ghost-Twittering as Part of an Online Networking Package

Corporate tweeting works best when combined with other networking systems such as Facebook and LinkedIn. Offer complete packages that let companies and individuals outsource their entire online networking strategies to you.

Price Flexibly

Twitter is still relatively new and the value of Twitter to companies still isn't clear. Understand the minimum you're prepared to accept and negotiate, using a broad package to increase flexibility.

Target Fakes

Well-known companies and personalities will always be faked on Flickr. One sales strategy then may be to alert their agents and offer to tweet on their clients' behalf, ensuring that they retain control of their online image.

Winning clients can happen in any number of ways. An optimized and marketed website will certainly be one effective way of bringing in potential buyers and it might also be possible to make cold approaches to the communications departments of major companies. Suggesting that public relations and marketing companies outsource their clients' online networking strategies to you could also bring in some business.

For firms, you will need to emphasize the financial rewards that Twitter can generate, while for individuals, you'll need to stress the importance of keeping control of the client's image when anyone can create an account in their name. You can also try monitoring tweets for ghostwriting requests. Branding consultant Todd Roberts (@tcroberts) once issued a call on his timeline for a ghost tweeter.

Perhaps the toughest issue in winning clients though will be the pricing. Twit4Hire's rates range from £175 (around $282) per month for one tweet per workday to £2650 (around $4280) per month for 20 tweets every workday. That averages to £8.75–£6.63 ($14.13–$10.71) a tweet. Considering the volume of tweets required to maintain an account and the current lack of clarity about Twitter's commercial value, companies might consider that too high. Twit4Hire has reported difficulty translating leads into customers.

An alternative approach might be to emphasize the fact that managing a tweet account involves monitoring others' tweets and finding followers, as well as writing the tweets themselves. A fee based on an hourly rate then rather than per 140-character post might look more persuasive and ensure that you're earning a fee that you consider fair. Professional twitterers could also consider taking a share of the revenues raised from special offers placed in the timeline.

Getting Started

Take-up is likely to be slow. You'll have to start by building a website that promotes your services, then market that site. It would also be a good idea to have an active Twitter account of your own with plenty of followers—even if it doesn't promote your ghost-twittering services which you might want to keep confidential.

A Model to Follow

Ghost-tweeting though can be controversial, depending on how it's done. Few followers assumed that Barack Obama @barackobama was writing his own tweets (more were upset that the tweets ended with the campaign) and Britney Spears now makes clear who is doing her tweeting by adding ^ followed by the initials of the writer at the end of the tweet.

Each of those provides different approaches to ghost-tweeting though. It is possible to tweet openly on behalf of a busy individual if the timeline is used primarily as an announcement board rather than a branding tool. And it may also be possible to keep someone's tweets going on their behalf for set periods when they can't do it themselves, especially when you're tweeting about them. While offering to tweet someone's presentation isn't likely to bring in much revenue, it could deliver a valuable contact.

Perhaps the best model to follow though is Twit4Hire (www .twit4hire.com). Formed at the beginning of 2009 by David Brown, the company offers ghost-tweeting services to corporate clients, charging a number of different rates depending on the number of tweets commissioned each day. The company reported interest from six firms in its first week of business . . . and 50 job requests from twitterers.

15 MARKET YOUR TWEETS AS COMMODITIES

What is Marketing Your Tweets as Commodities?

DIFFICULTY

SKILLS REQUIRED

INCOME POTENTIAL

A number of services have popped up offering twitterers the opportunity to place ads in their timeline. Usually, those systems have carried a number of disadvantages. The payments tend to be relatively small, the ads themselves are intrusive and while you can filter out promotional posts that you don't want, you can't pick and choose the firms that you do want to do business with.

An alternative option then is to be exclusive.

Instead of working through a third-party ad clearing house and showing ads for a range of companies, many of which you might never have heard of, you can reach an agreement with one firm and agree to promote only their products on your timeline.

In effect, you'll have created a sponsored timeline—and you'd be able to negotiate the rates yourself, cutting out the middleman's commissions and agreeing to a remunerative fee.

There's only one problem with this strategy: it's very difficult to implement in practice.

How Twitterers are Marketing Their Tweets as Commodities

In fact, finding sponsors for timelines is so difficult that only one twitterer is known to have done it. Robert Scoble (@scobleizer) is a tech writer and blogger with a large following of his own. In 2008, he brokered a deal with Seagate in which he agreed to promote their hard drives on his timeline.

GEEKPRENEUR

The promotions took a range of different forms. Occasionally, Robert would place a post that said something like: "ADVERTISEMENT: Seagate hard drives rock. I was paid to say that, but I would have said it anyway." Occasionally, he would also discuss Seagate's products, especially when he visited one of the company's Chinese factories. And once he took part in a giveaway in which anyone who turned up at Times Square with proof that they had heard about the promotion in Twitter received a free Seagate hard drive. Another drive went to the person who had sent them the tweet.

The amount that Seagate paid Robert Scoble for this marketing has not been publicized.

How to Do It

Seagate was willing to work with Robert Scoble for a number of reasons but there was one overpowering motivation for them to do so: Robert already had a huge—almost cult-like following—among geeks.

Seagate's marketing message then would be reaching a large number of people, all of whom fitted the company's target demographic, and it would be coming from a highly trusted source.

Creating that sort of relationship with the public is going to be vital to attract a sponsor. You'll need to show that your timeline has lots of readers and that those readers actually pay attention to what you're saying.

That isn't going to happen quickly and it isn't going to be easy. Robert Scoble had been blogging for a long time before he started posting tweets on Twitter. He also had a clear subject—in his case, technology—and he was able to bring his loyal readers onto Twitter with him.

If you have a blog and a loyal, targeted readership then you're already part of the way there but the other part isn't simple either.

In addition to a relationship with an audience you also need to cultivate a relationship with a company. It will probably need to be the sort of relationship of trust that comes from person-to-person meetings rather than through email (conferences would do) so that the sponsor feels confident that they will get a return on their investment.

None of this is the kind of thing for which there's a ready-made template. If you provide solid, helpful, reliable information about

for Success

Admit that You're Being Paid

If you do succeed in persuading a firm to sponsor your timeline, don't try to hide it. Not only will that harm the trust that your followers have in you, but the fact that you have agreed to promote a firm is a powerful force. Your followers will assume that you've only agreed to do so because you believe in it.

And if you believe in it, they should too.

That's exactly the sort of influence that your partner is paying for.

Believe in the Product

That means though that you do have to believe in the product. To pick up sponsorship like this, you'll need to have a public that trusts you. And once you have that, it's always going to be more valuable than anything the company would be willing to pay.

(continued on next page)

for Success

(continued)

Keep it and you'll be able to continue earning from it with affiliate sales and product launches. Lose it and you'll have wasted years of work.

If you don't really feel that the company that wants to sponsor you produces the best product of its kind, skip it.

Be Creative

Don't limit yourself only to promotional tweets. Show that this is a product you really do love by taking part in giveaways and promotional events. If you can link your name to the product, you'll make yourself indispensable to the company.

your topic, you should find yourself building up an audience and a following.

If you attend conferences and events, and make the effort to network corporate executives, you should create the connections that can lead to sponsorship.

But the best way to land a sponsorship deal on Twitter will always be to take the opportunity if it arises.

Getting Started

Sponsored timelines work when the sponsor isn't just advertising on a Twitter-based billboard but paying for a relationship with an already-known brand.

Although Twitter is an extremely powerful branding tool, its limitations mean that it will always be easier to build that brand outside of 140-character tweets and on a website that allows you to provide more in-depth insights, as well as downloads, images and video.

You can still use Twitter to let people know about those new posts but it's likely that your blog and website will have to do the bulk of building the brand, while Twitter helps to give it momentum.

Once you have that brand—and the public that comes with it—it's a matter of identifying a company you want to work with and building the commercial relationship.

A Model to Follow

The only model to follow is Robert Scoble's timeline. Although he was criticized for his relationship with Seagate, the deal was completely open and he does seem to genuinely rate their products. His ads were obtrusive but also friendly and informal. They felt like a recommendation from a friend as much as a paid placement. And he took part in giveaways that deepened the connection between his own personal brand and the company.

DRIVE VALUABLE TRAFFIC TO YOUR WEBSITE

What is Valuable Traffic on Twitter?

Earning money on the Internet is all about turning users into cash. There are ways to do that directly on Twitter, but it's always going to be much easier to do it on a website where a range of different types of ads—units that pay per thousand impressions, pay-per-click ads and commissions based on affiliate relationships—can increase the chances that every user brings revenue.

But you first have to bring those users to the website and one of the first commercial uses to which twitterers put the service was as an adjunct to their own blogs, a way of informing their readers that new content had been uploaded or that special offers were now available from their pages.

It's a strategy that makes sense. For a site's regular users, Twitter provides a way to learn more about the publisher, receive sneak peeks about upcoming content and communicate directly with the people behind the site. And for the publisher, it's a much easier way than creating 350-word blog posts to offer new content and keep readers informed and active.

But Twitter also offers a rich source of valuable new users. According to an article published in *Time* in August 2008, 12 percent of Twitter's users earn more than a quarter of a million dollars a year while another 14 percent are "Stable Career" types. That makes them valuable readers for any ad-supported website.

Moving those users from Twitter to a website optimized for mon-etization takes some knowledge and skill. You have to know how to

for Success

Track Your Clickthroughs

Whenever you're trying to attract traffic to a website, it pays to keep track of the results so that you can see which strategies work best. That's true too when you're driving traffic through Twitter. TwitPwr (www.twitpwr.com) is one service that provides clickthrough stats based on your short URLs but others include Bit.ly (http://bit.ly) and BudURL (www.budurl. com).

(continued on next page)

monetize a website first and you have to know how to drive users. Neither of those tasks is particularly difficult and they have proven to be very effective but you do have to know how to do them—and how to avoid putting people off your Twitter stream altogether as you encourage them to take action.

What Twitterers Do to Drive Traffic

There are a number of different strategies that Internet publishers are using on Twitter to bring traffic to their sites. The simplest include the one URL that Twitter allows its members to place on their bio. Most new followers are likely to click through that link at least once in order to see who is doing the tweeting.

More sophisticated twitterers though tend make use of their backgrounds to show off their other URLs. By placing a list of all their websites on the left of the screen, they're able to tell their followers where else they can be found on the Web.

Although effective, backgrounds do have the disadvantage of not being clickable or dynamic. Readers have to type the URL directly into the browser, and they can't tell followers when a site has been changed or updated.

More usually though, publishers will announce new content on their websites by simply writing a tweet that includes the headline and a shortened URL, linking to the page.

How to Do It

The easiest way to drive traffic to a monetized website is to set up automated tweets using Twitterfeed (www.twitterfeed.com), a free service that turns RSS feeds into tweets. You can choose to include the title, the description or both and select from a wide range of different URL-shortening services.

That's very simple and there are timelines on Twitter that do nothing but rely on Twitterfeed to create their tweets and keep users informed about new posts. Darren Rowse, for example, a professional blogger, uses Twitterfeed on the timeline for his Digital Photography School blog, @digitalps. Darren has reported clickthrough rates for those tweets of just under 10 percent.

But that may be exceptional. A more typical example of the way that bloggers drive users to an optimized website is Darren's personal timeline at @darrenrowse. Here, links and blog updates are interspersed among Darren's other tweets. He keeps his timeline interesting by talking about his life, answering questions from readers and joining discussions.

The links don't look like advertisements. They look like announcements of small projects that Darren has just completed.

The best way to drive readers to a website then is to create curiosity by engaging people on Twitter. It's a long-term strategy, one that relies on creating connections by following and replying, and deepening those relationships by continuing to keep those people involved in your conversations.

This is particularly true for personal blogs. Blogs might be updated only two or three times a week and certainly no more than once per day. Twitter though is updated constantly, turning the blogger from an occasional friend to a constant companion. An announcement of a new blog post, inviting the follower to visit the website is received like an invitation to visit a friend's home.

Twitter works best—even as a channel for traffic—when it's used socially, and traffic on the site moves more smoothly when it's pulled not driven.

Getting Started

Driving followers to a website begins slowly. It starts by creating a website optimized for monetization, then moves through building followers with an interest in the content of your website and keeping them engaged with your tweets. A good sign of that engagement is a steady stream of replies and direct messages.

Twitterers looking for a short cut though, can log in to Twitterfeed. com, enter their Twitter details and RSS Feed URL and see their site updates appear in their timeline. Whether anyone will click on those links though will depend on the tweets that surround those links.

for Success

(continued)

Build Curiosity

There are shortcuts that you can use to drive followers through a link, such as discount codes and competitions, but these are strategies in their own right, with results and revenue potential of their own. Ultimately, the most effective way to drive traffic is to treat Twitter as an extension of the website: create good, engaging content. Scatter the links naturally and followers will click because they want to.

A Model to Follow

Darren Rowse at @digitalps and tech guru Robert Scoble at @scobleslinkblog provide examples of automated timelines that rely on Twitterfeed. But these timelines have around 8,350 and 1,700 followers respectively in comparison to the personal timelines at @problogger and @scobleizer. At time of writing, these have around 63,000 and 91,000 followers respectively, and are growing fast. Even with a 10 percent clickthrough rate then, those automated timelines would still be generating fewer clicks than a 3 percent clickthrough rate on a timeline that contains good content and loyal followers.

Kenneth Yu at @emailcopywriter, however, might well provide an example of how you can merge links to a monetized site into an active Twitter stream and still lose clicks. Rather than relying on the curiosity his tweets have created, he offers the same link repeatedly and pushes new links uncharacteristically hard.

Even a Twitterfed link, when placed in a good timeline such as Darren Rowse's can get results.

DRIVE TWITTER TO YOUR SQUIDOO PAGE AND EARN MORE AD REVENUE

What is Squidoo?

Squidoo (www.squidoo.com) is a series of Web pages that aim to provide guidance on a range of different subjects. Anyone can create a page and there are no fees for using the site. In fact, publishers can even receive a share of the ad revenue generated by the site as a whole, relative to the number of readers the page generates.

The pages (or "lenses" as they're called on Squidoo, because each lens focuses on one topic) are modular so creating them is simple and requires no knowledge of HTML or any programming language. Lensmasters are free to choose the modules they want, placing ad units, videos, polls and huge range of other types of content. Like blogs, they can also write explanatory articles, but everything appears on just one long page.

The service was created by Seth Godin and contains more than 900,000 lenses generating amounts that range from a handful of bucks to perhaps $10,000 a year for the lensmaster.

While the page-building is easy on Squidoo though, the traffic generation isn't. Five percent of Squidoo's profits are donated to charity and 50 percent redistributed to the site's lensmaster but those revenues depend on picking up lots of viewers—and Squidoo won't do the marketing for you.

Some lensmasters then have been turning to Twitter to build up a community from which they can send users to their lenses.

DIFFICULTY

SKILLS REQUIRED

INCOME POTENTIAL

Tips
for Success

Create a Good Timeline

Squidoo is only one way in which you can monetize and benefit from a Twitter timeline. To gain all of the benefits though, and to maximize the benefits that can come through Squidoo, you will need a good timeline. Write tweets that contain interesting information, insights and links to news pages. Answer questions and become a part of the topic's discussions on Twitter. Your Squidoo page will then become an adjunct to that discussion.

Go Trivial

TwttrStrm represents a huge potential opportunity for twitterers. In effect, it diverts the discussion away from Twitter, making it all available on one filtered page from which the twitter can earn revenue. But to earn that revenue you have to ask a good question.

(continued on next page)

How Squidoo Lensmasters Are Using Twitter to Increase Their Ad Revenue

Like blog publishers, Squidoo lensmasters are mostly using Twitter as a supplement to their pages. While blogs can be large and detailed, with long posts and plenty of pages, lenses tend to be relatively short and to the point.

That makes the extra content, dynamism and discussion on Twitter particularly valuable for lensmasters. Twitter lets them place links to news pages as they're posted, reveal the research and level of expertise behind the lens, and talk directly to readers.

Brian Manning (@brimanning), for example, is a software developer who creates programs for sports coaches. His tweets are fairly typical for a good timeline. They contain a mixture of broadcast tweets about his life and work, as well as plenty of replies and questions to other twitterers. That helps to build the community and engage his readers.

Occasionally though, Brian will also tell his followers that his Squidoo lens (www.squidoo.com/coaching-software) has been updated: "I just updated my Squidoo page: Coaching Software / http://tinyurl.com/cxgdft."

In fact, these kinds of tweets occur fairly regular on Twitter. Squidoo now provides an option that allows lensmasters to post to Squidoo automatically every time they update their lens.

It also provides a module that allows lensmasters to place their tweets on their lenses, and Squidoo's TwttrStrm lets them ask a question and create a special ad-supported page dedicated solely to the answers.

That's a particularly useful way to monetize your followers. Ask the right question of a large number of followers and you can expect a good percentage of them to answer. You can also expect some of them to click the ads on the answer page, giving you some extra revenue. Woodworker "Rockler Woodworking" (@rockler), for example, asked his followers "Woodworkers: Where you do sell your creations online and why did you choose that site?" The results, visible at www.squidoo.com/Woodworking-Sales-Online, was more than a list of sites. It was a discussion of the answers that appeared both on Squidoo and on Twitter.

How to Do It

Creating automated notices that appear in your Twitter timeline whenever you change a lens couldn't be simpler. The profile under the bio settings now includes a section for "Social Applications Settings" that asks for both Twitter and Facebook details. Enter your Twitter username and password. Whenever you publish a change to your lens, a link in the lens publication will ask if you want to post a notification on your timeline.

While that may be enough to send some followers through to your lens, you can increase your conversion rate by building suspense before you update. Tell your followers what you're working on and let them know that you will soon be posting new content on your lens. The curiosity created by the teasers should be enough to give you some extra traffic.

Creating a TwttrStrm page is equally simple . . . and just as challenging to optimize. Squidoo's TwttrStrm building page at www.squidoo.com/twttrstrm/hq allows you to pose a question, enter your Twitter username, create a hashtag for easy tracking, place the page in a category and even provide a keyword to make the page easy to find.

The result will be a single page on which all the results can be seen and which gives you a share of the revenues from the page's ads.

To be successful though, you'll need to have plenty of followers and ask a question that people will want to answer. Squidoo lists the top 50 TwttrStrm questions, and they can provide good examples to follow.

Getting Started

If you don't already have a Squidoo lens then the first step will be to register at www.squidoo.com. Choose a topic about which you can talk easily and start playing around with the modules and text. Be sure to read the lenses of top lensmasters to see what a good lens should look like.

If you do already have a lens, then you'll need to build up a large following. Only a small number of your followers will click through to your lens and only a fraction of them will click an ad. To make those followers pay then, you'll need to have a large number of them. Start

Tips

for Success

(continued)

The question itself will depend on the topic but often the most trivial questions—queries that demand the least from followers, such as "what is your favorite TV character?"—can bring the best results.

by looking for people who have mentioned keywords related to your topic, and start following and chatting.

A Model to Follow

Vince DelMonte (@LoseTheFlabNow), a fitness expert, uses his timeline to promote both his website and his Squidoo page. His timeline contains quick fitness tips, replies to other twitterers and posts to articles. It also contains automated notification of Squidoo updates to create a timeline that's both interesting and which drives followers to money-making pages.

MAKE THE NEWS WITH TWITTER

What is Making the News on Twitter?

Twitter's growing user base includes top executives, consultants, experts and celebrities. It also includes a number of writers, journalists and even reporters for national news networks. That means Twitter can also be a great way to put a story about your business in the news.

You do have to be careful here though. Rick Sanchez of CNN (@ricksanchezcnn) might have an active Twitter stream with around 90,000 followers which he uses to pick up comments for his show but he's unlikely to use it as a source for story ideas. In an organization as large as CNN, those stories are likely to be set by the producers and while a good idea might bubble up through Twitter it would have to be exceptional to beat all of the other options available.

Other reporters though might well be interested in talking to someone with a good story idea and who can promise a good interview—which is why so many public relations professionals are using the site and following the writers. Don Reisinger (@donreisinger), a tech columnist for CNET and others, has estimated that of his 9,200-plus followers, as many as ten percent may be PR professionals.

Get the approach right and you should find that Twitter can be a powerful adjunct to the press release for businesses looking for free publicity.

for Success

Make the Story about the Audience

The golden rule for winning publicity is to remember that the reporter doesn't really care about your news. He only cares about what your news is going to do for his audience. When you're trying to guide a conversation on your timeline towards a story that you want a reporter to cover, don't emphasize what you've been doing; talk about the effect that your achievement will have on the public. That's what the reporters who follow your tweets will want to know.

Aim for Bloggers

The reason that publicity works is that reporters need stories. They have pages and airtime to fill and they have to finding interesting articles to put in them. If someone can provide them with a good story, they'll cover it.

In general though, life is easier for reporters on large publications. It will usually be up to their

(continued on next page)

How Twitterers Are Making the News

Some twitterers attempt to win publicity simply by making a cold approach to the reporter by replying to one of their tweets. Ken Grant (@kengrantde), who works for a chromatography company in Delaware, for example, replied to NPR's 100 Days (a timeline created for one campaign, then deleted) saying "hey, I've got a great story for you in Delaware—what's the best way to send it?"

An approach like that might work when—like NPR—the news outlet is specifically looking for user-generated stories but in general, Twitter isn't a great place for making cold pitches.

Reporters don't expect it and few are on the site in the hope of receiving a 140-character press release.

A more gradual approach may be more effective and appears to be the strategy taken by most professional PR firms on Twitter such as those following Don Reisinger.

Instead of sending cold pitches to hopefully sympathetic reporters, they follow those reporters, post interesting tweets, engage them in conversation and win their trust. When they tweet about a client or a story that they hope a reporter will pick up, there's a better chance someone will be in touch.

How to Do It

The best way to coax reporters to write about you then is to follow the general rule on Twitter: write interesting posts, engage people in conversation . . . and when you're trying to win publicity, make sure that some of the people you engage are writers. As Kevin Dugan (@prblog), a PR blogger, has put it on Twitter, participation, not pitching is key.

That means that it's also important to read the tweets posted by those writers. Twitter has reporters covering topics as far apart as technology and relationships. Reading writers' tweets will tell you what subjects they're interested in so that you can pull them into a conversation using as the hook a discussion in which they've already expressed an interest.

Getting Started

As is often the case with Twitter, the first move is to find the right people to follow—and make sure that they're following you back.

Searching WeFollow (www.wefollow.com) for keywords such as "journalist" and "reporter" should give you a list of important people to follow, although you might want to avoid looking for more generic terms such as "writer" initially. Lots of people might describe themselves as a "writer" but not all of them are read.

If you're going to persuade someone to write about you, you want to make sure that it's someone who actually has a readership.

Once you've identified people who may potentially be interested in writing about you and your business, tweet about what you're doing, and as part of your tweets engage those writers in your discussions. Comment on their posts and retweet their own posts. Make yourself visible in their field of followers.

If you do want to contact them directly about something you're doing—perhaps because you want timely publicity to coincide with a release or to cover a particular achievement—don't present that information as a pitch.

Instead, ask the reporter what they think or bring it up in one of their discussions. On Twitter, subtlety is always more effective than a hard sell.

Tips for Success

(continued)

editors to come up with the story ideas and they're so inundated with press releases, their biggest problem is often picking which story to write about first.

That's not true for bloggers. Many blogs are one-man or one-woman shows who have to come up with article ideas, find people to interview and write up the story themselves. Bloggers might have smaller audiences than larger outlets—although they also might not—but they're much easier to interest in your story.

Give Thanks

Once you get publicity, don't forget to thank the reporter. That's not just good courtesy. It also provides a plug for the reporter's timeline and publication, and lets your followers know you were in the press.

A Model to Follow

The best examples to follow when looking for ways to attract the attention of the media on Twitter are probably PR professionals who use the site. Individuals and small businesses tend to make the mistake of pitching for attention, while publicity types create conversations around their topic that draws in writers and leads to publicity.

Kevin Dugan's follower list is a good place to find many of them, and it's noticeable that it also includes a number of writers.

It's also noticeable that Kevin himself doesn't pitch stories to journalists on his timeline. Instead he creates tweets that reporters might be interested in reading so that they can contact him if they spot what could turn into a good story.

19 NETWORK FOR INDUSTRY AWARD VOTES

What is Networking for Industry Award Votes on Twitter?

It would be nice to believe that when a competition announces a winner the best entry won. That's not always the case. Contests judged by a panel of experts are always subjective. The judges simply pick the entrants that they like the best. And winners that are selected based on a public vote are often not those with the best product, the most creativity or the highest craftsmanship. Like any election, they're often the people with the best vote drive.

It's often worth making the effort. Winning a competition can have tremendous effects on sales, branding and recognition. When Beth Dow won Blurb's first photography book competition—a contest judged by a panel—sales of her book quadrupled. Twitter itself received its first major boost after winning an award at SxSW in 2007.

Twitter is one place that competition entrants are using to persuade people to pull the online levers and help them pick up a prize.

How Twitterers Are Winning Industry Award Votes

Usually when someone is pitching for votes on Twitter to win a contest, they take the direct route. They ask their followers to vote for them.

When Kim Gray's (@kimgray) blog, for example, was nominated in the design category at the 2009 South African Blog Awards she simply placed a tweet in her timeline that said: "Please vote for me http://www.sablogawards.com . . . in Best Design Blog Category."

That's simple enough and with just 50-odd followers, most of whom are likely to be very loyal, there's a good chance that Kim won a number of extra votes.

It's not surprising that this is the approach taken by most twitterers hoping to win competitions. It's simple and direct, and it doesn't demand any more from readers than that they click a link, then click a second link on the landing page. At least one twitterer even pointed that out in the tweet to encourage people to vote.

But a vote call will be even more powerful if you can persuade your followers to retweet the request. While the percentage of people who care enough to vote will drop as the request spreads, the more people who hear about your competition, the more votes you're likely to receive.

One way to do that is to encourage people to put down the competition. When Casey Wright (@caseywright) was taking part in a social media "tweeple" tournament, he emphasized that his opponent was Barack Obama (@barackobama). Those who wanted to see the President lose were inclined not only to vote, but to tell other people to vote too.

Humor is another method. Darren Cronian (@travelrants), a travel blogger, encouraged people to vote for his site in a blogging competition by threatening to run naked in "YOUR street." That won several retweets too.

How to Do It

Winning the votes is as simple as asking for them. You won't need to do anything more complex than post a tweet urging people to vote.

It might be a good idea though to include the full URL rather than a shortened URL if you can squeeze it in. Short URLs are fine when the tweet explains where the link leads but including the full address of the competition both reveals some information about it and makes it look official.

The end result is that the link looks more inviting to click.

Getting Started

Clearly, the first step in encouraging people to vote for you in a competition is to enter one. There are all sorts of vote-based competitions on

Tips
for Success

Show that You Care

Most twitterers try to win votes simply by asking people to click through to the competition and push the button. Followers may choose to do that, especially if they feel a close connection to you. But they'll still be taking time out to do you a favor.

They're more likely to do that if they feel that you appreciate it and really do want their help.

So make a big deal of the competition. Tell your followers when you're nominated and say how cool it would be to win. Remind them of the competition occasionally and encourage them to vote.

But Don't Overdo It

When Gary Stager (@garystager) was nominated for a Shorty Award, his response was to post new tweets every few minutes urging people to vote for him, many of them directed at individual twitterers. Aside from making him look desperate and suggest that he didn't

(continued on next page)

Tips
for Success

(continued)

deserve to win the award on his own merits, aiming his requests at individuals suggested that he didn't want the votes of everyone else. Not a good strategy.

Make it Fun

In terms of publicity, branding and the appearance of expertise, online competitions can have serious consequences. But usually, they're meant to be fun. So treat them that way. Make comments about the other entrants. Joke about the competition itself. Show that while you'd love to win, you're really getting a kick out of taking part. You should find that your followers want to take part too—by voting for you.

the Internet and it will be important to find one that wins you kudos in your industry. One easy—and valuable—contest to enter though is the Shorty Awards (www.shortyawards.com), a new and open competition that acknowledges good tweeting.

At the very least it should win you plenty of new followers.

To enter the competition, you can complete a form on the competition's website or be nominated by someone posting a tweet that says, "@shortyawards I nominate @someone in category #news because . . .," replacing "@someone" with your username, "#news" with an appropriate category, and providing a good reason. As long as the tweet contains "@shortyawards," your username and the hashtagged category, you'll be nominated.

Then it's just a matter of making sure that everyone knows—and that your followers are voting for you and encouraging their followers to vote for you too.

A Model to Follow

Perhaps the best way to see how people are encouraging their followers to vote for them is to search Twitter for the phrase "vote for me."

What you'll usually find is straightforward requests but you might also be able to spot a few desperate pleas and a number of well-made wishes that pick up re-tweets.

Out of twenty of patsdragon's (@patsdragon) tweets, for example, only four did not relate to a charity pet contest and all of them were aimed at individuals rather than the mass of her followers. While her appeals did win a few votes, they were likely to have put off many people too.

Dale Cruse (@dalecruse), however, a wine geek, didn't just win votes by writing "Can I ask you to please vote for me at: http://tinyurl.com/5pyvja Thanks!" but he also won at least one retweet that praised his blog. The request was subtle and polite, but most importantly, it also came in a timeline that was filled with good, interesting posts. If you want to win, it helps to deserve it!

FIND A BETTER-PAYING JOB

20

What is Job Searching on Twitter?

Successful job searching is always about who you know as much as what you know. Job vacancies tend to be passed along by word-of-mouth often filling up long before they reach the jobs section of a newspaper, let alone a website, and for job-seekers letting people know that you're looking for a new position is usually the first step towards finding a new job, even before updating your resume.

That's what makes Twitter such a powerful tool for anyone who's just found that their job has been downsized or who wants to move their career up a notch. The links between twitterers make it very simple for information—whether it's news of a vacancy or an announcement that you're in the job market—to spread far and wide.

Laid-off Twitterers have found new jobs through the site.

What Twitterers Are Doing to Find Work

Twitterers are following a number of different strategies to find work through tweeting. Those with large numbers of followers have been known to simply announce that they now need a new position only to be inundated with interview invitations and receive an offer very quickly.

Other twitterers though are using one of the many services that have cropped up on the site that feed announcements of vacancies or which even match jobseekers with people who can help them to find new positions.

DIFFICULTY

SKILLS REQUIRED

INCOME POTENTIAL

for Success

Build the Network

Although there are plenty of timelines that promise career help in all sorts of ways—from advice to job announcements—the most valuable tool for finding a new job on Twitter is always going to be your network.

Even as you're contacting recruiters and sending resumes in response to the jobs you see, don't forget to keep building that network. It's likely to be your best shot.

Combine Twitter with Other Social Media Services

Twitter can be a powerful tool, but it's at its strongest when mixed with other social media services too. LinkedIn is the social media site that was really designed with careers opportunities in mind so bring the two together. Look for the people you follow on Twitter on LinkedIn, and vice versa.

They'll be able to see your career achievements, and you'll be able to see who's best placed to help you.

Successful job-seeking on Twitter then is often a combination of working your own network and actively seeking for information about jobs flowing through the site.

How to Do It

The best way to find a job on Twitter is to have a large number of followers who know what sort of work you do, and who appreciate it. That's not something that's going to happen overnight so it's a good idea to start early . . . before you need the job.

Twitter offers value to its members in all sorts of different ways but its ability to deliver work to those who need it has been proved. It does pay then, when you're operating your Twitter stream, to think ahead and consider how those followers could help you if your company went belly-up.

That means ensuring that you're tweeting to more than just your immediate friends and family. You might need to tweet to as many as a thousand people to receive a wide enough range of job leads for some of them to translate into an interview and one of them into the sort of offer that you're willing to accept.

And you have to write tweets that are interesting enough to keep that audience engaged. Those will be tweets about your life and your work, and they will need to be replies too to other people's tweets so that you're seen as an active participant in discussions.

People like to help people they like so to win work through Twitter you'll need to use the site to bank goodwill.

Other methods are a great deal easier and far more effortless, but they're also a lot less effective. Following the timelines of recruiters such as Jim Durbin (@smheadhunter) or Chris LaVoie (@RecruiterEarth) will open you up to all sorts of tips and advice about looking for work, and should give you a heads-up about leads too.

Engaging recuiters in discussions will also make them aware of who you are and what you have to offer. Just make sure that your bio looks professional and that your website is up-to-date. Any recruiter on Twitter is likely to click through to your URL to learn more about you.

You can find recruiters and headhunters easily enough by searching for both as keywords. Twellow also has a list of around 800 human resources professionals covering a wide range of specialties so making that initial contact should be very straightforward.

Looking for tweets tagged "#jobs" should bring you a pile of the latest job offers posted on Twitter and, perhaps more usefully, will also introduce you to job feeds such as JobShouts (@jobshouts), Actors and Crew (@ACTORSandCREW) and Narms Jobs (@narmsjobs) to name just a few.

And finally, Job Angels (@jobangels) is a kind of Twitter-based matching service that brings together job-seekers with volunteers who can help them.

Getting Started

Job-hunting on Twitter should ideally begin long before you need it. It should be a use of the site that's always on your mind as you're building your network and posting your tweets. Look for people in your industry to follow, try to build a large network with plenty of people in potentially helpful positions and keep them engaged on your timeline.

If you need a job now though and don't have a following of a thousand people or more, it may be a little late.

So begin instead by searching through the recruiters at Twellow for a headhunter that could be interested in your skills. Don't rely on them, but you can make the first contact on Twitter just in case they have something available.

You can then search for specific jobs on the site, follow any relevant job feeds and make monitoring the site for opportunities part of your daily routine.

A Model to Follow

The best example of job-seeking on Twitter is probably Warren Sukernek (@warrenss). A keen twitterer who, according to the Baltimore Sun, informed his 2,800 followers that he had been laid off. Within a week, the newspaper reports, he had a

(continued on next page)

A Model to Follow *(continued)*

dozen interviews, one of which turned led to his new job with a Canadian Web firm.

It's noticeable that Warren's timeline is particularly active. Most of his tweets are aimed specifically at other twitterers, showing that he's discussing rather than announcing, a practice that's more likely to bind his followers into relationship that could lead to help.

That level of activity may not be necessary to find a job through Twitter. It's certainly possible that one job posted on the site will be the one you need. But Twitter is a huge network so the odds aren't in your favor.

Building a large following as active and dedicated as Warren's will always be a better strategy.

LAUNCH A BUSINESS ON TWITTER

What Are Business Launches on Twitter?

DIFFICULTY

SKILLS REQUIRED

INCOME POTENTIAL

The hardest time for any business is immediately after it begins. There's no income, no customers and no one even knows you exist let alone whether your products and services are any good.

The first stage of a launch then is always to let the world know you're there.

The second stage is to begin building a relationship with partners and customers.

Twitter allows entrepreneurs to do both of those things and to do them for no cost other than the time it takes to create the tweets.

You can look for followers who could be customers, reporters and bloggers. Tell them what you're about to do and ask them what they think. You can receive feedback before the business launches properly so that you can iron out the mistakes early, and you can even find freelance employees and test new marketing ideas.

Although Twitter won't be the only channel a new business will use to announce its launch and build a customer base, it may well be the most enjoyable channel—and it will almost certainly be the cheapest.

How Companies Are Launching on Twitter

The simplest way in which businesses are using Twitter to spread news of launches is that they're working the news into their existing timelines. LadiesonTour (@Ladiesontour), for example, a portal about ladies golf, placed a series of messages on its timeline describing how the publisher

Tips
for Success

Start Tweeting Before the Launch

Tweeting about your launch should begin long before the launch itself. It takes time to build momentum and followers on Twitter so you'll want to start tweeting and chatting several months before.

Who knows, you might even find that the people you meet on Twitter help you to launch more successfully.

Look for Buyers, but Talk to Experts

Those followers should include both potential buyers—which will help you to hit the ground running—and experts in your field. But focus your discussions on the experts initially. They'll help to spark your ideas but until you've launched, you'll have nothing to offer buyers.

(continued on next page)

managed to get back in touch with an old friend who now runs a golf business and which ended by saying that "his golf biz will write for our new ladies golf magazine launching April!"

It was a very subtle way of preparing the audience for the launch of the portal's new product, creating both curiosity and excitement.

Beers Group (@BEERSGROUP), a part of Tyndale publishers, did this even more simply when it tweeted about the launch of a new book: "Beers group is excited about launching the Kurt & Brenda Warner book this June! It'll be a great read. More details to come . . ." The promise of more details is a small addition but it can go a long way towards building suspense and keeping readers interested.

And Web design firm, Alienation Digital (@alienation_), uses Twitter to tell people not just about its own launches but about the launches of websites created for its clients. Usually that just takes the form of an announcement and a link—which tells readers more about the company's own achievement than that of Alienation Digital's client—but sometimes, the notices are a little more sophisticated. When Alienation Digital was preparing to launch a new website for a large hotel group, it placed images of the site on its Flickr stream to give its followers a "sneak preview." That rewarded followers and made them feel that the new website was something particularly special.

Perhaps the most sophisticated use of Twitter to support a business launch though can be found in the timeline of Manoj Ranaweera (@ManojRanaweera), CEO of edocr.com, an online document publishing business.

Not only did Manoj use Twitter to let his followers know about his plan to prove his business concept then look for funding, he also uses it to promote his start-up networking services. Those tweets tell followers what his business is doing and place him at the center of a circle of entrepreneurs and investors.

How to Do It

Using Twitter to support your business then can be as simple as writing a tweet telling everyone that your business has launched. But it should really be a lot more complex than that.

Ideally, news of the launch should begin with hints and previews, building suspense and excitement, and enhancing the importance of what's to come.

It should then continue after the launch by asking followers for their opinion and, like one strategy used by Manoj Ranaweera, inviting followers to test the system—a practice than can save on the costs of quality assurance.

Twitter though is a dynamic service—followers will expect to see continuous updates—so while you only need one tweet to tell people that your business is now open, you'll need a lot more to keep those followers interested and turn them into customers and resellers.

Launching is only the first step on Twitter. The next step is to use the site for branding.

Getting Started

The best way to begin twittering about a launch is to build your following long before you actually need it. Post tweets that are related to the area of your business and enter conversations with other twitterers discussing similar topics. If you can show that you're serious and knowledgeable about your field, when you do come to launch, you'll already have the respect and trust of other people on Twitter.

You can then begin building suspense about your launch, offer sneak previews to whet people's appetite and pick up free feedback, then look to move from launch to branding.

for Success

(continued)

Build Suspense

And use that pre-launch time to build excitement about your business. One of the biggest challenges that new businesses face is building the trust necessary to do business.

If you can help people to feel that your business is special even before it's been launched you'll go a long way towards developing that trust right from the beginning.

A Model to Follow

Search for the keyword "launch" on Twitter and you should be able to see all sorts of different ways in which different businesses are announcing their own arrival as well as the creation of their new products and services.

Not all of those tweets though are likely to be successful.

The best examples are those whose "launch" tweets are preceded by tweets that prepare the ground by talking about the opening that's about to come.

(continued on next page)

A Model to Follow *(continued)*

Manoj Ranaweera's timeline though provides a great example of how launching a business on Twitter can develop from the initial commencement through to branding, networking and talking to investors and other entrepreneurs.

Just because you begin talking about your business, doesn't mean you have to continue that way, and your venture may need funds as much as it needs customers.

GEEKPRENEUR

CREATE AUTOMATIC UPDATES FOR HANDS-FREE REVENUE

What Are Automatic Updates on Twitter?

There are two kinds of tweets on Twitter. "Discussion" tweets engage other twitterers in conversation. Usually, they're formed as replies to someone else's posts and even as replies to their replies.

"Broadcast" tweets however are snippets of information. Usually, they take the form of a description of what the twitterer is doing now or what they're thinking about. But they can also be announcements of a new blog post, links to a news item or even interesting quotes. The twitterer might welcome replies to these tweets but posts like these are generally intended to convey information rather than spark discussions.

Timelines made up of nothing more than RSS feeds of new blog posts (like Robert Scoble's @scobleslinkbog) are one extreme example of the way in which a business can deliver information through Twitter but plenty of other companies are doing the same thing in very different ways.

Tweets like these might not make the most interesting reading, but when information changes regularly and customers need to be informed about those changes, Twitter can provide a very easy way to transmit updates in real time and improve service to customers.

How Companies and Services Are Providing Automated Updates on Twitter

The business and services that are broadcasting updates on Twitter vary tremendously. The Chandra X-Ray Observatory (@chandraxray), an orbital telescope, regularly tweets its altitude and position, informing

for Success

Broadcast, Don't Chat

One of the challenges with using automated updating systems is that most of the information that streams through Twitter—and across followers' mobile phones—is not going to be relevant to them. Readers are likely to dip in and out rather than follow the timeline closely.

Use one timeline for your community-building but keep your data separate.

Begin Easy

Coding an automated system could be difficult, and if you're going to hire a programmer, expensive too.

Start by entering the system manually into an RSS field to test the reaction. If you find there's a market for this kind of data, then think about automating the process.

(continued on next page)

its 350-odd followers that "Chandra is 79 km from Dao Timmi in Niger, at an altitude of 39,978 km." Heavens Above SF (@abovesf) tells San Franciscans when the International Space Station and iridium flares—the sun reflecting off satellite solar panels—are visible above their city. Heavens Above London (@abovelondon) does the same thing for London's astronomers.

More usefully perhaps, StationPortal.com (www.stationportal.com) provides InternetRadio (@InternetRadio), posting tweets that tell followers in real time what Internet radio stations are currently playing. Wsferries (@wsferries) was created to keep Washington State's ferry passengers informed about cancellations, disruptions and reservations. RedJets (@redjets) provides a similar service for the UK's Isle of Wight ferries, and Syd Traffic-City (@sydtraffic_city) provides traffic updates for Sydney, Australia.

And in an interesting twist, LaundryRoom (@laundryroom) tells residents at OIin College how many laundry machines are currently available, and the library at Waubonsee Community College (@wcctoddlibrary) tweets automatically the most recently checked out "New Book," usage stats from the printers and tosses in quotes from the librarians when not much is happening.

That's a huge range of different purposes served by automated updates. Some, such as the astronomical posts, are intended to do nothing more than provide an interesting service but others, such as the traffic and laundry reports, are meant to make life better for users and bring real benefits both to readers—who, through Twitter, can access the information on the Web or mobile phone—and to the provider who gets to deliver improved services at almost no extra cost.

How to Do It

Creating posts like these can be horribly complicated. The easiest way to do it would be to use a service like Twitterfeed or TwitterUpdater (www.twitterupdater.com) to bring the information into Twitter from an RSS feed.

But someone would still have to type the information into the RSS feed manually.

To create a truly automated system will require some smart coding, and exactly the kind of coding you'd need would depend on the information you'd want to provide. Olin College's Laundry machines communicate automatically with Twitter thanks to smart student programming. To create the same kind of system for your business's updates, you'll need to get to know someone who's handy with code.

Getting Started

That might suggest that the best place to begin automatically creating automated updates on Twitter is to start scouring ScriptLance (www. scriptlance.com) for suitable programmers.

But a better place to begin would be to look at your company to see what kind of information your clients and customers might want to receive.

Restaurants, for example, could tweet each time they took a reservation to let customers know how many slots were still available at certain times of days.

Rental firms could link their inventory software to Twitter to let clients know what kind of vehicles or movies have just come in and which are no longer available.

And no one yet has managed to link their Ebay auctions to Twitter, even though plenty of people are doing it with third-party software. There's an opportunity for professional Ebay sellers!

A Model to Follow

At the moment, most of the automated updates are being delivered by public services such as libraries and municipalities. That's because it's mostly large organizations that have a need to deliver large amounts of rapidly changing information constantly.

The Olin College laundry room is an exception. It provides limited services to a big market and prevents users from having to camp out in the room, waiting for a machine to become available.

That makes it a model for any business in which people have to wait, while the fact that all of its updates are completely automated shows that, once created, the service can be supplied entirely effort-free.

23 PITCH A BUSINESS IDEA ON TWITTER

What Are TwitPitches?

The ultimate challenge for any marketer has always been the elevator pitch. Could they sum up the value of their product in the time it takes for an elevator to finish its journey and the potential client to reach his floor?

Twitter has created a whole new version—and a whole new need—for the elevator pitch.

While it was always very unlikely that a marketer might bump into a potential buyer on the way to fourteenth floor, there are plenty of investors, reporters and customers hanging around on Twitter. Although the best way to build interest in a product or a business on Twitter is over time and through conversation, some twitterers are demanding that businesses pitch to them in one tweet.

That's 140 characters to get your point across.

The advantage, they say, isn't just the need to be clear and concise. It also ensures that the pitch is open and available for anyone to see and comment on.

For public relations professionals pitching story ideas to reporters, small businesses looking to set up meetings with investors at the sides of conferences and for companies hoping to attract the attention of big buyers, TwitPitching can be a simple and effective first move.

How Twitterers a re TwitPitching

TwitPitching is said to have been started by Stowe Boyd (@stoweboyd), a technology consultant who wanted an easy way to arrange meetings

GEEKPRENEUR

with start-ups at a Web 2.0 Expo. Instead of allowing them to clutter up his email inbox or force him to open Word to read their canned press releases, he instructed them to pitch to him on Twitter.

The pitch needed to have up to three stages.

First, companies had to pitch to him directly, describing the product in 140 characters. They could then, if they wanted to, send a second tweet containing nothing but a link that would take Stowe to a website, video, press release or anywhere else. And finally, they would need to send a third tweet suggesting a time and place for the meeting.

It didn't take long for Stowe to receive this tweet on his timeline: "MKraft @stoweboyd #twitpitch: #zude is a social computing platform. Users drag&drop, build media-rich websites. Mashup whole web. Big News @ Expo." It was the first twitpitch and it led to Stowe to set up a meeting with the company.

Later, the addition of a #twitpitch hashtag become incorporated into twitpitches as a standard making them easy to identify and find, while the practice itself spread from Stowe's timeline across the Twitterverse. Reporter Jackson Proskow (@JProskowGlobal), for example, has taken the same approach to invite businesses to twitpitch him their stories while other twitterers are simply adding the hashtag to summaries of themselves or their companies in order to attract the attention of cruising recruiters and investors. Cedric Chong (@cedricchong), for example, wrote this tweet early in his timeline: "specializes in ICT Research, Consultancy and Go-To-Market initiatives across 14 markets in Asia Pacific. #twitpitch."

Although a tweet like that is simple to write, costs nothing and makes the information available, the chances of it being spotted are relatively small. Twitpitches will always be more effective when directed at specific individuals.

How to Do It

Writing the twitpitch itself is simple enough. If you can distil your business, service or skills into 140 characters then you can create a twitpitch. The tough part is recognizing why you'd want to twitpitch and who you'd want to twitpitch to.

for Success

Include a Link

Stowe Boyd's original twitpitch format required the pitcher to include a link in a second tweet. That left space for more characters in the first tweet but it did make things a little clumsy. Using your pitch as a teaser and including a shortened URL so that the reader can learn more is perfectly acceptable too.

Keep it Public

It might be tempting to send a direct message instead of a public tweet, but it's considered bad form on Twitter to direct message someone you don't know. In general, pitches should be public so that other people can pick up on them, but if you want to keep it private, build the relationship first.

(continued on next page)

Although twitpitching started as a way for companies to meet with a tech consultant, the practice seems to have been taken up largely by PR professionals hoping to attract the attention of reporters without having to write press releases.

That may be effective and some reporters are certainly asking to receive story ideas as twitpitches but Twitter does allow any business owner to form a relationship with a reporter over time.

That gradual approach will take longer and require more work, but is likely to achieve better results. The best people to twitpitch to—for whatever purpose—will always be those who have asked to receive twitpitches.

For others, the best use of twitpitches might well be to request them. So companies looking for new employees or freelancers could ask for resume twitpitches and links to where they can see the full details. Reporters, of course, can ask for story ideas, and consultants and investors inundated with requests can use twitpitching to shorten the review time and filter out companies they don't want to see.

Getting Started

How you begin twitpitching will depend on what you want to do with your pitch. Trying to persuade a reporter that you have a story for him will require you first to follow plenty of reporters. You can find them on Twellow and by searching for "article" or "reporter" on Twitter's search engine. You should then search their tweets to see if they're accustomed to receiving twitpitches. Not all reporters will understand what the pitch is meant to be so preserve your twitpitches for those who have asked for them. For those reporters who haven't received twitpitches before, try replying to their twits and building a relationship with them before you suggest your story idea.

A Model to Follow

Because how you twitpitch will depend on why you're pitching, you'll need to choose an appropriate model to follow—and when you're looking for interesting examples, looking not at the people who are doing the pitching but at those who are receiving them will give you a much greater range of tweets.

For businesses, the pitches received by Stowe Boyd and listed not on his timeline—where they can be hard to find—but on his website at www.stoweboyd.com/message/2008/04/web-20-twitpitc.html provide plenty of useful models to follow.

Svetlana Gladkova (@profy), for example, sent this tweet to Stowe and found it good enough to win a meeting: "@stoweboyd Profy is a new blogging platform focused on social aspects of blogging and providing a blogger with all the tools in one place."

It was concise, described what the product does and gets directly to the point. That's all a successful twitpitch needs to do.

Tips
for Success

(continued)

Be Ready to Respond

Reporters in particular are likely to want to move quickly if they like your pitch so make sure you're around to respond to their replies. Make your twitpitch at the beginning of your Twitter session, not the end.

24 ENGAGE YOUR BUYERS WITH A REAL-TIME COMPETITION

DIFFICULTY

SKILLS REQUIRED

INCOME POTENTIAL

What Are Real-Time Competitions on Twitter?

Competitions have long been used as a marketing tool. Instead of giving away lots of low-cost items to anyone who wants them, you give away one high-value item but make potential customers compete to receive it.

Because entrants have to work to win the prize, the reward has a higher perceived value than a freebie. And because it's valuable, the competition can attract a lot of attention. Customers who might not otherwise have noticed a company will notice the prize and the business is able to reach new markets.

Twitter's ability to spread information virally makes it an excellent place to publicize competitions. Firms are using the site to tell their followers about their contests, and those followers often then retweet that information to their own followers, transmitting the company's name across the twittersphere.

In addition though, some companies are also making the most of Twitter's real-time environment to use the site as a unique platform for contests, and create a genuine sense of community among their followers.

Whichever method the company uses though, the result should always be sales, publicity and branding the value of which exceeds the cost of the prize.

GEEKPRENEUR

How Businesses Are Running Real-Time Competitions on Twitter

Most twitterers who place competitions on Twitter are simply using the service to publicize their contest and bring in more entrants. To tell its followers about a competition with a two-night stay in Scotland as a prize, UK Travel (@ukseries) for example, a British travel agency, posted this tweet: "Win a holiday in Scotland... last couple of days to enter. http://bit.ly/N6x4A #scotland #inverness #competition #holiday #hotel."

A tweet like this has a number of elements. It begins by stating the prize, the most important aspect of the competition; the update was posted a day before the deadline to create a real sense of urgency (readers will need reminding as the closing date approaches); it includes a URL to send users to a website; and it's got a bunch of hashtags, including #competition, to make it easy for anyone interested in the topic—or just looking for a freebie—to find.

The London Word (@TheLondonWord), does largely the same thing with this tweet: "Win one night stay at Strand Palace Hotel and see Joseph and the Amazing Technicolor Dreamcoat #London #Competition: http://cli.gs/P657hJ."

Glen Carlson (@glencarlson) though takes a slightly different approach. The prize he was offering was nothing more than payment for a service. He wanted a logo for his business so he used logotournament.com to invite different designers to send in their designs, promising to pay for the best. As submissions came in—and he received around 30—he blogged about them and tweeted about them too: "—my crazy logo designers have added a bit of 'global roaming' to the mix! Final rounds now . . . http://bit.ly/rJxHd."

That didn't just encourage other designers to submit their entries and give Glen a broader range of logos to choose from. It also turned the competition into a kind of reality show. His followers read his blog entries and gave their opinions about the designs he was receiving. Glen ended up with a useful competition and some dynamic, interesting content for his blog and timeline too.

Perhaps the most imaginative use of Twitter as a competition platform though comes from SmartyPig (@smartypig), the timeline of SmartyPig.com, a savings site. The company uses Twitter's speed

Tips
for Success

Keep the Tweets Public

The big advantage of talking about your competition on Twitter is that when people enter by tweeting, everyone can see the tweet. That gives you some very easy viral marketing. Make it clear then that questions about the contest and entries to it cannot be made by direct message. Only you can see those!

Measure the Value

Track the results of your competitions to see how many followers, customers and sales you receive as a result. Because you know exactly how much the prize cost you, you'll be able to calculate how much you're paying for each sale—and whether you're offering a prize that's too valuable.

(continued on next page)

for Success

(continued)

Start Small

Begin with a small prize so that you can gauge the percentage of followers who are willing to enter and retweet. You can assume that a more valuable prize will give you a better response but you'll have a baseline from which to judge the cost of your competition.

to run short, real-time competitions. The timeline builds up interest by explaining when the contest will take place and at the appointed time, tweets a trivia question. To enter the competition entrants simply need to reply to @smartypig with the answer. The first three randomly selected correct entries each won a $100 gift card.

For $300 then, SmartyPig was able to persuade its followers to place its name in their timeline, prompting the followers of those followers to click through and see the company's name. Ben Behrouzi (@BenBehrouzi) used this approach to create publicity for his promotional timeline. He simply asked people to send him a tweet asking to be included in the free draw for a Macbook Air.

How to Do It

The easiest way to run a competition will always be to take it off Twitter. Use your website as the place to explain the rules and entry details, and to talk about the prize too. Set a deadline somewhere in the distance, then use Twitter to keep entrants coming in, update about progress and create a sense of urgency as the deadline approaches.

If you want to run your competition in real time though, you'll first need a sizable number of followers. You want to be certain that enough people tweet while the competition is open to make the competition worthwhile. Test it first with a small prize. Offer a free download or a $25 Amazon gift card to see how many replies you receive. If you only pick up half a dozen or so, you might want to stick to an off-Twitter competition until your follow list builds up. Don't forget that even having 1,000 followers doesn't mean that all of those followers will see your competition.

Getting Started

Competitions usually begin by selecting the prize. The key to any competition is to make sure that the cost of the prize is outweighed by the value of the new customers. That's most likely to happen when the prize is valuable but costs you little. Free copies of your artwork, for example, can make easy prizes. The cost of gift tokens can be measured as accurately as cash—and are almost as desirable. Gadgets can be effective on Twitter too and prizes given away on the site have included a Flip Mino HD Video Camera as well as notebook computers.

You'll then need to decide how long you want the competition to run and how you want people to enter it. Different challenges can work in different ways though. Ask a question related specifically to your business and you'll reward your customers for their loyalty but exclude new customers. Ask the kind of question that anyone can answer and you'll make new leads feel more welcome.

A Model to Follow

When it comes to creating real-time competitions there are fewer more appropriate models than SmartyPig. The timeline runs regular contests and even when it asks questions that reward its loyal followers, it also takes the opportunity to pull new followers into its website. After asking which song was playing in the background during the first SmartyPig winners video in June 2008, SmartyPig gave a clue that the answer was in the blog archive. To win the competition then, followers had to visit the website, already creating value for SmartyPig.

25 TAKE ORDERS ON TWITTER

DIFFICULTY

SKILLS REQUIRED

INCOME POTENTIAL

What is Ordering on Twitter?

Answering questions and chatting with leads and customers, allows twitterers to show that they—and their companies—are approachable, friendly and personable. They can create the kinds of close relationships that lead easily to sales.

But usually, those sales take place away from Twitter.

The limited length of tweets makes closing deals and explaining features just too difficult to do on the site. It's usually more effective to direct followers to a sales page that can take the credit card details.

At least one company though has found a way to prepare orders sent in by twitterers.

How Businesses Are Taking Orders on Twitter

Most businesses aren't taking orders directly on Twitter. Instead, they're taking questions that can lead to orders. Maryann Bjordal (@Marystat), for example, a Norwegian twitterer, quizzed Adaline (@adalinemusic), a Canadian musician, about where he could buy her music. She couldn't provide him with a way to make the purchase over Twitter but she could tell him where he could download her album.

For any business, those are likely to be the sort of questions that should turn up fairly frequently—and should be welcomed. You'd just need to make sure that whoever is running the company timeline is

ⓖ GEEKPRENEUR

able to refer new customers to a sales page as well as answer queries about orders already placed.

CoffeeGroundz (@coffeegroundz) though, a café in Houston, Texas, took a very different approach, even if it wasn't intentional. At the end of October 2008, regular customer Sean Stoner (@maslowbeer) wanted to eat one of the café's breakfast meals but didn't have time to wait for the order to be made up. He sent this tweet to J.R. Cohen, CoffeeGroundz Operations Manager and the person responsible for CoffeeGroundz's timeline: "@coffeegroundz i want to pre order a bkfast wrap so i can zip thru drive thru to get back for gas man. c'est possible?"

The café replied by asking what he wanted on the wrap.

That might well have been the first time that Twitter was used to take an order and it's still noticeable that the payment and collection took place in the real world.

It's not hard though to see how other cafés, restaurants and pizza parlors—and other businesses too—could take orders in the same way.

How to Do It

The hardest part of taking orders on Twitter is likely to be letting people know that they can do it. Tech-savvy users might well be willing to place orders for home-delivered food on the Internet but it's likely that most diners still pick up the phone and dictate their choices to a member of the restaurant staff. It's the only way to be sure that they're getting their pizza without olives but with onions.

Twitter though would allow users to place their order equally efficiently and personally, but it's a new method, so you'd have to tell them how. And because customers are likely to be reluctant to supply their credit card details, even through a direct message, it's an approach that's likely to work best for items that can be picked up in person rather than delivered.

One option then might be simply to invite followers to place their orders ready for collection. Reminding them that an order placed on Twitter would enable them to skip the line could be all the motivation they need to get typing. And you could make the service even more useful by tweeting individual followers when their orders are ready.

Tips

for Success

Make the Orders Public, the Payments Private

The challenge with placing orders on Twitter is that the site is a public environment. That may be good for you: if followers can see that there are plenty of orders coming in for certain items, they may feel more confident about ordering those items too.

But they certainly won't want to make their payment details public too. You'll need to make clear that payments need to be made in person, through direct message or by telephone.

Encourage the Orders with Special Offers

Twitter is a great place for making special offers. Because they can be made in real time you can create a sense of urgency, and because Twitter still feels like an exclusive community (even though it's actually more open than Facebook), followers will feel that they're being rewarded for

(continued on next page)

for Success

(continued)

being part of your club.

Tell followers that you have five pizzas going for a discount and offer them to the next five followers to reserve one each, and you should get orders coming in.

Build a Community

One of the benefits of building a follower list around the kind of business that can receive orders on Twitter is that it creates a sense of community—and a sense of loyalty to the company.

CoffeeGroundz built on that sense of community to organize tweet-ups on its premises. Other businesses can do the same thing.

Getting Started

Perhaps the best way to begin is by asking your followers if this is a service that they actually want and would be willing to use. A polling app like Twtpoll (www.twtpoll.com) could let you gather data about whether followers would be willing to place take-out orders on Twitter if it meant they could skip the line. But you could also learn how many would be prepared to provide their payment details through direct message and take delivery, or even supply a telephone number so that you could call them back and receive payment by telephone.

Once you can see that your followers would be willing to place orders, you can start encouraging them to do so.

Make special offers such as a free soda for anyone who orders a pizza in the next half-hour or provide discounts for on-Twitter orders until customers are accustomed to using the service.

And keep reminding people that they can do it. If an order hasn't appeared in your timeline for a while—and there's a good chance that they'll be occasional—then post a tweet telling people about one delicious item on your menu or one great product that you can prepare, and suggest that they order it now.

A Model to Follow

CoffeeGroundz is the main model to follow for this approach even if its first order was made unintentionally. The order was placed though because a customer felt close enough to the business to ask if it was possible—and that's always a sign of a good timeline.

The reply to the request wasn't just positive though, it was also friendly, personal and public, and CoffeeGroundz built on the discussion that followed the order by organizing tweet-ups and events for its Twitter followers.

Even if it never receives another order on Twitter, that one order alone has given the café a standing with young, tech-savvy customers and made it the main watering hole for at least one kind of customer.

GEEKPRENEUR

PUT AFFILIATE LINKS IN YOUR TWEETS

26

What Are Affiliate Links on Twitter?

The advantage of driving followers to a website is that your own site can offer an endless range of different tools to monetize them. But it's also possible to place at least some of those tools in your own timeline.

One of the most controversial issues on Twitter, for example, is whether it's acceptable to place affiliate links in tweets.

Affiliate links take users to a sales page. Should those users then choose to buy, the seller is able to track the source of the customer and pay the referrer a commission. On websites, affiliate links can be one of the most profitable ways to make money out of visitors.

But affiliate links always work best when they're worked into text and appear as a genuine recommendation from someone the reader trusts. Tweets of just 140 characters aren't long enough to provide the sort of balanced review needed to build that trust so affiliate links in a timeline do run the risk of looking like spam.

That won't just result in a failure to make a sale, it's likely to lead to a loss of followers and could even provoke Twitter into closing the account.

But if it is done carefully, affiliate links may just be one of the most rewarding ways to monetize followers.

What Affiliate Marketers Are Doing on Twitter

Affiliate marketers are working on Twitter in two different ways.

The affiliates themselves are simply inserting a text statement, together with a shortened affiliate link, into their Twitter stream.

DIFFICULTY

SKILLS REQUIRED

INCOME POTENTIAL

for Success

Be Relevant

Only offer affiliate products that are directly related to the subjects of your tweets. If you generally discuss sport or your life as a party entertainer, then suddenly tossing in an affiliate link to a book about working from home might strike your followers as strange. It also won't convert well.

Work the Recommendation into the Conversation

Affiliate links always work best when they come with a recommendation, and that recommendation has to be honest and personal. Instead of thinking of an affiliate tweet as a stand-alone post then consider it as the culmination of a series of tweets that make up a conversation. So you could spark a conversation that describes the success you had recently playing a video game and praise the joystick. When someone asks what kind of joystick you were using, you'll have an opportunity to offer the link.

(continued on next page)

Some sellers though are also providing the tweets to their affiliates. An affiliate with an active Twitter stream is sent a marketing email that includes a link. If the affiliate agrees, he can click the link and an affiliate tweet appears automatically in his timeline.

It's an approach that takes a little preparation and some smart coding. And it hasn't gone down too well among twitterers, mostly because the affiliate tweet itself tends to look too much like a commercial.

But that doesn't necessarily mean that it won't be effective. The ability to persuade a large number of other twitterers to place your affiliate link in their timelines might still produce a large number of clickthroughs and plenty of sales.

How to Do It

The mechanics of adding an affiliate link to a timeline are simply enough. Once you've created an affiliate relationship with a seller—Buy.com seems to be particularly popular with some twitterers—you'll be able to create your own affiliate links (links to a product page that also contain your affiliate number so that the seller can trace and reward you). Toss that link into a URL-shortening services such as TinyURL.com and you'll have a channel through which followers can reach a sales page and earn you revenue.

That's the simple bit. The tricky bit is to insert the link into the timeline in a way that doesn't look like spam and does persuade readers to use it.

There are plenty of examples of the wrong way to do it. Klaatu (@klaatu) is one twitterer who simply tosses affiliate links into his Twitter stream. Although he adds the occasional comment and he doesn't surround the link with hard sales copy, readers have little reason to click the link.

And because they're so dull, followers have little reason to read them either.

A better example is the way in which Scott Jangro (@jangro) worked an affiliate link into his Twitter stream. After seeing a request in a friend's stream about which coffee grinder to buy, a topic that Scott had discussed previously, he recommended the model he owns . . . and used an affiliate link to help others see what he was discussing.

The advantage of this approach was that it was relevant, personal and recommended. The product was related to a topic that Scott's followers were used to discussing and he was able to recommend it honestly.

In general then, the best approach to using affiliate links is to use them naturally. Work them into your conversations so that they look like personal recommendations, not promotions.

Getting Started

Begin by becoming an affiliate. Amazon.com is probably the best place to start, even though the commissions are not particularly high. The range of products is very wide and the brand is trusted enough to make up for the low payments. You can sign up by clicking the "Join Associates" link at the bottom of Amazon's home page.

Once you have your affiliate link, look for requests among your followers for product recommendations. If you can't recommend a product based on your own personal experience then point out that you've heard the product was good. But don't recommend an item if you don't know whether it's worth buying.

Compare Direct Tweets with Indirect Tweets

The two questions surrounding affiliate advertising on Twitter are whether it's acceptable, and whether it's effective. If affiliate advertising is acceptable on blogs there's little reason it shouldn't be acceptable on Twitter too, provided it's done properly. But that doesn't mean it will be effective. One school of thought, in fact, suggests that twitterers are better off linking to a Web page where they discuss the product in detail before providing an affiliate link. Much depends on the topic though so it's worth trying both approaches and comparing results.

A Model to Follow

In October 2008, Internet marketing guru Joel Comm sent an email to his affiliates asking them to tell their Twitter followers that copies of his AdSense book were available for free download. His email also included a link that allowed them place a tweet recommending the book automatically in their timeline.

The promotion provoked some controversy, and Joel conceded that affiliates who had the best results were those who changed the text surrounding the affiliate link and made it more personal.

An alternative approach though is to create a timeline that consists of nothing but personally recommended products. Flashlight Worthy (@FLWbooks) does this with a stream of book recommendations. This approach does require products that need to be refreshed frequently (so coffee machines might not work, but music and computer games could).

It's also worth noting that Flashlight Worthy passes followers through its own website where followers can read more about the product and see a more inviting ad.

27 MAKE DIRECT SALES ON TWITTER

DIFFICULTY

SKILLS REQUIRED

INCOME POTENTIAL

What Are Direct Sales on Twitter?

Twitter has its disadvantages. While the short posts and open reply system make the system easy to use and the conversations available to anyone who wants to join them, 140 characters is not enough to make a persuasive sales pitch.

A website will always be a more effective place to promote goods and take orders.

Much has been made, for example, of Dell's ability to sell around a million dollars' worth of refurbished computers through Twitter. But it sells another $14.95 billion through other channels.

Selling directly on Twitter then means playing to the site's strengths: its immediacy and its directness. Websites, even stores, are only updated occasionally. Twitter though can be updated constantly, allowing followers to feel that they're being told of great deals as soon as they come in.

Users will still need to reach a website to review the product and place their orders but by following a timeline that delivers news of bargains, they can feel that they're being informed of fantastic opportunities.

What Direct Sellers Are Doing on Twitter

There are relatively few direct sellers on Twitter. For businesses, the site works better as a community, branding and public relations tool than as a direct sales channel. Where it is being used to generate direct

GEEKPRENEUR

sales though, twitterers are creating timelines dedicated to bargains and positioning themselves as a source of attractive deals.

Attempting to work direct sales messages into personal timelines runs the risk of making the messages look like spam and putting off followers who will then choose to unfollow.

It is important to note though that the most effective direct sales timelines on Twitter also ensure that their tweets are still personal and directed. They might not place sales announcements around their general tweets but they will place information around their sales messages. And they monitor the twittersphere for questions about the sort of products they have available, and make relevant suggestions that everyone can see.

How to Do It

The methods used to make direct sales vary for individuals and businesses. Large companies using social media for marketing purposes may appoint large teams that work through a number of different sites at the same time, from Facebook to YouTube. NetApp, for example, is said to have diverted 20 percent of its public relations budget to social media while Dell has 20 different Twitter accounts, of which only two are used to generate direct sales.

A business looking to use Twitter as one more sales channel then can create a timeline specifically to announce deals on products, and keep it separate from its news and information timeline. Updates should be made regularly enough for followers to consider it the main source for bargains related to these products.

Clearly then, the company will need a source of bargains and a steady stream of deals and products. For DellOutlet (@delloutlet), which offers refurbished computers, that's simple enough. But in general, this is a strategy that works best for large retailers.

Individuals can earn from direct sales in a similar way by also creating a dedicated timeline. Without a stream of products of their own, they might find it harder to source bargains but an Amazon affiliate, for example, could look for discounted items in a selected category and tweet about them, inserting their affiliate code.

Artists and craftspeople who tweet about their work can also announce that they've completed a work and that it's now available for

for Success

Keep It Personal

Even a timeline dedicated to direct selling still needs to have a personal feel to it. Readers need to imagine that there's a real person behind the tweets, someone they can contact, query and talk to, not some corporate announcement machine. Personal recommendations, comments and asides aren't just fine in a direct sales timeline, they help to make sales.

DellOutlet, for example, frequently answers questions from other Twitterers about specific models and deals, pointing out where they can find them. That kind of public conversation alerts other buyers to the same bargains.

Combine Different Channels

Most direct sellers on Twitter use microblogging as just one method of reaching buyers. They may also have Facebook accounts where they run groups, for example, or encourage buyers to sign

(continued on next page)

for Success

(continued)

up for email newsletters to receive weekly updates. Twitter allows them to talk directly with buyers but the other channels provide a greater range of communication options.

sale. Erick Baque (@Eroica), for example, a fantasy artist and writer, occasionally lets her followers know when a new painting is hung and ready for purchase.

Both companies and individuals though do need to use the first person to make the most of Twitter's personal feel. Even DellOutlet, which is clearly a corporate account, feels like it's coming from a real person—a salesperson.

Getting Started

Companies that already have a stream of bargains about which they want to alert the public need to do little more than create a dedicated Twitter account and start building followers. Usually, that means following others who will then follow you in return, but it's notable that DellOutlet, perhaps the most successful direct seller on Twitter, has almost 120,000 followers but only follows 21 people . . . all related to Dell.

Although it is possible that DellOutlet began by following people then unfollowed once it was strong enough to stand alone so that its other accounts stood out in its follow list, it's more likely that the company's name alone and the value of its offers are enough to bring followers.

Most direct sellers though will need to start following people and posting bargains. Monitoring tweets using a service like Monitter (www.monitter.com), which lets users track keywords as they turn up on Twitter, will also allow them to jump into conversations, make offers and bring in new users.

A Model to Follow

DellOutlet is always going to be the model to follow for direct sellers. That's not just because it's known to have an enviable amount of sales but also because its timeline is a great example of how a commercial timeline should operate.

Although the posts are business-oriented, directing customers to the products they want to buy, promoting the company's email newsletter and announcing bargains, Ricardo Guerrero, who created the account, also manages to keep it personal. Followers find it approachable enough to ask direct questions—and he answers them.

Those principle will always form the foundation of a successful sales timeline.

Amazon's Twitter service (@amazon) doesn't do that, and suffers. Instead of setting up separate timelines for different product categories so that followers only see tweets on subjects that interest them, the company offers products that range from vegetarian cookbooks to clothes to computer accessories. Most of the tweets appear to be automated and none of the tweets are replies to potential customers.

The service was only launched in mid-February 2009, making Amazon relatively late to Twitter and it's possible that the company will improve but in the meantime, the absences from Amazon's timeline provide great examples of the importance of communication and directness—as well as attractive offers—when selling through Twitter.

28 CREATE PROFITABLE EMAIL LISTS WITH TWITTER

DIFFICULTY

SKILLS REQUIRED

INCOME POTENTIAL

What is List-Building on Twitter?

An active timeline filled with interesting tweets and discussions with followers will create a close community around the twitterer's brand. That's a valuable asset but it still has to be monetized, and on Twitter, that's not always easy.

One hundred and forty characters is not a great deal of space to make an offer or deliver a sales pitch.

That's why it often makes more sense to approach a community of followers away from Twitter and through a traditional system.

There's nothing particularly new about email marketing. What is new is the ability to use Twitter to harvest those emails, and online marketers are doing it in all sorts of creative ways.

What Twitterers Are Doing to Build Lists

Twitterers are using a range of different tactics to persuade their followers to leave their email addresses on websites.

The simplest strategies involve nothing more than creating a tweet telling their followers about the site and urging them to sign up. DMI (@DMIEvent), a firm that trains disaster management professionals, simply posted a tweet that said "Don't forget to sign up to our training sessions August 11-13" and included the link. Interested followers would no doubt register; casual followers or those unwilling to commit five months in advance would have ignored the tweet.

Internet marketer Taheera Tucker (@TaheeraT), however, created a sense of urgency with her invitation. She tweeted: "If you like to make money I highly suggest checking this out http://www.knowledge exploit . . . Next Big Launch is March 14th! Sign up 4 free."

By writing her tweet the day before her "Next Big Launch" Taheera forced her followers to decide quickly to sign up, and by mentioning that registration is free, she suggested that her followers will be receiving something of value for nothing.

An alternative approach is actually to give away something of value in return for signing up. Blogger and investor, Ernie Varitimos (@AppleInvestor), urges his followers to register by promising them a free investor report every trading day and a free Zen ebook that they can download.

How to Do It

There are two important factors to bear in mind when trying to persuade people to sign up on a website.

The first is the offer. People will only be willing to hand over their email addresses—and risk filling up their inboxes with unwanted messages—if they feel they're getting something they want in return. Lots of Twitter-based marketers emphasize that what they're offering is "free." But Internet users have long expected everything they find on the Web to be free.

Much more effective is to stress the value of the information they will be receiving. Emphasize its rarity, its effectiveness and the extent to which it has the potential to help the reader achieve his or her goals.

The second thing to consider is that on Twitter, hard selling doesn't work. That's what makes the offer so important. Readers of your tweets will be following you because they consider you a friend. They find your tweets interesting, they want to learn more about the information you make available through your posts, and they want to have the opportunity to discuss your topics with you directly.

The tweet that invites followers to register needs to look like it's doing the followers a favor . . . and the sign-up page itself should also be as personalized as the tweets. Ernie Varitimos' registration page at www.zacharybass.com/about/subscriptions/sign-up, for example, continues to use the first person, just like his Twitter timeline.

for Success

Use Double Opt-In

The biggest risk involved in using Twitter to harvest emails is that once you start sending out emails, you'll be accused of sending spam. Few things kill a marketer's reputation faster than an accusation like that.

Use the double opt-in method that requires subscribers to click a link in an email before they're added to your list and make it clear that you won't be selling your list but that you might be informing them of special offers as they turn up. And don't forget to include an unsubscribe link in every message you send.

Make the Reward Clear

When followers are already receiving good information from you through Twitter, they might wonder why they should bother signing up to receive more information by email.

Emphasize the length of the information that they'll be receiving after registering. Ebooks are a good reward. They pack far more detail than a

(continued on next page)

Tips
for Success

(continued)

140-character tweet, can be used to promote other goods and services, and they're relatively cheap to produce.

Don't Push Too Hard

No one on Twitter likes a hard sell, but followers will register because they like you. Keep even the squeeze page personal, and be prepared to discuss the newsletters and books that followers will receive after registration. It's a much more natural way to arouse curiosity and raise interest.

Getting Started

You'll need a few things before you can begin collecting emails of followers on Twitter.

You'll clearly need a lot of followers, but you'll also need a registration page, the ability to collect and store email addresses, and a reward for signing up.

The registration and database will take a little programming but the requirements are fairly clear. If you can't do it yourself, there are plenty of programmers available who can and quite a few website plugins that can do the same thing too.

Much harder will be preparing the reward. The easiest option is to issue an email newsletter at regular intervals that provides solid information while also leaving room to make profitable offers. Those offers could be products from your own site, but they could also be affiliate products created by other companies.

Of course, once you have those addresses, you can also send unique marketing messages whenever you broker a deal or release a new product.

A Model to Follow

Ernie Varitimos at @AppleInvestor provides a great model for anyone looking to turn followers into email-based customers. As befits someone who mentions on his bio that he's a Zen Buddhist, Ernie's strength lies in his holistic approach.

All the parts of his timeline work together to inspire followers to sign up.

So the tweets he provides in his timeline offer truly valuable information: stock tips and financial analysis, which suggest that his email-based material will be even more valuable. Most of his tweets too are conversations with other twitterers, rather than broadcasts, an level of engagement that is more likely to build the kind of close relationship that translates into responses. And Ernie doesn't push his registrations hard, relying instead on the power of his free gifts and his own personality to build registrations.

PUT ADS IN YOUR TIMELINE

What Are Timeline Ads?

DIFFICULTY ➡

SKILLS REQUIRED ➡

INCOME POTENTIAL ■ ■ ➡

Twitter itself currently makes money only by going cap in hand to investors. That's changing but in the meantime, some smart companies are looking for ways to incorporate ads directly into twitterers' timelines, generating a commission for themselves and paying the twitterers for the space and the opportunity to place sales messages in front of their followers.

Magpie (www.be-a-magpie.com) invites twitterers to sign up on its website. Using AdSense as a model, it then attempts to match the keywords in its ad inventory to the main subjects of twitterers' timelines. Advertisers pay on a cost-per-mille basis (as opposed to only paying when someone clicks on a link in the ad), so twitterers are paid based on the number of followers they have.

All advertising messages contain "#magpie" so that readers can see that they're advertising messages, and account holders can choose the frequency with which the ads are shown. The default setting is one ad for every ten tweets that they post themselves.

The idea of incorporating ads into Twitter is, however, controversial. Twitter is a conversation more than a magazine so ads may be more annoying in a timeline than on a Web page. The effectiveness of the ads still isn't clear, the reaction of followers may be to turn off—at least until the ads become widespread—and initially, at least, inventory may be so small that ads aren't particularly relevant. A quick search for the latest ads to appear on Twitter seemed to bring up frequent jewelry ads, a tea promotion and some tech ads, and they appeared even on time-

for Success

Track Your Followers

Unlike other ad systems, optimizing your Magpie ads won't earn you more money but it should help to prevent you losing money by keeping your followers on board. Just as smart publishers track changes to their pay-per-click ads to make sure they're bringing in as much money as possible, so smart Magpie users will need to track their follower numbers to make sure that their ads—and the way they're using them—won't reduce their readership.

Pay Attention to What Comes Before and After the Ad

Blending ads into a website is always a key element of optimization but Magpie's ads don't allow the same sort of color, font and positioning options common in other ad systems. Instead, you'll have to make sure that the timeline resembles the ad by posting similar tweets around it.

(continued on next page)

lines that appeared to have little connection with the subject beyond an occasional related reference.

Nonetheless, the money may make signing up worthwhile. Magpie provides an estimate of future earnings based on the size and topic of the Twitter account. Mark Hopkins (@rizzn) of Mashable was told that his 3,500 followers could bring him as much as $200 a month. Although that's not going to allow him to give up his day job, it would be a nice monthly bonus for tweeting—something that he was planning to do anyway.

Provided, of course, that the ads don't bring that number of followers down.

What Magpie Publishers Are Doing to Maximize Their Timeline Ads

At the moment, there seems to be little evidence that twitterers are doing anything to optimize their income from Magpie. Most have simply signed up for the service and allowed Magpie to place its ads in their timeline.

That's likely to be a mistake and one that's likely to be rectified the more advertisers—and publishers—sign up.

How to Do It

Earning from Magpie is as simple as signing up at www.be-a-magpie.com and choosing how often you want to receive your ads.

Earning without irritating your followers though, will take a lot more effort.

Online publishers have generally found that advertising systems pay best when they're used carefully. The ads need to match the content and the units need to be blended into the page.

They also need to select the right number of units for the page of content.

GEEKPRENEUR

But optimization is usually important for ads that pay-per-click. If the publisher doesn't make the ads visible—while making them appear as useful as content—readers won't click and the publisher won't earn. Publishers are motivated to optimize.

The fact that Magpie's publishers earn regardless of whether anyone clicks might suggest then that they have little reason to consider how their ads appear. But too many ads in a timeline, and especially too many irrelevant ads that contribute nothing to the twitterer's statements and replies, are likely to reduce the number of followers. Twitter users have already reported unfollowing people who use Magpie. That will lead to lower income and more importantly, weaken the power of a timeline.

At the moment, too few people are using Magpie for different strategies to have been tested and for the best practices to have emerged but it's likely that Magpie will be least disruptive in timelines that contain plenty of links and hashtags. Although each Magpie ad is prefaced by "#Magpie," the presence of similar-looking tweets should help the ads to blend into the page without looking disruptive.

Getting Started

Begin by registering at Magpie's website. Make a note of the number of followers you have before the first ad appears. The risk of using Magpie is that your followers might be put off by the ads so you'll need to know how much damage—if any—the ads are causing.

It might also be a good idea to choose the least frequent option available on Magpie initially, at least until your followers are used to seeing the ads.

You'll need to approve the ads before they appear which will give you an opportunity to make sure that they're appropriate, and to create tweets of your own that resemble them.

Tips
for Success

(continued)

In the run-up to the appearance of an ad, create other tweets that contain hashtags and links so that the Magpie ad doesn't stand out too much on the page.

Work on your Followers

The two criteria used to price ads are the topic of your tweets and, more importantly, the number of followers. There are probably too few advertisers to make targeting high-paying keywords worthwhile, but it will always pay to dedicate a certain amount of time to building your followers.

On average, you can expect Magpie to pay just under two cents a follower.

A Model to Follow

Although few twitterers have so far bothered to optimize their Magpie ads, one twitterer who has produced a stream in which the ads are well-blended is Dave Weinberg (@Daves_Deals).

The stream offers little more than a series of Twitterfed posts from a number of different sites around the Web. Although it's not personalized and there's little sign that the timeline is being used to converse rather than announce, it does have a little under 700 followers. (It's uncertain though how many of them are actually reading the posts.)

More important is that the tweets that Dave posts look very similar to Magpie's ads. But Dave's timeline streams nothing more than ads. Donna Jackson (@wisequeen) uses her timeline to chat and discuss. She manages to blend her Magpie ads by the simple expedient of choosing an ad that fits her timeline: an ad for tea.

TURN YOUR BACKGROUND INTO A PAYING BILLBOARD

What is a Paying Background?

Magpie places ads in twitterers' timelines but the timeline isn't the only valuable spot on a Twitter page. Users have already discovered the value of the background as a place to list their URLs, place their own and product images, and build their brand.

The space on the left of the timeline is a useful piece of Twitter real estate.

Twittad takes this principle one step further, by allowing twitterers to rent out their background. They can make their pages available, list the number of followers they have and the length of time they want to rent their page, and demand a fee.

At the moment, prices do not seem particularly high but range quite broadly. Sales appear to have been made at levels from one to ten cents a user and, more interestingly, for durations that range from one week to one month with little change in the overall price of around five to seven bucks.

That might reflect the uncertainty surrounding the value of this kind of advertising. Unlike most online advertising systems, including Magpie's, Twittad cannot allow users to click through the ad, making effectiveness difficult to measure and forcing the advertiser to rely solely on the ad's branding power.

And while timelines with lots of followers can charge more money, advertisers are aware that not all followers look at the pages of those they follow, preferring instead to read their tweets in a client such as TweetDeck.

DIFFICULTY

SKILLS REQUIRED

INCOME POTENTIAL

Tips
for Success

Count the Costs

Advertisers can ask Twittad to create their ads for them but few of the backgrounds are as attractive as those twitterers have been creating for themselves. They also prevent the twitterer from providing more URLs to their own website. The o pportunity cost involved in taking a background f rom Twittad needs to be weighed up against the small payments you could receive in return.

Create Dedicated Timelines

Rather than place an ad in your own timeline, a better option might be to create special timelines that earn from advertising. Focus your tweets on a topic so that it becomes a source for information, news and comments on that subject. You'll keep your personal timeline clean while being able to earn relatively easily from background advertising.

But it does appear that some sales are being made even if they're not being made for giant sums. For twitterers looking to monetize a commercial timeline then, Twittad could well be one option to add a little more cash each month.

What Publishers Are Doing to Earn with Their Backgrounds

There are still relatively few Twittad backgrounds floating around on Twitter, suggesting that the idea still hasn't entirely taken off, neither among twitterers nor among advertisers.

Interestingly though, those timelines that are using the system are often those with an obviously commercial bent and which have names such as CafePharma (@cafepharma) and TravelSaving (@travelsaving). Other timelines that have been selected by advertisers were those with a clear theme.

In general, the more targeted the subject of a timeline's tweets, the greater the chances of finding an advertiser, and the more the publisher will be able to charge.

How to Do It

Signing up for Twittad is simple enough. But like any advertising system, the real challenge lies in making the most out of it. While it is possible to simply place your timeline on Twittad and make it available for sponsoring, advertisers will want to make sure that they're putting their ad in front of people who may become customers.

Dina Fierro (@eye4style), for example, one of the first people to rent out her background through Twittad, describes herself in her bio as a "beauty and fashion blogger." The fact that her 1600-plus followers are people looking for style advice—and not just information about what she's eating or doing right now—made her timeline attractive to IndieSmiles (www.indiesmiles.com), an independent fashion site.

That's certainly one way to make the most of Twittad: create a timeline that's dedicated not to what *you're* doing but to what a particular sector is doing, such as fashion, sport or stocks. You might include relevant RSS news feeds in your timeline as well as your own comments on the latest events.

Look for people who have used related keywords in your tweets and add them as followers to build your own follower list.

Sometimes though, even a criterion that appears to be fairly irrelevant can be enough to win the attention of an advertiser. Sandra Staub (@spot23net) won an a placement from the Germany-USA Career Center based, apparently, on the fact that she tweets in English to a primarily American audience even though she's based in Germany.

The question that anyone considering using TwittAd needs to ask though, is whether it's worth it. With typical prices as low as one to two cents for a follower, you'd need over a thousand to make more than about twenty bucks a month. At the same time, you'd be giving up real estate that could bring benefits of your own and damaging the appearance of your Twitter page.

A better strategy then might be to create half a dozen or so commercial timelines dedicated to particular topics, supply them mostly with RSS feeds to make the updating as simple as possible, and follow widely to bring in followers. Although there's no guarantee that you will manage to sell advertising space on those pages, they could net you a total of a hundred or so dollars a month.

Getting Started

You can sign up for Twittad at www.twittad.com. After completing the registration form, Twittad will tell you whether your timeline matches one of its categories. If it doesn't, you'll need to add it to Twellow, a kind of Twitter directory.

Twittad will then provide a valuation of your timeline through its site whatsyourtweetworth.com (www.whatsyourtweetworth.com). It's not entirely clear what it's basing its valuations on but the figures do provide a general guideline for the amount you might want to charge.

Finally, you'll be able to describe yourself on the site in a way that appeals to advertisers (make your timeline's topic clear) and even include an AdSense unit with your information to pick up a little extra income.

A Model to Follow

Dina Fierro's timeline at @eye4style is a good example of a Twitter account that's capable of attracting advertisers. The bio makes clear that it's about beauty and fashion, and she's active enough to indicate that her timeline has a number of dedicated followers. It contains a combination of conversations with followers, comments about fashion and links to her own blog.

Those users of her blog may be important too. By allowing advertisers to see more information about the sorts of topics you're likely to cover, you make it easier for advertisers to understand what sort of followers they're likely to be marketing to. You will also help them to feel that they're getting a bargain. A cost-per-mille ad on a website may cost a great deal more than the five or ten dollars for two weeks or even a month that you could be receiving from Twittad, even though they're placing their name in front of the same people.

Cafepharma also provides a good example of a dedicated commercial timeline. Linked to a site for pharmaceutical sales professionals, the timeline uses news feeds from Twitterfeed for hands-off updating, and has rented out its background through Twittad.

GEEKPRENEUR

HELP CHARITIES ...
AND ADVERTISE
YOUR BUSINESS

What is Advertising Your Business by Helping Charities?

The main problem with advertising on Twitter is that the site works best when twitterers use it for personal communication. While websites and blogs are fairly static, tweets are conversational. Twitterers tweet, reply and discuss.

And just as few people would enjoy talking to someone who repeatedly tells them to try a product for which they receive a commission, so inserting ads in to a timeline may be regarded as rude and disruptive.

Unless it's done for a good cause. AdCause (www.adcause.com) gives twitterers who are willing to rent space on their timelines the opportunity to donate some of their profits to a list of charities. These include the American Red Cross, the American Cancer Society, National Endowment for the Arts and CarbonFund.org. On registration, you can choose the percentage of your profits that you want to give to each.

Of course, you could do this with your profits anyway if you wanted to, in which case you wouldn't be restricted to AdCause's lists. But at least the donations are automated and it might just prevent a few followers from running away at the sight of your ads.

The remainder of the system though works in a very similar way to Magpie. Publishers sign up, describe their timelines and select the duration and frequency of the ads they receive. They can also set their own fee, and it's interesting that the prices here seem to range even more broadly than on Magpie. While one twitterer with just over 800 followers is demanding $150 for a month's placement every ten tweets,

DIFFICULTY

SKILLS REQUIRED

INCOME POTENTIAL

Tips
for Success

Invest in a Good Profile

To attract advertisers you'll need a good timeline, which takes time and effort to create. But you'll also need a good adspot description and bio. Don't pass directly over those. Empty fields or descriptions of what you look to do in your spare time rather than information that's relevant to advertisers will make them feel that their placement won't be effective.

Give Away (Some of) the Profits

AdCause differs from Magpie in making it easy for publishers to donate percentages of their profits to a range of different charities. You might prefer to choose a different charity of your own but tell your followers that the ads that appear in your timeline support a charity and you should reduce the number that choose to unfollow.

other twitterers are demanding $7.50 for a similar duration every fifteen tweets to just over 600 followers.

Advertisers can look for suitable placements from among the twitterers available, reject the price demanded and make an offer of their own, and insert their ads into that twitter's timeline. The ads come without a revealing hashtag but you can expect them to have a link.

What Charitable Publishers Are Doing on Twitter

One of the advantages of AdCause is that the site is very friendly for advertisers who can easily browse the list of publishers. In addition to the price the twitterer is demanding and the duration and frequency of the ads they're prepared to run, advertisers can also see the number of followers each publishers has and the number they're following.

Those two figures are important. Advertisers know that an easy way to build up follower numbers is to follow a lot of people and hope that they follow in return. They're also aware that just because someone has chosen to follow a timeline doesn't mean that they'll actually read the tweets. A timeline with a large number of followers but which follows a small number of people is likely to have interesting content and followers who actually read the tweets.

Creating a timeline that's that interesting isn't easy to do. It's usually done by people who already have a standing in their field, even if it's only as a blogger. People will follow them because they expect to receive inside information from an expert.

Much easier is to create a bio and adspot description that stands out on the list of publishers and attracts attention. Not all twitterers are doing this but those who are doing it are using a number of different strategies.

In the adspot description, for example, publishers tend to point out the frequency with which they post—an important metric not otherwise obviously available to publishers—and describe the subject of their tweets. Some also point out that their tweets are republished on other social media sites such as Facebook, and also appear on their blog, increasing the number of viewers.

That's all valuable information that may help to justify the figures of $150 and even $750 demanded by some twitterers.

The bio too, which appears as a floating layer when the advertiser places the cursor over the TwitterID on AdCause, allows publishers to offer additional details about themselves, including keywords that advertisers might want to target. Not placing such a bio makes a publisher look less than serious.

How to Do It

The registration process is simple but to stand a good chance of being targeted by advertisers, you'll need a timeline that's updated regularly and has plenty of followers.

The best way to make a timeline work is always to build relationships with people. Reply to tweets, ask questions, create connections and become the center of a network of like-minded people.

Twitter is something like a party, and the twitterers whose timelines will be worth the most to advertisers will be those who can dominate their corner, draw a crowd and keep them attentive.

Publishers on AdCause do ask for relatively large sums but to justify those demands, they need to create good content and market themselves carefully and seriously on the site.

Getting Started

You can sign up at www.adcause.com as both an advertiser and a publisher. The registration process is straightforward—if a little buggy—but little help is given to creating an effective profile.

That's important so take the time to search as an advertiser to see how other publishers are presenting themselves. You should find that it doesn't take too much to stand out and draw the attention of advertisers.

A Model to Follow

DaniellsDesigns (@DaniellsDesigns) is the timeline of a jewelry artist and photography student who uses her timeline to promote her Etsy store. She also tries to earn as much as she can through advertising on Twitter.

So her background has been bought by Twittads, which uses it to promote their services, and ads for AdCause turn up every ten tweets.

But DaniellsDesigns' tweets, which have just under 10,000 followers (she follows slightly more), are engaging. She takes part in conversations, talks about her designs and to customers, and perhaps most importantly, also throws in the occasional advertising tweet for one of her own products: "Etsy sellers!!! wear your shop on your wrist! http://tinyurl.com/djueac."

The result is that while followers can still feel that they have an opportunity to talk to the artist, they also recognize that the stream is commercial . . . and the ads from AdCause look like a natural part of her timeline.

EARN FROM ADS IN YOUR TWEET LINKS

32

What Are Ads in Tweet Links?

Ever since Twitter hit the headlines with its award at the 2007 SxSW event, people have been wondering how the service will find a way to make money. Will it put ads in timelines? Will it charge for corporate accounts? Will it force users to pay per tweet?

Twitter's founders, happy with their private investors, have always been cagey, saying that they're focused on building up users and getting the service right but in the meantime, other companies are exploring a number of different options, some of which are less intrusive than others.

HootSuite (www.hootsuite.com) is a remarkably useful Twitter app that lets twitterers manage multiple accounts. That's hugely valuable for business owners that might have personal twitter accounts, marketing accounts and customer service accounts and want to be able to post to all of them without having to log out and log in again.

But since March 2009, HootSuite also allows its users to earn from AdSense. The ad itself doesn't appear in the timeline but in the bar that appears at the top of the page when a reader clicks a link shortened by HootSuite's URL shortener.

That keeps the ad unobtrusive: it doesn't appear in the timeline itself. On the other hand, the ad will only be shown to people who click the link, its location in the top right-hand corner of the page may mean that it's easily missed, and more worryingly, HootSuite also says that half the time, it will place one of its own AdSense units in that slot in order to keep the service free.

DIFFICULTY

SKILLS REQUIRED

INCOME POTENTIAL

Tips
for Success

Optimize the Format

One of the most effective ways to improve clickthroughs on AdSense units is to blend the unit into the page. Users tend to ignore ads, but if they feel that the information in the ad unit is part of the site, they're more likely to click the link.

Google allows AdSense publishers to change the ad units' color schemes

(continued on next page)

Tips

for Success

(continued)

and even the font of the ads. NDTravel was smart enough to make use of this option, changing the background color from the standard gray to white so that it looks like part of HootSuite's bar and not like an ad. In general though, it's a good idea to keep the links blue—it's what users expect—but the best results come when the ad format matches the content on the Web page.

Follow the Stats

AdSense lets you create channels so that you can track the results of your ad optimization. Create a channel for your HootSuite ads and you'll be able to see exactly how many clickthroughs your receiving each time the ad is shown. Combine that information with the statistics provided by HootSuite and you'll be able to see which tweets generate the most ad views and which kinds of ads generate the most revenue.

Go for the Retweets

AdSense units usually only pay a few cents for each

(continued on next page)

Nonetheless, Google's AdSense is probably the most reliable and effective advertising system on the Web, and the service costs nothing. If you're going to include links in your tweets, then this could be a good way to earn from them.

What Link-Based Advertisers Are Doing on Twitter

By March 2009, HootSuite's 15,000 members had served over 1.6 million shortened URLs. Each time a reader clicked on one of those links, they were taken to a page topped with a bar that included an ad for a charity. They can also now include a half-banner Google AdSense unit.

Although Google has done an outstanding job of matching ad inventory to the content on a website, the challenge with AdSense has always been to optimize the ads so that they blend into the page and invite clicks. There are numerous strategies to do that and HootSuite's users are only now beginning to figure out what works best on Twitter.

One strategy is likely to be the frequency with which the ads are served. Both ArsenalFans (@arsenalfans), a stream that provides information about the Premier League soccer club, and NDTravel (@NDTravel), which tweets about travel locations, include a shortened link in each of their tweets. Those links include AdSense, increasing the chances that if one tweet doesn't result in an ad click, another will.

The quantity of posts then—as well as the quality of the content on the Web page—will be an important part of earning with these AdSense units. That's particularly true when half of your ads will only benefit HootSuite.

How to Do It

Placing your ad in your HootSuite bar is reasonably simple. Register at www.hootsuite.com and add all of your Twitter profiles. That won't help directly with your AdSense earnings but it will mean that you can easily include your AdSense units on all of your accounts.

You'll then need to click the Settings tab at the top of the page, paste your AdSense code into the field provided and choose which accounts will include ads in their links. Clearly, the more accounts on which you place AdSense units, the more you're likely to earn. Click "Save Google AdSense" and when you place a shortened URL in your tweet, your ad will be served—half the time.

Getting Started

To begin earning with AdSense in the links you place on Twitter, you'll first need an AdSense account. You can sign up at www.google.com/adsense. The process can take a day or two so use that time to read Google's Terms of Service carefully. AdSense pays a small amount of money for each click on an ad so it's important not to click your own ads or encourage others to do so for you. Either of those actions will get you banned from AdSense very quickly—an expensive mistake.

Once you're approved, you'll be able to choose your ad format, receiving a few lines of code that are intended to be pasted into a website. AdSense has a huge range of different formats to choose from, but HootSuite allows just one kind of ad in its bar: the half-banner.

That's the code that you'll be pasting into your HootSuite account and which will be generating the ads that appear in the bar.

Tips

for Success

(continued)

click so they work best on sites with lots of traffic. Few twitterers though have more than a few thousand followers of which only a fraction will click on the link. Only a fraction of them will click the ad—and half of the ads they see will benefit HootSuite.

To try to expand the range of your ads then, urge your followers to re-tweet the post with the link. The ad that appears will still be yours but every re-tweet will put the link in front of another audience.

A Model to Follow

DiscoverWine (@discoverwine) is an example of one very easy way to profit from AdSense in HootSuite links. The timeline itself consists of little more than announcements from blogs and websites about wine. Sometimes the tweets contain the hashtag #wine for easy searching but none of them appear to contain any original content. The timeline simply acts as a kind of RSS feed for wine enthusiasts who want to be informed about wine reviews and articles.

That makes the timeline very easy to produce . . . and very easy too to replicate across a range of different fields. So it would be possible to create a series of timelines about beer, vegetarian cuisine, coffee, tea and bread, draw up a list of websites about each topic and tweet about new content on each site.

Using HootSuite, it would be possible to manage all the accounts from one place, and it's even possible to schedule the tweets in advance. Once you've built up a strong enough follower list, you wouldn't need to do any more than spend an hour or so every day adding the day's tweets . . . and wait for the checks to arrive from Google.

33 MEASURE YOUR MARKET WITH TWITTER POLLING

DIFFICULTY

SKILLS REQUIRED

INCOME POTENTIAL

What is Polling on Twitter?

Twitter's user base can make a fantastic source of knowledge. Whether you point your question at one particular expert or ask all of your followers and invite answers, you should be able to find solutions to a wide range of problems.

And trolling the site for keywords related to your business should give you an idea of what people are thinking and saying about your products and services.

But sometimes you want a general answer to a specific question. You want to conduct a poll to discover which of a number of options customers or users would like the most.

On websites, that's always been possible to do with a simple polling script. It's now also possible to conduct the same kind of multiple choice poll on Twitter . . . with one advantage. As the question is passed around the site, not only will you be picking up more answers to your question, you'll also be spreading the name of your business across Twitter.

It is important though to remember that Twitter users are a fairly self-selecting bunch of people. A professional polling company would make sure that the answers it receives come from a representative sample. On Twitter, you're only going to be receiving responses from people tech-minded enough to use the site.

While that might limit the usefulness of the responses, it should still provide a valuable way of picking up some helpful information—and employing some viral marketing too.

How Twitterers Are Polling on Twitter

Twitterers are generally taking two approaches to using Twitter to create polls. Perhaps the simplest is to create the poll on a website and use Twitter to bring in some extra votes.

This is the approach taken by Paige Waehner (@exerciseguide), About.com's exercise guide and a personal trainer. Each week, she places a poll on About.com, and uses Twitter to promote it.

The kinds of questions that Paige asks though are really a service to her readers. Questions like "Do you exercise when you're sick?" or "How is the economy affecting your workouts?" enable her readers to see other people's answers. In effect, she's using a poll as another form of content, and Twitter as a source of readers.

Twitterers who are really looking for usable information and want it specifically about other Twitter users tend to use a Twitter-based tool, such as Twtpoll (www.twtpoll.com).

This is a free app that allows you place a question in your timeline with a link that brings people back to Twtpoll's website to choose the answers. While it's possible to market the question page separately, the advantage of Twtpoll is that it's focused primarily on Twitter's users. The kinds of questions being asked through Twtpoll range from simple decision-making such as whether to buy a computer game or save up for a vacation, to which kind of programming language a tech twitterer's followers tend to use.

How to Do It

Creating a question on Twtpoll is very simple. The app asks you to enter your Twitter name, then create your question in 140 characters. That's not always easy, so you might want to think carefully about the phrasing.

You'll then be able to place the answers in a separate field, using individual lines for each answer choice. You can enter as many answer choices as you wish and even allow respondents to select more than one answer.

Then it's a matter of clicking the "Create Poll" button and waiting for the answers to roll in. As they arrive, they'll appear as a pie chart which also displays the number of votes for each answer choice.

Tips

for Success

Create Large Samples

The biggest disadvantage of using Twitter for polling is that the sample is going to be relatively small and unrepresentative. The advantage though is that it's fairly simple to broaden the sample, and in doing so market your own business too.

Simply asking your followers to retweet your question is one strategy that you can use and adding #twtpoll to your question will also make it easy to find on search results. There may well be people who want to read the latest questions created on the site and see if they can answer them.

You could also try picking a particularly contentious issue. Sports questions do well because fans have strong feelings, even if there's no scientifically correct answer. Questions about which programming language or content management system tend to get plenty of answers too because developers can be loyal to one or the other.

(continued on next page)

Tips

for Success

(continued)

Find a controversial issue to ask your followers and you'll learn a little more about them and there's a good chance that your question will be passed around by each side too in the hope of ensuring that their side wins.

Keep the Question Simple

It is noticeable that many of the polls on Twtpoll have had relatively few respondents. One of the reasons may be that the follower list was too small so few people saw it but another may be that the question was too complex. The easier the question is to answer, the more answers you'll receive. More than three answer choices is too many.

Getting Started

With the help of Twtpoll, creating a poll shouldn't take more than a few minutes. Much harder will be coming up with a meaningful question that can help your business and which people will also be willing to answer.

Those two points aren't unrelated. Followers are most likely to take the time to answer if they feel that their responses are going to have an effect. They want to believe that they're contributing to something valuable.

Unless they're making their opinions known about sport, which turns up frequently in polls and picks up good responses.

It's also noticeable though that interspersed among questions about teams and predictions are plenty of tech questions too, such as Mike Ellis's (@dmje) simple "Joomla or Drupal?"

Drupal won big, which might not say much about Joomla but it does say something about Twitter's users . . . especially as the poll received about 150 more responses than Mike has followers.

A Model to Follow

ClickOptimize (@click_optimize) is a Web design and online marketing company that also created one of Twtpoll's most popular polls. The question itself was very simple. It asked respondents to choose of two YouTube videos they preferred: "Which of these two videos do you like more? #lonerider"

The videos were promotions for a local beer company. The hashtag made the question easy for the beer's loyal customers to find while the two answer choices contained links to two one-minute clips which were short enough to enjoy without demanding a great commitment from the viewer.

The result was that ClickOptimize was able to get an objective opinion about two marketing options.

No less importantly, it was also able to spread both its own name and the name of its client across Twitter.

GEEKPRENEUR

PASS OUT TWITTER COUPONS AND LAND MORE SALES

34

What Are Coupons on Twitter?

Dell put Twitter on the map as a business service with the revelation that it generated over a million dollars issuing discount coupons across the site. But Dell isn't the only firm to recognize the value of offering exclusive deals to the kinds of customers who are so loyal that they're willing to follow the company's posts.

Other businesses, from travel companies to online retailers, are also interspersing their tweets with special offers that reward followers, make them feel as though they're part of an exclusive club and which generate sales.

Twitter might have been designed as a way of telling other people what you're doing, but when it's used by businesses as a way of telling their customers how they can purchase goods cheaply, it's been proven to be extremely beneficial—and it's a system that can be easy to use too.

DIFFICULTY

■ ■ ■ ➤

SKILLS REQUIRED

■ ■ ➤

INCOME POTENTIAL

■ ■ ■ ■ ■ ➤

How Twitterers Are Issuing Coupons

Twitterers are generally using two approaches to issuing coupons on the site. DellOutlet (@delloutlet), for example, simply places codes in its tweets, and suggests that twitterers enter the discount code when they make their purchase.

The link in the tweet leads to the product page.

An approach like this works well for Dell because followers know that they can expect to see discounts in the company's timeline and because Dell already has sales pages available for all of the products in its inventory.

Tips
for Success

Customize the Coupon Page

TwtQpon allows users to redesign their coupons to match the look and feel of their own websites. There is a fee for this service but you can pay as much or as little as you want, so the results should always cover the costs.

The advantages are that the coupon will look more professional, more trusted and more persuasive. You'll be able to remove twtQpon's logo from the top of the page (although a smaller version will still appear at the bottom of the page), replacing it with your own. You should find that overall, you make more sales.

Use #twtqpon

While some twitterers may look for polls to review, even more are likely to search for coupons to use. Include the hashtag #twtqpon and make your offers easy to find.

(continued on next page)

For smaller firms though, creating special squeeze pages to convert leads with discounts may take some effort. Many twitterers then are using TwtQpon (www.twtqpon.com) to issue their Twitter-based discount coupons.

Created by the same people who provide TwtPoll, TwtQpon lets twitterers post a tweet that describes the discount, adding the discount code and a link. They can also upload an image. The tweet appears with a shortened URL that takes the reader to a page designed to look like a traditional coupon. The coupon is decorated with the uploaded image and contains a button linked to the seller's website where users can make their purchase and redeem their discount.

For an extra fee, sellers can also customize the coupon page to make it look like part of their own website.

How to Do It

Like Twtpoll, TwtQpon doesn't require registration. Anyone can reach the site, enter their Twitter name, type in their coupon title then make their offer in 140 characters. Upload an image and add the URL of the sales page to create the coupon itself, then it's just a matter of adding an expiry date to create a sense of urgency and hitting the "Create a Twitter Coupon" button.

All that's left will be for you to collect the orders and ship the products.

That's the easy bit. TwtQpon makes the coupon itself a breeze to create and place online.

The hardest part of making a discount offer on Twitter though is knowing which items to offer and ensuring that as many people as possible reply to them.

One way in which Dell adds a little power to its coupon codes is by warning its followers that a new discount is about to be released. Before it posts its new discount code, Dell Outlet might send a tweet that says something like "Another Twitter Exclusive coupon coming! Not combinable w/other coupons, valid online only, limit 2/redemption."

That's an approach that not only creates a sense of anticipation about forthcoming discounts but it also entices followers to retweet, virally marketing the offer.

Getting Started

Creating coupons on Twitter begins not with the coupon itself but by choosing the right product.

Combining different Twitter strategies can be very helpful here. Use Twtpoll to ask which of your products your followers find most appealing or how much they would be willing to pay for them, then use the results of the poll to choose the appropriate products and discount size.

So you could run one poll that asked "Which of these products would you most like to buy?" and list three of your top-selling items in the answer choices. When you have your result, you could then run a second poll that asked, "How large a discount would persuade you to buy ___?" and offer three different sized discounts in the answer choices to get an idea of how many extra sales a 10, 15 or 20 percent discount code would produce.

When you finally create the discount code itself using TwtQpon, you'll already know what to expect.

A Model to Follow

Although it's certainly a good idea to keep an eye on the way Dell Outlet (@delloutlet) uses coupons another good example comes from The Franklin (@thefranklin), a science museum in Philadelphia.

Like Dell Outlet, The Franklin too creates anticipation by announcing in advance that a coupon code is coming. When the coupon is placed on the site though, not only does the offer provide real value, it's made to look like a special reward for the museum's Twitter followers: "BUY 1 GET 1 FREE— TWITTER EXCLUSIVE DISCOUNT (EXPIRES 4/3/2009) @ http://twtqpon.com/l3gt6v #twtqpon."

The hashtag makes the coupon easy to find, even by people who aren't following the museum's tweets, the expiry date creates urgency, and even the use of upper case makes the coupon stand out against the museum's other tweets.

for Success

(continued)

Build Anticipation and Urgency

Discount coupons may well work by themselves but there are a couple of strategies that will increase their power. The most frequently used is to limit the validity of the coupon. You want people to decide to buy now ... before they forget. TwtQpon allows you to enter an expiry date on your coupon so use that option to limit the discount for just a few days and force your followers to make their purchase as soon as they see the coupon.

You can strengthen that sense of urgency by making the offer feel like a rare event. When DellOutlet announces that a discount is coming they make it feel like a special occasion— and again, something that people should make the most of.

35 TAKE DIRECT PAYMENTS ON TWITTER

What Are Direct Payments on Twitter?

DIFFICULTY

SKILLS REQUIRED

INCOME POTENTIAL

Twitter doesn't allow its users to send text messages longer than 140 characters so it's not surprising that it also doesn't provide a way for twitterers to transfer money across the network.

TipJoy (www.tipjoy.com) is one service that aims to fill the gap.

Twitterers don't actually send payments—or even payment details—through Twitter. Instead, they announce through a tweet that they're paying another twitterer a certain amount of money, usually less than $10 and often a micropayment of around $1. TipJoy records the promise and credits the funds to the recipient. That recipient can then either extract the funds or pass them along to someone else.

Payments can be entered into the system by creating an account at TipJoy and transferring money by credit card or from Paypal. The site itself earns revenue by charging a 3 percent transaction fee.

That fee though is only levied when the credit is extracted as cash. So someone who receives money through TipJoy and uses it to pay someone else pays no fees. But someone who regularly cashes in their credits could find themselves losing 3 percent of their income to TipJoy.

That's painful enough—although no more painful than receiving money through Paypal—but even more difficult will be persuading people to send you the money in the first place.

How Twitterers are Collecting Payments

The format for sending money through TipJoy is very flexible. For the payment to be completed, tweets need to contain a payment keyword, a transaction amount, and a recipient. The keywords are: 'rtip', 'p' and 'give' (which can occur anywhere in the tweet) and 'tip', 'pay' and 'tipjoy', which must occur within the first three words of the tweet.

The transaction amount must be preceded by a dollar or pound sign or be followed by 'c' for cents or 'p' for pence.

The recipient can be a Twitter username beginning with @, a URL beginning with 'http:' or an email address. Often payers will also indicate the reason for the payment.

So a typical TipJoy payment might look something like this: "p $1 @geekpreneur for great blog post."

In theory, TipJoy's payments can be made in return for anything, and the site discusses the possibility of being credited for Web content as one example. In practice, persuading Internet users to pay for anything is difficult and most of the uses appear to focus on charity fundraising. TwestivalFM (@twestivalfm), for example, raised around $5,000, much of it through TipJoy. Trading Goddess (@tradinggoddess) asked her followers to donate through TipJoy to help someone in need to buy a cheap car. She even used TwitLonger.com (www.twitlonger.com), a service that allows people to post messages longer than 140 characters to explain in more detail: "Would someone care to @tipjoy me $25.00 for my friend's car I will give you th... Read More: http://is.gd/tfvV"

Some brave souls though are trying to receive commercial payments through TipJoy. Swedish singer Sofia Talvik (@sofiatalvik) posted that she was considering receiving payments for album and mp3 sales through Twitter with TipJoy. There's not a great deal of evidence to suggest that many people are lining up to buy her music through the service, but it's hard to say if that's because of the music or because they prefer not to use TipJoy.

Another creative use came from Almighty God (@almightygod) who asked for tips in return for forgiveness: "Anyone interested in buying indulgences? For a small price you can have a sin forgiven. payments via http://tipjoy.com/."

How to Do It

Making payments on Twitter is very simple but there's a good reason that most of the payments made with TipJoy on the site have been for causes: you can't deliver the goods on Twitter.

Tips
for Success

Give Away Value

TipJoy makes asking for money easy, and it makes pledging money easy. But it doesn't make persuading Internet users— a group of people who have become used to receiving content for free—easy. One way to get around that is to give away products on your site that appear to have higher value. Instead of asking for a tip for your content, suggest that people pay a dollar or two to download an ebook, a report or a music track.

The content could be the same—or just a little longer—but because it's downloaded instead of read online, it feels more valuable.

Give to Charity

Tippers will also give to charitable causes, whether those are organizations such as Wikipedia or individuals in need. Tell people that you'll be a donating a percentage of the tip to a charity, and you might just be able to up your conversion rates.

So asking people to donate a small amount to help someone in need or to support a good cause can be very effective because the payer doesn't expect to receive anything in return. And the pledge itself is very quick and simple to make (although feeding money into the system itself could take a little while longer)

While a fan may be tempted to pay an independent artist for her songs through Twitter, most people prefer to pay through the same channel they use to pick up the product. TipJoy though does supply a range of APIs and buttons that sellers can place on their websites, allowing their users to make the payments on their site.

Users can click on the button and make the pledge through Twitter, allowing TipJoy to record the transaction and credit your account.

All you'll have to do is give them a reason to make the payment.

And that's the really difficult bit. Tip jars on websites aren't new. Bloggers have been asking for payments through PayPal for years . . . and on the whole, not receiving them. Ads tend to bring in much higher payments. But if you have a lot of users and they're generous types then you might be able to pick up a little extra cash with TipJoy.

Getting Started

To start collecting money with TipJoy, you don't really need to do any more than ask for it. You don't need an account or register with Tipjoy to begin receiving funds.

If you do sign up though, you can add a button or a create an API to place on your site . . . and hope that people pay.

A Model to Follow

Most of the money transfers—or at least transfer pledges—made with Tipjoy appear to have been spontaneous. Twitterers are promising funds to good causes or to friends who have given good advice because they feel like it and because it seems fun.

The only working model for demanding money is Trading Goddess's request for donations towards a cheap car for someone in need. Commercial recipients tend to rely on buttons and the generosity of their readers.

MARKET AN APP, EARN AS AN AFFILIATE

36

What Are Affiliate App Earnings?

TweetLater (www.tweetlater.com) is a Twitter API that offers twitterers a wide range of features intended to make tweeting easier. They allow twitterers to automatically follow people who follow them, track keywords and unfollow automatically those who stop reading their posts.

Most significantly, it also allows twitterers to schedule their tweets.

Although most tweets will be posted on the spur of the moment, being able to book posts in advance can be very helpful, allowing at least part of a timeline to run automatically. Some twitterers have used the service to plan posts of tweets that contain affiliate links while David Griner (@Genny_Spencer) has even used the service to post a 70-year-old line-a-day diary written by a relative without having to post daily.

Much of TweetLater's functions are free but the company also offers a wide range of additional services for a monthly fee of $29.97. As subscribers, TweetLater's users can manage multiple Twitter accounts; view tweets written by selected followers; colorcode their tweets; delegate tweeting to support staff and ghostwriters, and much more besides.

In effect, the program offers a complete production and management suite for Twitter.

And to bring in buyers, TweetLater also has an affiliate program that pays 40 percent of the subscription fees of referrers and 5 percent of the earnings generated for referred affiliates.

You might not be making money from your own tweets, but you'll still be making money from Twitter.

DIFFICULTY

SKILLS REQUIRED

INCOME POTENTIAL

for Success

Make Recommendations

The best way to increase affiliate referrals is always to actively recommend the products you're offering. Review TweetLater, explain how it works and tell your followers the results you're having with the service.

And be honest. If TweetLater isn't helping, no one will pay for it anyway. If it is helping, then sharing the news will only help to deliver sales.

Target Your Audience

Your Twitter followers will be one audience that's easy to reach but to put your affiliate link in front of people who aren't yet following you on Twitter, you'll need track them down.

Keyworded articles will help and so will contributing to forums but you can also try creating miniblogs that focus on Twitter issues and placing your affiliate links there.

How Affiliates Are Earning Affiliate Revenues by Marketing an App

Almost immediately after TweetLater launched its affiliate program, twitterers began complaining that direct messages containing affiliate links for the site were turning up in their inboxes.

Even TweetLater thought that was a bad idea.

Direct messaging has became the chosen channel for all sorts of automated messages and spam too. They don't just allow the sender to talk to a follower confidentially, they also allow the sender to post sales messages without filling their own timeline with sales material.

The result is that direct messaging has become almost entirely ineffective—and that applies equally to TweetLater affiliate links sent as direct messages.

But clearly, Twitter users are going to be the prime market for TweetLater affiliates. Place a link on a website and you can't be sure how many of your users will have a Twitter account. Put a link on Twitter and you can be certain that all your followers have one!

Shelagh Jones (@shelagh) placed an affiliate link to TweetLater in her timeline, allowing everyone to see it. That can be difficult. In general, ads in timelines are obtrusive and not very popular with followers. Shelagh got around that problem though with a tweet that put the affiliate link into an account of her own experience—exactly what tweets are supposed to contain: "I've just upgraded to TweetLater Pro—works really well, especially as I've Twitter account for each business. http://bit.ly/A2Za."

It is notable though that immediately after posting that tweet, Shelagh was criticized for not pointing out that the link generated affiliate earnings. Responding to those criticisms gave her another opportunity to recommend TweetLater: "Hi! Should have said—link to Tweetlater is affiliate link. Free version's good, Pro is much better, with free trial for 7 days at moment."

Of course, none of that means that you can't place affiliate links on websites. MerchantCircle Marketing Advisor, Bob Centracchio, placed an affiliate link on a forum in response to a marketing question, and pointed out one of the system's benefits: "I have over 1300 contact on twitter http://twitter.com/nomad1ne I can connect with and Twitter on Auto Pilot! Cool stuff . . . take a look . . . free tiral offer!"

And that's always going to be the best way to benefit from an affiliate link, whether it's placed on Twitter or on a website: make a genuine recommendation of a product that you enjoy to people who trust your opinion, and you should find that you generate referrals.

How to Do It

Anyone can register for TweetLater's affiliate program but while picking up your code will be relatively simple, generating referrals will take some skill. Although all of your followers will have Twitter accounts, only a small percentage of them will have the kind of business accounts that make paying almost $30 each month worthwhile. And it's likely that you'll have far more readers on your website or blog than followers on Twitter.

The best strategy then might well be to promote TweetLater both on Twitter and on your website.

On Twitter, talk occasionally about the benefits of using TweetLater. Show your followers how it works, mention when you've used it and share your experience with it. If your followers feel that your tweets are teaching them something, they'll feel easier about seeing your affiliate link placed alongside those messages.

And the same is true on your website. Write articles that talk about twittering in general and TweetLater in particular. Describe what you're doing with it and teach people how to make the most of the service. You might well find that you're picking up both referrals and new followers.

Getting Started

You can sign up for TweetLater's affiliate program at www.tweetlater. com/affiliates. You'll just need to complete a number of basic fields and enter your PayPal details to receive your affiliate code.

At the moment, TweetLater doesn't seem to have any buttons, badges or banners to promote its service but there's no reason why you couldn't create your own to add to your Web pages as well as inserting text links into your articles and tweets.

A Model to Follow

There are few good examples showing smart placement of TweetLater affiliate links but Shelagh Jones tweets did do a couple of things worth copying: they recommended TweetLater based on her own experience with the service; and they were served to a targeted audience. Do both of those things, and you should be able to pick up some regular referrals.

GEEKPRENEUR

SELL YOUR TWEETS AS A BOOK

37

What is Tweet Publishing?

Tweets are perhaps the most disposable of literary forms. Although Twitter keeps posts in its database apparently ad infinitum, and it's possible—and sometimes necessary—to search through the archive of old updates, tweets aren't really meant to stick around. They're intended to be read as they're posted . . . and then forgotten.

In part, that's because tweets aren't meant to have a narrative. They simply describe what you're doing at one particular moment or they share your opinion about some particular issue.

That might mean that reading all of a timeline's tweets from beginning to end could be pretty dull. But it's possible that Twitter won't keep every tweet forever, and there's always the chance that your tweets could be lost.

There is also the possibility that with a bit of careful editing, people might actually want to read all of your tweets, especially if they're filled with interesting insights and valuable information.

It's unlikely that you'll be able to persuade a publisher to bring out a copy of your tweets—you'd certainly find it a hard sell—but it is possible to self-publish your tweet book. You could then give them away as bonuses on your website and at your talks, hand them to clients or even try to sell them.

How Twitterers Are Publishing Their Tweets

Very few twitterers are taking the time and effort to produce books of their tweets. One person who has done though is James Bridle (@stml), a former publisher. He used Lulu (www.lulu.com), a print-on-demand

DIFFICULTY

SKILLS REQUIRED

INCOME POTENTIAL

for Success

Publish the Discussions

Because many tweets are responses to other people's posts, a timeline only shows one half of a conversation. That can make for some pretty surreal reading. One solution is to ask your conversation partner if you can include their tweet in your book so that readers can follow the discussion. They're unlikely to refuse, but you should ask.

Create a Twitter Diary

There are all sorts of ways to edit your tweets but one option is to extract those tweets that function as a diary and turn those posts into a narrative arc. Even in a Twitter book, readers will want a beginning, a middle and an end.

(continued on next page)

publishing service, to produce a single copy of what he describes as the first volume of his tweets in order to see whether it was possible to "make a traditional diary/journal in retrospect."

His conclusion was that it was possible, even though the kerning—the space between the letters—did come out a little strange.

James had no desire to sell his book and admitted that it would have made little sense to anyone other than himself, but it did generate plenty of interest from other twitterers, including some requests from people who wanted to hire James to create their books for them.

How to Do It

While print-on-demand services like Lulu and Blurb (www.blurb.com) make printing the books very simple, extracting all of your tweets from Twitter does take a little skill.

The simplest option is to continue hitting the "More" bar at the bottom of your timeline to pull up your tweets at a rate of 20 at a time. Select all and you'll be able to copy all of those tweets . . . together with Twitter's navigation links, your bio, timestamps and your follower data. You would then need remove all of that extraneous data using your text editor's Find and Replace function.

James Bridle however wrote a short script which pulls down all of the tweets automatically at a rate of 2000 an hour. His book consisted of 4100 tweets and stretched to 270 pages, so the text for a similarly-sized book would take around two hours to produce using this method. James makes the code available at http://booktwo.org/files/booktwo-gettweets.txt.

To use it, you'll first need to register to use Twitter's API at http://apiwiki.twitter.com —and know what to do once you get there.

Or alternatively, if you don't want to cut and paste your tweets or fiddle with the code yourself, the API page lists developers available for independent work. One of them should be able to help you for a small fee.

Once you have the raw text, you'll need to edit it by making sure the tweets are in chronological order, removing timestamps—they'll still show up even in James Bridle's script—and perhaps deleting tweets that aren't relevant.

That's perhaps the toughest part of turning your timeline into a printed book. A volume that included every tweet you posted would be accurate but it might not make for a particularly interesting or useful read. One that only included your wittiest aphorisms or your discussions related to your particular topics could be more valuable but demand more careful editing. You'll need to know what you plan to do with your book so that you can create the sort of content that will do the job.

And finally, printing the text is fairly simple. A 250-page hardcover book, with dustjacket, will cost about $23 to produce through Lulu and requires little more than uploading your files. Blurb (www.blurb.com) requires users to create their books with its own software and a similar book would cost a little more at $26.95 for 241-280 pages.

Getting Started

The act of publishing your tweets in book form begins with extracting your text from Twitter's website—either by copying and pasting or by using Twitter's API. But the process itself should begin before you start putting in the work.

You first have to know what you want to do with your book.

Most twitterers who print out their tweets will want to do it to preserve their posts for themselves. Online text is ephemeral; a book can last forever. If you want to make money out of your book though, you'll need to work a little harder. You'll need to produce a volume that other people want to read.

A book that reveals how to complete certain kinds of tasks—selling software, building decks, writing code, etc.—and written in 140-character stages might sell, for example. Discussions about how you overcame a life challenge such as an illness could work too.

You can also think of your book as a branding tool, something you can give away to clients and customers. Whatever you plan to do with your book, make sure you know its intended use before you create it.

Tips
for Success

(continued)

Ditch the Chronology

Twitter publishes tweets in chronological order, but you don't have to. Another way to publish your tweets is to group them by subject. That might make the book easier to use and the information more valuable.

A Model to Follow

James Bridle is the model to follow and you can see photographs of his "Tweetbook" in the Books collection of his Flickr stream at www.flickr.com/photos/stml. James only created one copy and it was only intended for his personal use but he has created a method that others can follow.

James' choice of bookcover is particularly notable. He took a picture from the New York Times Review of Books, which would have given him some copyright issues if he had decided to distribute the book, but it does show the importance of using a good cover.

Just make sure that yours isn't protected by copyright!

GEEKPRENEUR

CREATE
—AND SELL—
A TWITTER APP

What Are Twitter Apps?

While Twitter has been focusing on creating a service that simply allows users to post and read messages, other developers have been using Twitter's API to expand the range of features available for the site.

The list of applications already available is enormous. Twitter's Fan Wiki at twitter.pbwiki.com/Apps lists hundreds of them from Twitter desktop clients like Ada (madan.org/ada/) and TwitTray (kwitcherbitchen.org/twittray) to Diabetes Tracking tools and YiqYaq (www.yiqyaq.com) which turns tweets into audio channels. Altogether, more than 2000 apps are believed to have been created by Twitter's fans.

In practice, only a fraction of them are in regular use. Timestamps in timelines show not just when a tweet was posted but which app the twitterer used to write the post. Clients like Twhirl, Tweetdeck and Tweetie turn up far more frequently than Toro for Twitter or P3:PeraPeraPrv.

Developers might be finding Twitter's API relatively simple to use and the site's growing user base a tempting market but they still face the challenges of persuading people to use their app . . . and even harder, monetizing them too.

With a good idea, a friendly interface and impressive design though, both are possible and have happened. If you're a developer with an idea or have a plan and are prepared to work with a programmer, it could happened for you too.

DIFFICULTY

SKILLS REQUIRED

INCOME POTENTIAL

Tips
for Success

Think about the Money

Creating a Twitter app might be fun but it will certainly be hard work, and if you're not a developer, you won't be enjoying that work either. As you think about how you'd like the app to function, make sure you also include how you want the ads to appear, whether you can sell it as an iPhone app or the chances that people will actually pay to download it to their desktops. (It would need to be exceptional to do that!)

Solve a Problem

Twitter bought Summize because the company's own search engine was pretty poor. It made more sense to buy a good one than to create a new one from scratch. Look for firms that could link up well with Twitter, build an app that bridges the gap between them, and there's always a chance one of the two companies will bring you on board.

How Twitterers Are Creating Apps

Apps are created using Twitter's API at twitter.pbwiki.com. Anyone can register, join the community and start creating their tools. For developers, it's all very straightforward, fun and challenging.

For Twitter users who don't know the difference between an API and an apple pie though, it all looks horribly complex and a surefire way to make millions of people angry by breaking Twitter. (You can't do that, but you can get very confused.)

Although the apps themselves are created using a range of different programming languages (Ruby on Rails is particularly popular, and Air often turns up as a platform), the monetization strategy is fairly uniform.

Most apps don't have one.

Like Twitter itself, the bulk of apps appear to have been built with little thought given to how they might make money. The result, of course, is that few do. They fulfill the developer's goal of meeting a coding challenge, helping others to get more out of Twitter, and perhaps providing a showcase for the programmer's skills and talent. But they don't deliver revenues.

There are exceptions however. Just as one top app on Facebook has been reported to pull in funds of over $700,000 a month, while others are said to top a million dollars in monthly income, so a few app developers on Twitter have managed to turn their tools into cash.

Usually, that means waiting for a large company to buy them out. Twitter bought Summize, for example, integrated its search engine into the site itself and took on the five developers who created it as employees. Seesmic, a company that specializes in video-based social media, bought Twhirl.

A number of companies are also looking at other revenue models such as advertising and paid downloads. HootSuite takes 50 percent of the income from AdSense units placed in its browser bar, and Twittelater offers an advanced version of its iPhone client for $4.99.

How to Do It

Apps are usually created by the developers who came up with the idea but if thinking is more your thing than coding, then it is possible to work with developers who are ready to code for cash—or, if you can persuade them that the idea is good enough, for a partnership.

Once the coding is done though, the real work begins. You have to market and monetize it.

The best form of marketing for a Twitter app is always going to be viral on Twitter. Ask tech-minded twitterers with large followings such as Stephen Fry and Robert Scoble to test-drive your app—or even less famous users with large followings—and tell their followers what they think. Make sure it's added to the wiki's list and push the website too.

Ultimately, good apps should sell themselves. Summize wasn't the first search tool available for Twitter. But it was the best, and that was what delivered the buyout.

Relying on a big company to make you an offer though is a pretty precarious route. It's much better to look at ways of making money yourself then hope to make your life easier by taking all the cash in one go if someone does come along. Twittelator's (http://www.stone.com/iPhone/Twittelator/) use of a free model that lets people get used to the tool and enjoy using it, then offering an advanced model that costs a fee is one good way to turn an app into cash. Advertising, when placed unobtrusively, can also work but does require lots of viewers to generate reasonable amounts of revenue.

Getting Started

There are so many apps already available for Twitter that it's best to begin not by registering for the API and starting to code—or look for a developer—but by looking at the apps available and trying to spot a gap in the market.

That gap could be a need that no one is meeting but it could also be a service that simply isn't working as well as it should. Either way, there's little point in creating an app when there's a good one already available!

A Model to Follow

The best model to follow when creating an app is probably HootSuite. That's not because it's made the most money. Summize might well hold the record for that although with no statistics publicly available, it's hard to tell.

But HootSuite has produced an app that's genuinely useful, was good enough to win a Shorty Award for Best App, and it's also found a way to monetize its service.

Regardless of what your app does, that combination of usefulness, customer loyalty, publicity and a monetization strategy will all go a long towards ensuring that your app brings in revenues.

GET REAL
FINANCIAL AID

39

What is Financial Aid?

DIFFICULTY

➡

SKILLS REQUIRED

■■➡

INCOME POTENTIAL

■■■➡

Financial aid is money provided by colleges and the Federal government to help students pay tuition fees and meet their living expenses. The amount provided and whether it's paid in the form of loans or grants varies from school to school, as do the requirements.

In fact, financial aid can be both hugely important in determining where a student can study and horribly complicated to win. Just as taxpayers turn to professional accountants to make sure that they pay the lowest levels of tax possible, so many parents turn to professional financial aid advisors to make sure that their assets are arranged in a way most likely to deliver the largest amount of assistance.

The difference between a carefully submitted report and one completed without a great deal of care can be several thousand dollars each year the student is in college.

There are plenty of sites on the Web that deal with financial aid, explain how the system works and what parents should be doing. But like taxes, financial aid differs from family to family.

Websites provide general information but Twitter can allow a parent to keep up with the latest developments and, more importantly, talk to a financial aid expert directly.

How Twitterers Are Finding Financial Aid

In February 2009, Christopher Penn (@cspenn) a financial aid expert, was invited to take questions from callers during a broadcast on

for Success

Use Twitter's Experts as Guides, Not Gurus

The sorts of questions that parents and students will have about financial aid are likely to require long, complicated answers. Twitter isn't really the forum to go into a great deal of detail, which may be why experts tend to take the questions off the site and onto their own websites, or even onto televisions shows.

Perhaps the best approach then is to consider the experts on Twitter not as sources of information but as people who can tell you where to go to find the information you're looking for.

You'll have to do a little more work, but you're less likely to be disappointed by the results.

(continued on next page)

CNBC's "On the Money." He posted a tweet inviting parents trying to adjust their financial aid mid-year to contact him to ask their questions on-air. Blogger Susan MacDowell saw the request and sent him her brother's details. Her brother called into the show, Chris gave him some tips and an hour after sending an email to his daughter's college using those suggestions, he received a message back from the college informing him that the award had been increased.

That was a very concrete example of how Twitter helped someone to save thousands of dollars, but it was also relatively rare. More usually, the conversations take place on Twitter itself. Concerned parents read the tweets posted by financial aid experts and ask them questions directly. Christopher Penn even invites parents to tweet in their questions with a hashtag so that he can answer them in his regular podcast.

With Twitter providing an open environment in which it's easy for anyone to find a relevant expert, it's no wonder that parents are using the site to ask financial aid experts about their situations.

How to Do It

Twitter might be an environment in which anyone can meet and contact almost anyone else but the communication channels are fairly limited. Financial aid is a complex thing and the kind of questions that parents and students run into while completing their FAFSA are unlikely to be answered in 140 characters.

Usually, that means that the sort of answers financial aid experts provide tend to point to places where they can find more information rather than go into the sort of details that can solve a specific problem.

To get the most out of the financial aid experts on Twitter then, keep your initial question general. Make it a question that the expert should be able to answer fairly easily and in doing so, help others—and show off his own knowledge too.

Once you've done that, you can try shooting him or her a direct message with your specific question.

Having already entered a discussion with you once, there's a greater chance that the advisor will be willing to address your query, or at least tell you where you can look to find the answer.

Getting Started

Using Twitter as a source for information about financial aid begins by finding experts to follow. Twellow is a good place to look, and you can find a reasonable list under the category "Financial aid."

Twellow lists twitterers in order of the number of followers so those at the top of the list are likely to be the people supplying the most useful information. Christopher Penn's information, for example, is always helpful, and he has been known to respond to other people's tweets even when they haven't contacted him directly. When Jamie Trias tweeted that she wouldn't be able to go to college without a full scholarship, he responded by sending her a free book that he hoped would help.

Once you're following the financial aid experts on Twitter—and the list of active professionals isn't huge—read the tweets for a while (they're packed with interesting information) then shoot out your question to one of them.

If you don't receive a reply try direct messaging another of them. Repeat the question too many times in your timeline and not only will your tweets look dull but other experts will feel that if someone else didn't answer you, they should probably avoid the question too.

And for these types of issues, direct messaging might be more appropriate anyway.

A Model to Follow

Susan MacDowell's brother wasn't on Twitter and he didn't see Christopher Penn's tweet himself. But he does provide a model to copy for two reasons.

First, he wasn't afraid to ask a question even though he might have found it a little embarrassing.

More importantly though, he put the advice that he heard into action right away. Financial aid doesn't have to be too complicated but the deadlines are important and it often pays to move quickly, file early and implement professional advice. Susan MacDowell's brother did all of those.

Tips
for Success

(continued)

Read the Tweets

Financial aid isn't something that tends to change dramatically, but it is affected by the economy, by changes in the law and by the colleges themselves. Reading the tweets of financial aid experts—and even the timelines of the colleges—can alert you to changes in deadlines, as well as to new and unclaimed scholarships.

Sometimes reading can supply as many answers as asking.

Follow Parents and Students

Financial aid experts tend to be experts on financial aid as a whole, but you can also ask questions of students who have gone through the process at the college you're applying to. Twitter is also a great place to form of a community of parents.

You might well find that they're the biggest experts of all.

40 WIN EYEBALLS WITH A TWITTER NOVEL

DIFFICULTY

SKILLS REQUIRED

INCOME POTENTIAL

What is a Twitter Novel?

SMS-sized messages might not appear to be the best medium for a novel. It's hard to build suspense and atmosphere in 140 characters, and persuade people to keep reading. But it's happening. In Japan, half of the ten best-selling novels of 2007 were delivered through mobile phones, many of them written not by established writers but by teenagers texting between classes.

For readers, keitai shousetus (as mobile phone-based novels are called in Japan) are a convenient way to read fiction. They can dip in while standing on the train, reading the story in short bites and without having to carry a book around. For authors, they represent a particular type of literary challenge. The stories can be delivered directly to an audience but they have to be created in tiny, laconic segments that enable new readers to join in and follow easily.

As always with novel-writing, the monetization is going to be even harder than the writing. Only a small percentage of traditional novels make money. While a number of Japanese mobile phone stories have sold well, there's no sign yet that any of the Twitter-based novelists have generated income from their stories.

But some of them have developed relatively large followings, allowing the writers to tell publishers that they have an audience. The novels themselves could later be printed as books, and it may be possible to link to ad-supported websites or use product-placement.

GEEKPRENEUR

How Twitterers Are Writing Novels

There are a number of twitterers writing novels on the site and in a number of different ways. N.L. Belardes is creating Small Places (@smallplaces), describing his story in short sections of text.

Matthew Richtel, a New York Times reporter, is taking a slightly different approach by writing a novel in real time, and Novels in 3 Lines (@novelsin3lines) is posting three-line narratives in the style of French writer, Felix Fenéon.

Most interestingly though, UK publishing company Penguin experimented with a project called "We Tell Stories," placing six books by six different authors on LiveJournal, Google Maps and Twitter. The Twitter-based story, available at @Slicequeen was perhaps the least successful. The author created two different accounts—one for the main character and one for the character's parents. But the largest of the two still only gathered slightly more than 100 followers.

How to Do It

The size of the tweets is a challenge but it's not the biggest difficulty with story-telling on Twitter. One of the biggest criticism's of the Twitter-based Penguin story, Slice, was that readers coming in late had to catch up by reading the episodes in reverse chronological order.

Not only do readers have to put up with 140-character chapters, they also have to endure reading a book backwards.

As we'll see in the next chapter, a better approach then may be to look not at novels on Twitter but at characters. Fans of television shows have created timelines for their favorite characters, including Peggy Olson (@peggyolson), Don Draper (@_DonDraper) and a couple of Betty Drapers (@BettyDraper and @Betty_Draper) from the AMC show Mad Men. Unlike the novels on Twitter, these timelines don't have a storyline or a narrative arc so readers aren't forced to search back through old tweets and reconstruct the plot. Instead they attract readers based on the strength of the characterization, allowing them to dip in and out without worrying that they missed the beginning or can't return if they're away too long.

for Success

Think of Soap Operas, not Novels

It's not the size of the posts that's the problem for Twitter-based novels but the fact that people will be coming in in the middle of the story. Soap operas and television drama shows have solved this problem by creating strong characters and multiple, overlapping storylines. When thinking about how to structure your Twitter-based novel, look to soaps and dramas like *The Sopranos* and *Mad Men* to see how the writer's cope with latecomers.

Use HootSuite

HootSuite is an invaluable tool for Twitter-based fiction writers. It will let you handle multiple accounts and also to send out tweets at fixed times. Instead posting your story in blocks of tweets, you'll be able to prepare them in advance and spread them out during the day.

(continued on next page)

The biggest challenge though will be monetization. There is currently no model for successfully monetizing a Twitter novel, but other twitterers have used methods that could be used in a Twitter-based novel too. While Magpie's ads could be seen as too intrusive by readers, Robert Scoble has allowed product placement in his timeline—a practice used on the YouTube drama LonelyGirl15. It would also be possible to expand the story beyond Twitter, including links to ad-supported websites.

Getting Started

Creating any novel always begins not with the first words but with planning the storyline and defining the characters. For a novel that is going to be based on Twitter, that's particularly important.

You'll need to know who your characters are, how you'll cope with a Twitter timeline's reverse chronology and whether your story will have a traditional beginning, middle and end or meander on based on the strength of its characters.

Once you've created the framework for your story, you can then create the Twitter account, paying particular attention to the bio and the background to give your novel atmosphere, and start tweeting.

And finally, you'll need to bring in followers. You might want to wait until you have a few tweets up first before you do that—so start the novel slowly—then follow readers of other Twitter-based novels and anyone working in the story's subject area.

A Model to Follow

Slice might not have worked as a Twitter-based novel, but Penguin's experimentation did create models for other writers to follow. In particular, the company didn't just use the micro-blogging service to publish its story but also incorporated full-length blogs and Google Maps.

Twitter might provide one way of publishing a narrative but if you're online, there's no reason why you shouldn't make use of all of the tools available on the site.

If all you want to do though is put a story you've written onto Twitter and benefit from it, then N.L. Belardes' Small Places has managed to gather an impressive audience of around 3,000 from less than 600 updates. His story contains no replies to readers so there's no audience participation, but he does occasionally break into the story to tell readers when the novel has been mentioned in the press and to offer links to his websites and other writing.

N.L. Belardes might not be earning directly from Small Places but it is attracting attention and giving him new readers.

Tips
for Success

(continued)

Make it Real

One of the differences between Twitter and a novel is that novel readers suspend their disbelief when they open a book. That doesn't happen on Twitter. Twitter's re aders expect the tweets they see to have been written by real people.

Give your characters real lives and the time and space to develop. Answer—in character—questions put by readers and give them interests outside the storyline.

41

BECOME A HOLLYWOOD WRITER BY TWEETING A CHARACTER

DIFFICULTY

SKILLS REQUIRED

INCOME POTENTIAL

What Are Characters on Twitter?

Whenever an author creates a set of characters, he or she owns the copyright to them. In theory, that means that no one else can develop those characters or write them without their permission. Fan fiction though, in which fans of the character develop storylines of their own, can be beneficial for the rights owners. They help to form a community around the series and foster loyalty to the brand.

Provided it's done for fun and not for profit, rights owners such as television companies have learned to stand back—and sometimes even participate by interacting with the fan-authors—rather than shutting them down.

Fan fiction, which is usually published on websites, has now appeared on Twitter. Characters from AMC's show Mad Men," from Buffy the Vampire Slayer," from The X-Files and from many other fictional series, including comic books, Star Wars and Star Trek are all present on Twitter and tweeting as though they were real people.

It's a phenomenon that didn't initially have a smooth journey. AMC wasn't pleased to find that its characters had been brought to life on Twitter and in a way that was beyond its control, and attempted to shut the twitterers down. The network was eventually persuaded by it publicity company that it was better to enjoy the free advertising than try to fight it.

How Twitterers are Creating Characters

Tweeting fictional characters began with Paul Isakson (@paulisakson), Director of Strategy & Insights at space150 (www.space150.com), a digital relationships company, who put Don Draper on the site. He eventually handed control of that timeline to AMC but not before inspiring PR executive Carri Bugbee (@carribugbee) to set up a timeline for another "Mad Men" character, Peggy Olson (@peggyolson). Carri won a Shorty award for her portrayal of the show's rising star and has been praised by AMC for the accuracy of her characterization.

Other characters though have been represented with varying degrees of fidelity to the original. Buffy Summers (@buffysummers) of "Buffy the Vampire Slayer" is portrayed on Twitter with a similar degree of accuracy and interacts with other characters from the show. Darth Vader (@darthvader), on the other hand, is more of a satire than a representation.

Each of these timelines has been created for fun, and none of the twitterers appear to be generating revenue from it (although the rights owners may certainly be benefitting from the free advertising.)

Carri Bugbee though has found a way to generate revenue from her character tweeting by setting up Supporting Characters (www.supportingcharacters.com), an agency that offers character twitterers for entertainment companies.

How to Do It

Carri Bugbee has talked about the extensive research that went into creating Peggy Olson on Twitter. She would watch each show twice and transcribe Peggy's speeches in order to get the voice right and the vocabulary exact.

To think of topics to discuss though, she would also spend a great deal of time reading the tweets posted by other fans, especially the day after the show was broadcast. She wanted to know what topics they were discussing, which issues they thought the most interesting and which aspects of Peggy's character they were focusing on.

for Success

Stay in Character

Carri Bugbee made a name for herself for the degree of loyalty she showed her "Mad Men" character. Betty Draper (@bettydraper) went one step further by keeping in character even off Twitter. Instead of using email, she typed and mailed a letter to Twitter co-founder Biz Stone, thanking him for the site.

When you're tweeting a character, that closeness is the ultimate test of the timeline's success.

Pay Attention the Day after the Show Broadcasts

Tweeting in character is important, but you'll also have to tweet on topics that engage your audience. The best time to understand what the show's fans are interested in is the day after the show broadcasts.

Read what people are saying about the episode and try to make sure your own tweets relate to those topics.

(continued on next page)

The timeline itself is very dynamic with plenty of in-character replies to questions posed by other fans and to other characters in the show too, an important part of building followers and creating a realistic atmosphere while maintaining accessibility.

Carri has criticized the tendency of other shows to create lifeless character timelines that consist of nothing more than RSS feeds or news announcements with no interaction and without following other twitterers.

While the tweeting itself should be fairly simple then, the research may be time-consuming. The marketing of an agency will be even harder. Carri has the advantage of winning an award for her character tweeting so one option may be to create a similarly realistic character, then pitch to join her agency.

Getting Started

But the hardest part of all may be to take the first step of finding a character, especially one that hasn't been taken already. Of those already on Twitter though, many are fairly dormant, leaving you free to set up a similarly-named character—changing the position of the underscore, for example. There is more than one Don Draper on Twitter.

Another option is to search for the names of TV series that are being discussed on Twitter and whose characters aren't yet on the site. That should ensure that you don't create an obscure character for which there's no audience.

Having found a character you can use though, the next step will be to do the research: watch a lot of television and make a note of the character's vocabulary and phrasing. Then read tweets about the show to see what people are discussing and make your appearance with an optimized timeline.

A Model to Follow

Carri Bugbee's Peggy Olson is always going to be the model to follow, even though Buffy Summers and the other vampire-slaying characters are also very good. Peggy Olson's timeline though combined dynamic tweets and replies to fans and other characters with very close attention to detail.

The result was that the timeline's followers really felt that they were actually talking to a real person, and because she was following them back, they felt that she was interested in them too.

Carri's idea to monetize this strategy is also important, and while winning those contracts isn't going to be easy, it is an approach that others could follow to target TV shows in other markets or even books and movies.

Tips
for Success

(continued)

Look for Flagging Characters with Large Followings

Although you might struggle to find free characters who are able to build an audience, there is one relatively simple s olution. Tweeting in character can be hard to do in the long run, and many character twitterers find their enthusiasm flagging after a while.

If you can find a character whose posting rate is beginning to fall—or who hasn't posted at all for a while—but who has a large following, DM the twitterer and ask if you can take it over. If they're loyal to the character but no longer want to tweet, they might just agree. Carri Bugbee picked up a number of character timelines this way.

42 MARKET YOUR SOCIAL MEDIA SKILL WITH A UNIQUE TWITTER DIARY

DIFFICULTY

SKILLS REQUIRED

INCOME POTENTIAL

What is a Diary on Twitter?

When blogs launched, they were intended to function as online diaries. Bloggers, a term created by Evan Williams (@ev), one of Twitter's founders, were supposed to be publishing accounts of what they were doing and thinking.

Microblogging was supposed to be blogging in miniature, with posts about the writers' daily lives limited to just 140 characters.

In practice, just as blogs became a new way of publishing a wide range of different kinds of content, so microbloggers began using their timelines in a number of different ways, not least to chat with other microbloggers.

But there may be a value too in taking Twitter back to the origins of blogging and using the site's chronological structure to create—or re-create—a record of daily life.

How Twitterers are Writing Diaries

For the most part, of course, twitterers aren't writing diaries. They might be describing what they're doing (sometimes in painful detail) but the real value of Twitter comes in answering questions, receiving replies and becoming an active member of the site's community.

One twitterer who is placing a diary on Twitter is David Griner (@griner), a social media strategist for ad firm Luckie & Company. David's own timeline is a standard, well-written Twitter presence, filled with plenty of replies and comments, insights into his own life and descriptions of his work. But David also runs @Genny_Spencer, a timeline for which the bio reads: "This is the real line-a-day diary of a young farmgirl in 1937. It is maintained by @griner." Above the bio, a link leads to a page on David's blog, www.thesocialpath.com, on which he explains that the tweets are taken from a line-a-day diary that was written by his great-aunt, Genevieve Spencer, when she was a young teenager on a small farm in Illinois. The diary was originally written between 1937 and 1941.

The diary breaks a number of rules for good twittering. Genevieve Spencer doesn't follow anyone. Nor does she reply to anyone. That can lead to a dry, impersonal timeline but because this timeline is unusual in not being live, it does keep it honest too.

For once, the value of the timeline for its followers isn't in its dynamism or its variety but in its insight into a bygone age.

The value for David Griner though is a little harder to quantify, but it mostly comes down to branding. As a social media strategist, David is able to use the timeline to bring followers to his own personal stream and to his website. He gets to show off his expertise and brand himself as an expert on social media.

For someone who makes their living out of online marketing, that's always going to be valuable.

How to Do It

This isn't going to be an easy model to repeat. David Griner created @Genny_Spencer after his family came across his aunt's old diary, and his sister commented that the short entries looked like the Twitter of the day.

Few other families are lucky enough to come across such a valuable resource.

That means to repeat this strategy, you might well have to re-create a fictional diary. You could base it on old photographs, reminiscences from relatives or stories you've heard while tracing your genealogy.

One option could be to focus on a particular event or period in a relative's life. Genevieve Spencer's diary lasts for a set number of years and describes a historical period from one person's perspective. A diary that attempted to repeat this strategy could look at a relative's war service or their first years in the country. If you can target a particularly

for Success

Use TweetLater

David Griner doesn't post a new tweet every day. Instead, he has placed all of the tweets in TweetLater so that they're posted automatically. While that means a lot of work at the beginning, it also means that once the tweets are loaded, he can leave the timeline to run itself.

Because timelines are best when they're dynamic and should include interactions with other twitterers, it's not always a good idea to pre-book tweets. But historical diaries are static, so you can just post, leave and enjoy the benefits.

Know When You're Tweeting

Genevieve Spencer reveals rural life in the years just before America's entry into the Second World War. For that reason, it becomes a valuable historical document as well as a good read. It's the history that's the attraction so make sure you know the period before you start tweeting.

(continued on next page)

interesting period, you should be able to inject a little drama into your timeline.

Extracting the benefits from the timeline will be harder. David Griner places two links on Genevieve Spencer's timeline that bring followers back to him. One leads to his own timelime and the other to his blog. It's also notable that the timeline itself relates directly to his work as a social media strategist.

To enjoy similar benefits then your timeline should reflect aspects that are important to your field of expertise too. That could be something as simple as taking a chance to show off your creativity but you could choose a historical period or event that relates directly to your business. A designer, for example, could create a diary that describes the founding of his grandfather's textile business. A photographer could recreate his great-uncle's post-war studio. And a writer could simply use the timeline to show off her character-creating skills, linking back to her own timeline and her website.

Getting Started

The first step will always be choosing the person to feature in your Twitter-based diary. Because few families have line-a-day diaries lying in their attics, that will take some thought.

And having made the choice, it will also require a lot of research.

The value for readers in these kinds of diaries is in the historical detail. For David Griner, that came naturally as part of the source material. For someone re-creating a diary, it will have to come through reading history books, watching documentaries and films, and visiting museums. It's those small things—the type of telephone, the make of lens, the clothes—that add color to the timeline and make it interesting.

A Model to Follow

Genevieve Spencer's timeline is clearly the model to follow for these kinds of timelines but pay attention not just to the timeline and the tweets themselves but the way that David Griner users the timeline to bring readers back to him. He might have set the timeline up as a way of sharing an interesting family document but it's clear that publishing his aunt's notes also demonstrates his own social media expertise.

Tips
for Success

(continued)

One Day, One Tweet

A timeline without interaction is usually a little dull, but keeping your posts regular can help to keep readers interested. They'll know when to expect the latest updates and they won't feel that they're being overwhelmed with broadcast tweets.

43 BUILD A TWITTER CITIZEN PUBLISHING HOUSE

DIFFICULTY

SKILLS REQUIRED

INCOME POTENTIAL

What is Citizen Publishing?

One of the reasons that Twitter has so captured the public's imagination has been its ability to report events far faster than the mainstream media has been able to. From terrorist attacks in Mumbai to planes crashing in the Hudson River, twitterers on the scene have been able to report events as they were happening.

Those twitterers though aren't posting their reports for any reason other than their desire to share the news.

News publishers though, want to make money. That's created a dilemma for mainstream media outlets who find that they're being scooped on breaking stories. On the one hand, Twitter has become a valuable resource for information that they can't pick up easily themselves. On the other had, for audiences, Twitter is also a rival, pulling viewers away from television screens and newspapers to computer screens and mobiles phones.

The compromise made by some publishers has been to use Twitter as a source of individual pieces of information which it then collates, checks and analyzes.

Of course, the outlet still has to make money out of that new Twitter-based content but for publishers with good ad models or even information products, using Twitter's crowdsourcing to pick up new has been shown to result in unique and valuable new content.

How Twitterers are Becoming Citizen Publishers

The best example of a publisher that used Twitter to create unique content was TechPresident.com (www.techpresident.com), a crosspartisan blog that looked at how the 2008 presidential candidates used the Web and examined the impact of user-generated content on the campagn.

For the Iowa caucuses though, TechPresident did something new. It created a Twitter timeline called @iowacaucus and invited twitterers across the state to tweet in the results as they happened.

Together, those posts made it clear which way the election was going, and Patrick Ruffini (@patrickruffini), one of TechPresident's contributors, was able to post very early in the evening —and long before the mainstream media—that the results were trending towards an Obama victory.

How to Do It

Using Twitter to crowdsource stories requires two elements: you'll need a story that can benefit from Twitter's crowdsourcing power; and you'll need a way to monetize the story your contributors produce.

TechPresident's choice of a caucus worked because it relied on reporting a real-time event that was happening over a scattered area. Because the mainstream media struggled to place reporters in so many different locations at the same time, Twitter was able to offer a viable solution. Elections then are clearly one type of story that can be reported in this way because they happen in many different places at the same time.

They're also pre-planned, another essential element in crowdsourcing stories. While it may be possible to use crowdsourcing to report on reactions to an event—taking tweets from twitterers in colleges after a shooting, for example—it takes time to find twitterers in the right areas and persuade them to post replies to your timeline so that you can analyze the information. Finding buyers to report from stores as important new gadgets are launched could work, as could sports competitions and multiple demonstrations such as 2009's tea parties.

Once you've chosen a story, you'll need to search Twitter for suitable reporters. Twitter's search engine allows searches within a set dis-

Tips

for Success

Analyze the Data

When an event happens, your competition isn't going to be the mainstream media, it's going to be Monitter. Lots of people will be tweeting anyway and using hashtags to make it easy for other Twitter users to follow.

Your advantage won't be the information that will be trending on Twitter anyway, it will be what you do with the kind of information you're collecting and what you do with it. Use your timeline to ask searching questions of your reporters and make sure you're ready with analysis and commentary as soon as it becomes clear how the event is trending.

Blow it up

The benefits of a crowdsourced story like this will be the extra publicity, the growth in readership, the perception of your publication as serious and dedicated to original content, and money from advertising, subscriptions and product sales on your pages.

(continued on next page)

But you'll have to let people know you're doing it.

Make sure that your readers know what you'll be doing. Urging your reporters to ask others to contribute too should help to spread the word.

Be Creative with the Benefits

Crowdsourcing a story in this way will take some effort. Like much of Twitter use it should be fun and interesting but it will take time and organization. Be creative in your revenue-generation to ensure that you make the most of that work. Look for sponsors, write up the commentary as a commercial report or push ads hard on the results page.

tance of a specific location. Finding twitterers interested in your topic and close enough to report on it then shouldn't take too much effort.

Ideally, you'll want your reporters to reply to your dedicated timeline but you can also create a hashtag to capture all of the comments on the event once it begins.

The last stage will be the hardest. You'll need to analyze the data you bring in and, trickiest of all, monetize it.

TechPresident benefited primarily from the publicity that beating the mainstream media brought them. Ensuring that the page discussing the results is optimized for ad revenue will be important and you could also combine this strategy with others, running a sponsored or ad-supported stream on the website in the same way that Glam.com did during the Oscars.

Getting Started

TechPresident has its own timeline at @techpresident but to report on the IowaCaucus, it created a separate timeline, allowing it to communicate directly with its reporters on that one topic and attract followers who only wanted to follow the caucus.

Begin then by creating a timeline dedicated to the event you want to cover. Use the bio to make clear who controls the timeline and link to your website—you'll want to benefit from the extra followers, after all—then begin searching for twitterers in the right locations to contribute to your data collection.

A Model to Follow

TechPresident's timeline @iowacaucus is clearly the model to copy but another interesting example—even if it wasn't organized in quite the same way—took place in May 2009. When Stephen Fry visited Bletchley Park, the site of Britain's World War II code-breaking center, his tour was tweeted by the park's supporters who joined him at the site. The result was a massive boost in publicity for the park's museum which was trying to raise funds. Fundraisers then could try inviting a celebrity to visit a site and tweet about it to bring in extra money.

GO VIRAL
ON TWITTER

What is Viral Marketing on Twitter?

Twitter has become a favorite of marketers for two reasons. First, the kind of close community that businesses can build around their timelines can deliver sales, feedback and enormous branding power.

But a company's followers also follow other people and have followers of their own. That means that a good marketing message can quickly spread across Twitter's network putting the name of the business in front of thousands of other people even if the company's own tweets have relatively few followers.

That kind of viral marketing is extremely valuable, and on Twitter, it's done through retweeting—placing your message in someone else's timeline with your attribution so that other people can see it.

Persuade your followers to retweet your posts and you'll be able reach a much broader audience, win more clicks on your links and pick up more followers too.

How Twitterers Are Going Viral

Retweeting happens when a twitterer has posted a particularly interesting tweet . . . or because he or she has asked for the post to be retweeted.

Dan Zarrella (www.danzarrella.com), who describes himself as a "social and viral marketing scientist," has done some careful research on the characteristics of tweets that have been retweeted.

Tips

for Success

Be Polite

The word "please" occurs five times more often in tweets that contain requests to retweet than in other kinds of tweets, and for good reason. When you're asking someone to do something on your behalf, it pays to be polite.

Pick your Moment

According to Dan Zarrella, retweets are most likely to happen on Mondays, Tuesdays and Wednesdays and to occur during work hours. Retweeting beats working, it seems.

Reciprocate

What goes around on Twitter comes around too. Some twitterers have found that people are more likely to retweet for people who retweet for others. Do some retweeting of your own.

He found that retweeted posts are more likely than other tweets to contain the word "you," to refer to blog posts and to include links. Talking directly to your followers, tweeting about your new blog post and linking to it, it seems, doesn't just encourage your followers to click through to your site, it can also win you completely new readers too.

But in terms of the content of those retweeted posts, Dan also discovered that many of them were particularly valuable and that value came in four different forms. They could contain or point to Web content that offered instructional information; they could provide news, especially breaking news; they could provide warnings, particularly about Twitter-based phishing scams; and they could tell people how to pick up free gifts or win prizes.

Include tweets like these in your timeline and you'll increase the chances that your followers will retweet for you too.

How to Do It

So the type of content you include in your tweets will be important. The more valuable and practical your tweets, the more likely your followers are to share them. Place a good how-to on your blog, offer a free sample of your product or warn people about a competitor's service, for example, and you might just win helpful retweets.

You can also ask people to retweet your post.

There's nothing wrong with doing that. In fact, Dan Zarrella found that many retweeted posts contained a request either that the tweet be sent on or for help—or for both.

Of course, getting retweets is only the beginning. You also have to benefit from all that extra attention, and that takes a little more thought.

On the one hand, any retweeted post will also bring you new followers. The etiquette of retweeting requires twitterers to say who posted the original so as well as clicking the link in the tweet itself, people will also click through to your timeline to see who wrote the original. That should increase your readership.

But you also want those followers to act on that tweet and in a way that benefits you.

Including a link to your website will bring your site readers and perhaps ad clicks.

Giving away free gifts should bring you plenty of retweets and also give new customers a feel for what you can do. An ebook that shows off your expertise, for example, could make for a simple gift that would back-end those new readers into making a purchase. Stever Berardi's (@photonaturalist) offer of a free ebook about wildflower photography from his website, for example, won retweets and brought readers to his website.

To make it easier for people to retweet, you could also use PleaseRT. me (http://pleasert.me/). Although not really necessary, the site allows twitterers to enter a tweet that they'd like to be retweeted. The tweet then appears with RT at the beginning and a link at the end which, when pressed, pastes the tweet into the reader's text box ready for retweeting.

The retweet link though may well compete with the content link so readers may end up having to choose between retweeting and clicking!

Getting Started

The best way to begin retweeting is to give it a try. The only penalty for failing to make a tweet go viral is to be ignored—and no one will know.

If you have a website, the easiest method would be to create an article that provided solid, practical information—such as the best way to photograph lightning or how to cook a soufflé. If you can imagine someone paying for a class that would teach them the same skill, you can be confident that the information is valuable.

Post a tweet that says something like: "New Blog Post: How to Cook a Soufflé. http://bit.ly/65are. Please RT!" then keep an eye on search results or by tracking your name to see how many retweets you receive.

Alternatively, you could also begin by monitoring a news site for an item of breaking news related to your industry. Place the headline in your timeline with a request to retweet and as it spreads across Twitter, it will carry a link back to your tweets.

A Model to Follow

TweetRank (www.retweetrank.com) provides a list of twitterers ranked according to their ability to win retweets. Although the positions change fairly frequently, perennial chart-toppers include marketer Guy Kawasaki (@guykawasaki) and Mashable's Pete Cashmore (@mashable).

To some extent, both of these popular twitterers can win retweets without asking for them simply because of who they are. Their posts are seen as important enough—and interesting enough—for readers to want to pass them around anyway.

But it is noticeable that the posts that win the most retweets are those that contain links.

Twitterers will share tweets but they're much more likely to share good blog content . . . especially when it comes recommended.

PICK UP VALUABLE INSPIRATION FOR YOUR CONTENT IDEAS

What is Valuable Inspiration on Twitter?

The rise of Twitter has affected bloggers in two contrasting ways. A number of bloggers have noted that they're blogging less and tweeting more. Tweets are much less demanding, take less time to write than full-length blog posts and can even be posted on the fly from a mobile phone.

At the same time though, bloggers have also found that being able to take part in discussions has inspired them to create new blog posts. They can see which topics people are discussing most and poll them to try out different ideas. They can even ask readers directly what sort of topics they'd like to see covered on the blog.

All of that is fortunate because while it is possible to make money on Twitter, it's much easier to monetize a blog. Put the two together and you can end up with a more powerful blog with more readers, the kinds of articles that more of your users want to read—and higher income too.

DIFFICULTY

SKILLS REQUIRED

INCOME POTENTIAL

How Twitter's Bloggers Are Getting Inspiration for Their Content Ideas

On December 5, 2008, Dr. Ves Dimov (@AllergyNotes) wrote on his timeline that he was "rarely blogging any more but still Twitting." He also added that this was becoming "typical."

Two days later, he wrote this tweet: "I have at least 4–5 blogging ideas for next week from Twitter. This is working unexpectedly well. I never expected to find Twitter useful."

Tips

for Success

Use Polls

In addition to tapping his followers for blog post ideas, Darren Rowse also runs frequent polls. Those give his followers an easy way to interact with his timeline, tells Darren what other people think . . . and they can also function as the source of entirely new blog posts.

When you find that the majority of your followers prefers one choice over another, you can write an original post that publishes the results and tries to explain them.

Think about the Money

Being able to create new blog posts without having to think too much about it will certainly be valuable but you still have to monetize the readers that blog post will bring.

When you get the ideas, try to match them with affiliate products you recommend and make sure that the topic isn't going to bring up low-paying pay-per-click ads.

(continued on next page)

That's no less typical. Before they began using Twitter, bloggers were forced to dream up ideas for all of their blog posts by themselves. They wrote about topics that interested them . . . and hoped that they'd interest other people too.

Sometimes it worked and a blog took off. Sometimes, the publisher misjudged his or her audience and a post—and perhaps the entire blog—dived. And almost always, bloggers have run into the problem of sustaining a blog once the ideas have begun to dry up.

Twitter has helped to solve that problem for bloggers by allowing them to talk directly to the readers and to listen in on the conversations that other people interested in their topic are discussing. They can see where the points of contention are and what people are saying.

That can all be done simply by reading the posts on Twitter. But bloggers are being a lot more proactive.

David AvRutick (@davrutick), the President of folding kayak company, Folbot, asked his 1000-plus followers directly what they wanted to read on his blog: "Have to think of a blog topic. Any ideas?"

Darren Rowse, perhaps not surprisingly, takes a similar approach but with a little more sophistication. With almost a hundred times more followers than David AvRutick, he can expect a much greater response so his request for help with blog posts ideas took the form of an invitation for questions: "Am taking some questions for posts next week on ProBlogger if you have any—reply them with #pbquestions."

The use of the hashtag meant that Darren would able to find all of the questions his followers posed—and revealed that he was expecting them to come in large numbers.

How to Do It

The easiest way to use Twitter as inspiration for blog posts is to read the discussions taking place on the timelines of other people in your field. They'll tell you which issues are currently causing controversy and allow you to weigh in one side or other of the debate.

Follow the people taking part in the discussion so that they follow you back, and when you announce in your timeline that the post is up, there's a good chance that they'll click through to see your take on the issue.

That's particularly true if you make the effort to send them a direct message, ask for their take and include their quote in your post. There's an even better chance then that they'll also rush to tell other people about it.

If you want to ask your followers to send in their own suggestions, do include hashtags to make them easier to find. Darren Rowse's hashtag, #pbquestions, referred to questions for ProBlogger and was unique to his request so they wouldn't be confused with any other search signifier.

Do be aware though that what one person finds interesting, others may find dull. Just because someone comes up with a suggestion or a question, it doesn't mean that you have to address it. Comments from followers can spark your inspiration but they don't have to set your blog's agenda.

Getting Started

The best way to begin using Twitter for inspiration is to get reading. Look for people talking about issues related to your topic and see how the debates are flowing. That will give you people to follow and it will also show you how interest in various aspects of your topic differ from one follower to another.

If your follower list is relatively small—David AvRutick-sized rather than Darren Rowse-sized—you should be able to predict the kinds of suggestions your followers will offer.

Tips *for Success*

(continued)

Share the News

Once you've written the post, don't forget to tell everyone in your timeline. Everyone who suggested the topic is almost guaranteed to like it but you can also ask them to retweet it and bring yourself some new readers.

A Model to Follow

The biggest model to follow for using Twitter for blog inspiration is Darren Rowse. Darren had already created a name for himself as a professional blogger with Problogger website (www.problogger.net) and his book, "ProBlogger: Secrets for Blogging Your Way to a Six-Figure Income."

The large following Darren has built up on Twitter acts as an extension of his blogging empire, allowing him to interact directly with his readers. His secondary timeline, @digitalps, is an easy way to send followers to his new blog posts, while his main timeline at @problogger tells people more about how he blogs and what he's blogging about.

Their reactions alone can tell Darren a great deal about the issues that are confusing his readers and about which they'd like to learn more. Sometimes you don't need to do any more to find blogging inspiration on Twitter than talk to your readers.

---

46 SELL YOUR BOOKS

DIFFICULTY

SKILLS REQUIRED

INCOME POTENTIAL

What is Book-Selling on Twitter?

Creating a novel on Twitter—and trying to earn from it—will always be a struggle. But Twitter does offer some fantastic resources for novelists. Published writers, in particular, with books to their name and sales on Amazon to build can keep their fans engaged and encourage more purchases, especially of their new books.

But there's plenty for aspiring novelists too. Publishers and agents have already discovered the power of Twitter and are offering tips and answering questions on the site. Although you'll still have to write query letters and put together proposals in the traditional way (and handle the traditional rejections), Twitter can provide the contacts and information that can point you in the right direction and give you a head start.

How Authors Ae Using Twitter

Top-selling fiction writers are fairly rare on Twitter. While there's no shortage of non-fiction authors promoting their books, top-selling novelists tend (for the moment, at least) to be steering clear. Look for @johngrisham, for example, and you'll only be offered Twitter's "Suspended" notice, a sure sign that someone who wasn't John Grisham had been squatting the account—but also a sign that the novelist himself isn't using it.

Plenty of writers though certainly are making the most of Twitter and they're doing it in a number of different ways. James Rollins

(@jamesrollins), author of a series of thrillers as well as the novel based on the film "Indiana Jones and the Kingdom of the Crystal Skull", tweets about his writing progress and the books he's about to release, rustles up support for his entries in writing competitions, offers tips for aspiring writers, and answers tweets from readers. It's all straightforward Twitter stuff, but it does have the effect of turning his readers into a community—exactly the kind of thing that's likely to encourage them to keep buying.

Other authors though are taking an even more proactive approach to selling their books on Twitter. It's no surprise that Joel Comm (@joelcomm), author of a book on marketing with Twitter, has used a number of different strategies to promote his work. He scans for mentions from people who say they've read it, thanks them and encourages them to post a review on Amazon. He runs competitions urging people to send in pictures of themselves holding the book to enter a draw to win a camera. And he even organized a day-long tweetathon which, while it benefitted a charity, also helped to promote his book launch.

And a third way that authors are using Twitter is to keep make their first forays into the publishing world. Literary agents such as Colleen Lindsay (@ColleenLindsay), Greg Daniel (@DanielLiterary) and Jennifer Laughran (@literaticat) are offering suggestions and tips about querying, and employees at publishing companies as large as Random House (@AnnKingman), Wiley (@apackard, @chriswebb and @elleinthecity) and Portfolio/Penguin (@davidmoldawer) are also on the site. Although many of them are tweeting about their lives rather than the book business, their tweets can offer valuable insights into what's happening in the book world, how to query and what publishers are currently looking for.

They might just be able to answer your questions too.

How to Do It

If you're already an author and just want to use Twitter to keep your readers together, informed and interested in between releases, then you shouldn't need to do too much more than keep an active timeline. Place a link to your stream on your website so that your readers know where to find you on the site, and you can also try placing a blog post on your book page at Amazon that contains your Twitter name too.

Tips
for Success

Take Testimonials

Twitter is stuffed with short, perfect testimonials by readers who have enjoyed the books they've read. Whenever someone writes a tweet saying that they enjoyed your book, thank them for the compliment, invite them to place a review on Amazon . . . and ask them if you can include the tweet in your sales material.

Talk to Readers

Readers want to feel connected to a writer. That's why they turn up to book readings and signings. Think of Twitter as a giant book reading and you can collect at least some of that goodwill. Answer their questions, be prepared to discuss how you work and the characters you're creating. Make sure they know too, when your next book will come out.

(continued on next page)

Tips

for Success

(continued)

Plan Your Campaigns

The best tweets are often those posted spontaneously but that doesn't mean you can't also plan a Twitter-based campaign. If you've got a book coming out, prepare your followers in the weeks before your launch by talking about it often. Once it comes out, mention how well it's selling and thank people who mention it for their praise so that everyone else can see it's being recommended. Organize a competition to keep the sales flowing and once it's been out for a while, offer a couple of chapters for free to mop up doubters.

Try to use your tweets to answer the kinds of questions that readers ask at book readings, such as what's inspiring you at the moment and how you work. While giving away plot secrets might not be a good idea, you can use Twitter to create suspense by offering sneak peeks into your characters' lives and development.

If you're looking to promote your book on Twitter and encourage sales, you'll need to take a lot more action. First you'll have to build your own follower list by following people who have mentioned books similar to yours in their tweets. You can find them by searching for the author's name at search.twitter.com. Engage them in conversation so that they know who you are and make sure that your bio includes your book titles and that the link leads to your book's Web page. Once you've built up a decent-sized follower list (around 1,000 is a good place to start but that will take a little time and some effort), you can begin pushing the book a little harder with giveaways and competitions. Offering free chapter downloads can be one useful way of showing what your book is about and winning plenty of retweets.

And if you want to contact agents and publishers, it's just a matter of following, reading and asking your question. You can find a list of literary figures on Twitter at www.highspotinc.com/blog/2008/12/a-directory-of-book-trade-people-on-twitter.

Don't expect to receive an offer from a publisher on Twitter but do use it to pick up some extra information.

Getting Started

The first step in selling a book on Twitter is always to write it! Bear in mind that the methods that authors are using on the site can be just as effective for self-published authors. Publishing companies tend to leave much of the book marketing to the authors themselves so if a method can work for established authors such as James Rollins, it can be just as beneficial for self-published and print-on-demand writers. Use Twitter to build a following and encourage people to buy and read.

A Model to Follow

When it comes to actively selling books on Twitter, it's hard to beat Joel Comm who uses all of the marketing tools available. His book, Twitter Power, was sold with free access to a four-week webinar, details about which he posted frequently on his timeline. He timed his tweetathon to match his book launch and included plenty of references to his book in the tweetathon's publicity material. He ran a competition encouraging people to send in pictures of themselves holding the book so that others could see that people were buying it. And every time someone mentioned the book on Twitter, he thanked them and asked for a review.

James Rollins though doesn't push his books quite so hard but he did put a great deal of effort into winning votes for a writing competition. His tweets tend to be more about how he works and what he's working on—a good way to build a friendly relationship with his readers.

47 ORGANIZE A TWITTER CONFERENCE

DIFFICULTY

■ ■ ■ ➡

SKILLS REQUIRED

■ ➡

INCOME POTENTIAL

■ ➡

What is a Conference on Twitter?

For entrepreneurs, there are few places that can deliver a more powerful networking punch than a conference. Not only will you get to hear some important speakers sharing their knowledge, providing some valuable behind-the-scenes information and delivering a preview of the next great products coming down the pipeline, you'll also get to make some very valuable contacts.

In fact, it's often the ability to pick the brains of other delegates that can be the most important aspect of a conference. Those conversations can open up new opportunities, joint ventures and even partnerships.

Nothing can replace that face-to-face contact. But Twitter does do a pretty good job of providing a channel through which those communications can take place.

If Twitter is the Internet's watercooler then Twitter-based conferences—or "chats"—are like departmental meetings. Anyone with an interest in the topic can take part, the subjects are laid out in advance and the gatherings themselves are limited in time.

Although they're not likely to result in direct income, they can deliver some extremely valuable information.

How Twitterers are Organizing Conferences

It might be possible to argue that conferences on Twitter are happening all the time and spontaneously. The entire site is a conference at which multiple conversations are happening and anyone can join in and drop out at any time.

GEEKPRENEUR

When a conference, or chat, is organized though, the conversation is much more focused. The organizer will set a specific time and duration for the meeting. The topic of the conversation may be defined with a list of questions laid out on a website, and the transcripts of the entire exchange posted for others to see once the event has closed.

The result should be an airing of expert views that anyone can later browse through and benefit from.

The best example comes from Tim Beyers (@milehighfool), a freelance writer and co-founder of #editorchat, a weekly Twitter-based conference for writers and editors.

His conferences take place at the same time each week, last around 90 minutes and are intended to provide a way for writers and editors to discuss issues related to their business. Topics have included the importance of SEO when writing for the Web, whether Web writers should be paid more or less than print writers and whether editors are being more flexible about word count. Contributors have even included John A. Byrne (@JOHNABYRNE), Executive Editor of BusinessWeek and Editor-in-Chief of BusinessWeek.com.

All contributions must include the hashtag #editorchat to enable easy, real-time tracking but anyone is welcome to contribute.

How to Do It

Organizing a conference like this isn't easy. You'll need first to make sure that you have enough relevant followers and interest to make it worthwhile. Although even a focused chat with just three twitterers could still have value, the more participants you can gather, the wider the range of views and insights you'll be able to pick up and the more valuable the conversation will be.

You'll also need decide which issues you want to discuss. Tim Beyers tends to go for five topics and invites contributors to post their own ideas as comments on the conference's blog. And that, of course, means you'll need to set up a blog to supplement the conversations and provide a static venue (as opposed to Twitter's dynamic platform) where participants can collect the information.

During the conference itself, you'll need to make sure that everyone stays on topic and that enough time is left to cover all of the questions.

Tips
for Success

Make Introductions

Begin each conference with an introduction. Introduce yourself and ask everyone to introduce themselves too. During a conference, participants aren't going to be able to click through to everyone's profiles and read all the bios so seeing a stream of mini-resumes flowing past will be very useful . . . and a lot quicker than doing the rounds of the coffee room at a real conference.

Accept Help

The hardest part of running a conference like this will be keeping it going over time. Not only will you have to give up a sizable chunk of time each week to take part in the conference, you'll also have to think up issues to discuss, type up the transcript and chair the discussions.

Make sure that at least some participants are prepared to lend you hand so that the ideas stay fresh and that you don't get tired out. A good conference group is one

(continued on next page)

for Success

(continued)

that continues after the founder has moved on.

Invite Special Guests

A conference is only as good as the people who choose to take part. While you'll want as many people as possible to participate, go out of your way to bring important people in. If you know of influential people in your field who are on Twitter, invite them to join your next conference.

By being on Twitter, they've already shown that they're approachable and social, and by taking part in the discussion they'll get to show off the degree to which they're willing to help. You'll get to create an even more valuable discussion.

And finally, you may want to create and post a transcript of the entire chat so that a record is available of the discussion.

Getting Started

Starting a conference like this will probably be easier than maintaining it once you get going and you've covered the most pressing issues.

To begin, sound out your own followers about whether they'd be interested and ask what times and what issues they'd like the discussion to cover. Next, set up a specialized blog that can function as a kind of center for the conference where people can leave permanent comments and make contributions on a static page.

Any of the free blogging services such as Wordpress (www.wordpress .com) or Blogger (www.blogger.com) can work fine.

Once you've done all that, it's just a matter of waiting for the big day, introducing yourself, asking everyone else to introduce themselves . . . and getting the ball rolling.

A Model to Follow

Tim Beyers' #editorchats are the ideal model for anyone considering organizing a conference on Twitter.

The quality of the participants is certainly important, with twitterers that range from editors of leading publications to hopeful freelancers weighing in with their experiences. But it's really the level of organization that impresses most.

Setting up a conversation on Twitter really isn't difficult at all. The site, after all, was designed for open communication. But to make that discussion valuable, focused and available for future reference does take a certain amount of work and effort. Tim Beyers has managed to create a template for on-Twitter discussions that anyone—anyone who is prepared to put in the time, that is—can follow and benefit from.

MARKET WITH A SPECIAL TWITTER DAY

What is a Special Twitter Day?

Businesses have long set aside certain times to market specifically to one niche market or drum up extra business at otherwise quiet periods. Clubs are known to have ladies night, for example, while bars have regular happy hours. Both of those strategies use discounts to tempt customers and fill seats.

Some businesses on Twitter are doing something similar. They're setting aside a special day to reward people who follow their tweets. The rewards may range from a simple discount to a free gift to a chance to win a complete three-course meal.

But the principle remains the same: one group of customers is rewarded for their loyalty and the company gets to pick up some extra business.

With Twitter though, the rewards can go even further than a few extra customers. Because Twitter still has an exclusive, cool image, businesses that are on Twitter and which are willing to reward their followers get to benefit from that image too.

How Twitterers Are Creating Special Twitter Days

Businesses on Twitter that are creating special Twitter days seem to be largely those in the restaurant and catering business. Perhaps that's not too surprising. Restaurants and cafes have a steady flow of customers, certain days that are busier than others and the flexibility to make simple special offers.

DIFFICULTY

SKILLS REQUIRED

INCOME POTENTIAL

for Success

Create Urgency

Once you've selected a day to promote, it's a good idea to keep to it. Followers will be able to fit it into their routine, and may even become regulars. But you can still pressure followers to make their decision quickly. Fuel demands that its customers make an early commitment in return for the possibility of receiving a large reward. Other options though may be to boost the offer—with perhaps a free dessert or a complementary drink—to anyone who reserves in the next half-hour.

Twitter is a real-time forum so making use of that dynamism may produce extra sales on Twitter day.

Tie It to Twitter

Twitter has a brand and image of its own, one that combines friendliness, efficiency and community. All of those characteristics can be helpful to a company too. One option then is not just to bring twitterers into your business but turn them into

(continued on next page)

Tony and Alba Pizza (@TonyAlba_Pizza), for example, a pizza parlor in San Jose, put on a Twitter Monday night special with this post: "Hey again it's Monday Night $5 off XLG or FAMILY. Say you want the Twitter Monday night Special."

That's very simple, and Riley's Café (@RileysCafe) in Cedar Rapids does something similar with its Twitter Tuesday. Discounts have included "a $5 coupon good towards our night menu when you mention "TT" and of course eat!" and even 25 percent off the entire menu.

Fuel (@fuelrestaurant), a restaurant in Vancouver, takes a slightly different approach with its Twitter Thursdays. Anyone mentioning Twitter while making a reservation is placed in a draw to receive a three-course meal for free.

Although the offer itself changes from venue to venue what all of these deals have in common is their simplicity. To take advantage of the offer, followers don't need to clip a coupon, enter a code or do anything special at all. They just need to mention the discount when they make their booking or place their order.

How to Do It

That means that creating special Twitter days couldn't be simpler too. You'll just need to post a tweet that describes the discount on offer and explains what followers need to do receive it. Fuel's "Reserve before 5pm for your chance to win dinner for 2 on us! Call 604 288 7905 & mention twitter! The winner will be revealed upon arrival" is an excellent example. It describes the prize and lays out precisely how to win it.

This tweet also does something else though. By forcing followers to book before 5pm, it creates a sense of urgency. Followers who might have left their choice of where to eat until later will have to make a commitment by late afternoon.

And that, of course, means that the restaurant will have a clearer idea of how their evening's going to look halfway through the day instead of halfway through the evening.

The only challenges will be making sure that as many people as possible see the offer. Building up lots of followers first will help, and asking for re-tweets can be useful too. More challenging though will be coming up with an offer that's both affordable and attractive.

Riley's Café's 25 percent discount might have been too generous. It won the business some local press coverage, which might have made the whole thing worthwhile, but it's noticeable that later offers were lower in value. Starting big to attract attention then working your way down may be one effective strategy.

Getting Started

To begin creating a special Twitter day for your business, you'll first need to identify a day you want to promote. As cafes and restaurants tend to be quieter at the beginning of the week than at weekends, that shouldn't be too difficult a decision.

You'll then need to choose the kind of bargain you want to offer. At the moment, businesses are offering all sorts of different benefits so the best strategy is to list a number of different options and track the results of each one in turn. Every business is different but you should be able to see which offers produce the best results.

A Model to Follow

There are all sorts of different models to follow to create a special Twitter day but perhaps the best is Fuel's.

The restaurant appears to have put a great deal of thought into its offer and although potentially expensive, it is only given to one customer, and it gets results. The winner of one free meal had canceled a reservation at another restaurant in order to put themselves in the running.

Note how carefully the timeline describes its offer, how it creates urgency and how it also maximizes the benefits. A report of the result of one of its Twitter days was written up at Kitsilano.ca, a website for local events, helping the restaurant to spread the word even further.

Your special Twitter day doesn't have to be marketed only on Twitter!

Tips
for Success
(continued)

a community based around your business once they arrive.

Encourage people to continue tweeting in your establishment and you'll turn your offer into an ad-hoc tweet-up, help people makenew friends, give them a fixed place to meet . . . and create loyal customers.

Add Local Followers

Although in theory any business can make use of a special Twitter day to encourage sales on one day of the week, in practice, the businesses that use this approach tend to be cafes and restaurants with quiet moments and which are dependent on local clientele.

That makes it vital those businesses have local followers. Twitter's s earch function allows results to be restricted geographically. If you're looking to bring in foot traffic make sure that you follow local twitterers—and that you're providing enough interesting traffic to make them want to follow you.

49

SQUAT SOME TWITTER REAL ESTATE

DIFFICULTY

SKILLS REQUIRED

INCOME POTENTIAL

What is Squatting on Twitter?

Back in the days of the Internet bubble, a few lucky speculators found themselves on the receiving end of giant checks after registering a valuable domain name. Sex.com, for example, was sold for $14 million, Business.com for $7 million and even GarageSales.com changed hands for $110,000. Considering that those names originally cost less than $10 to purchase, the sales represented an impressive return on investment.

Today, those investments aren't so easy to make. The best names have long been taken so to own a top name, you'd have to buy from the investor who got there before you. But Twitter is still relatively virgin territory. There are plenty of good names still available and while the value of a Twitter timeline is still unclear, that's usually the best time to stake your claim.

How Twitterers are Squatting Names

Mostly twitterers are squatting names on the site badly. Twitter has specific rules against name squatting and moves quickly to suspend accounts that don't meet its regulations. It's not necessarily the principle of holding a valuable name on Twitter and selling it later for a profit that Twitter seems to have a problem with so much as the practice of spamming.

Twitter specifically outlaws "unauthorized serial account creation," "unauthorized mass account creation," "aggressive following,"

GEEKPRENEUR

"extremely imbalanced follower/following ratio" as well as repetitive updates, timelines that contain too many links and those that receive lots of spam complaints.

The people at Twitter also tend to move pretty quickly so timelines such as @dvd and @notebooks bring up nothing but the "account suspended" message. A better bet might be to do what the owners of @notebook and @clothes have done . . . which is nothing.

They've registered the name but done nothing to develop it. While that may make valuing the name difficult, it does mean that they're not in danger of losing it through spamming.

The best option though is to monetize the name's timeline as much as possible. Twitter does allow timelines with automated feeds so it is possible to add posts without any great effort. Most of the tweets at @fashion, for example, are fed from ShoppingBlog.com. Should the blog choose to sell the timeline one day, they'll be able to point to their 9,000-plus followers as a sign of its value.

It's not clear that the owners of @fashion are interested in selling though. That can't be said of Jeremy Vaught, owner of @music. His timeline is active and contains both quotes and replies to other twitterers. It has around 760 followers, even though he's only following one person and posted about 25 times, a good sign that the name alone is good enough to bring in readers.

And the name of his timeline is "Your Brand Here," while his bio says "I had plans for this in the early days, now I'm willing to lease it if you are interested." Even the link leads to a page on his blog that offers the timeline for sale or lease.

How to Do It

Registering a valuable timeline name on Twitter will be as simple as coming up with a good name and reserving it. Bear in mind that each timeline you reserve will need a separate email address though, and consider too that while Twitter does not allow "mass" or "serial" account creation, it doesn't define what those terms might mean. Play it safe and try not to reserve more than a handful at one time.

The bigger challenge will be deciding what to do with the timeline you've created. While the simplest option is to do nothing and hold onto it until you're contacted by a potential buyer—the equivalent per-

Tips
for Success

Build Followers

Even if you've only created a timeline with the intention of selling it one day, do make the effort to make it active. Whether the buyer wants the timeline to place ads or market his or her own brand, they should be willing to pay more if they can see that it comes with a ready-made audience.

Use Phrases

Registering Twitter's names is so easy—and the site is growing so quickly—that it's possible that many of the best names will have gone already and you'll be stuck with a thesaurus looking for useful words. Hyphenated and compound domain names tend to be pretty poor substitutes, but on Twitter—where followers don't actually need to reach the timeline to read the content—they can work fine.

If you can't think of a good word, a two- or three-word phrase might do fine too.

(continued on next page)

Tips

for Success

(continued)

Let People Know you're Selling

Because the buying and selling of Twitter names isn't yet established, you'll need to tell buyers that your timeline is available for sale. You can certainly do that with a message in your bio but remember that that might put off followers who won't want to build a connection with someone who isn't going to be staying. Keep the tweets automated and impersonal, and while you might struggle to build buyers, you should make the exchange a little easier and do it without alienating followers.

haps of a parked domain—it's likely that you'll be able to ask for more money if you can show that your timeline has followers and a revenue stream.

That's the difference between selling a domain name and selling a developed website.

You might be able to build followers by offering automated headlines from a blog that you own on a similar topic—like @fashion does—or you could use RSS-based headlines from other sources linked to the original site. Provided it's interesting enough to build up followers, your timeline should build up value.

Once you've got the followers, you'll need to make the sale. At the moment, timelines don't seem to have begun changing hands for money but there does appear to be interest in doing so. That interest is only going to grow as the value of Twitter becomes clear. And because you won't need to hand over any server data or do anything other than provide the buyer with the timeline's password, the exchange itself should be very straightforward.

Getting Started

The first steps in holding a valuable Twitter name are very easy indeed. You just have to register the name. It's a process that might take all of five minutes.

Before that though, you'll need to have thought of a good name and that's a little harder. Although there are still plenty of good terms available, investors aren't hanging around and they're being snapped up quickly. Google's keyword tool at adwords.google.com/select/KeywordToolExternal might help you to identify some good terms that you might have otherwise missed but remember that real value will come from developing the timeline before you sell it. It's possible that you'll earn more from a well-developed mediocre name than a well-titled but empty timeline.

A Model to Follow

Jeremy Vaught's timeline at @music provides a pretty good example of a timeline that's being offered for sale. The name is particularly meaningful and good enough to pick up hundreds of followers with very little effort. The tweets that he has posted though are interesting, preventing him from looking like a spammer and his bio, name and even his link show that he's prepared to broker a deal.

Alternatively, @fashion's automated tweets show how easy it can be to fill a well-named timeline with effort-free content ready for a sale . . . if the owner wanted to sell it.

50 PICK UP VALUABLE STOCK TIPS

DIFFICULTY

■■■■➤

SKILLS REQUIRED

■■➤

INCOME POTENTIAL

■■■➤

What Are Stock Tips on Twitter?

Among the millions of tweets posted and exchanged on Twitter every day is a lot of banal stuff. Descriptions of lunches and breakfasts are plentiful, as are reports on the music people are listening to, the books they're reading and the naps they're about to take. But plenty of valuable data is being shared too and some of that includes the kind of data that smart investors might be able to use to help their money grow.

Some of that information is advice supplied by experts—people who are supposed to know which way the market is moving and are willing to share their tips about companies on the up. Some of it though comes from the companies themselves. While it's unlikely that a major deal is going to be reported on Twitter first, reading between the lines, especially in tweets posted by executives, may provide clues about how a company is growing . . . or why it's about to shrink.

It might not be wise to base an entire investment strategy on Twitter, and it's always worth investigating tips and information that appear on the site through other channels. But Twitter can certainly be one place to research investment options.

How Twitterers Are Picking up Stock Tips

The most basic way to pick up stock tips is by finding someone on Twitter who discusses the market, and follow them. You could use Twellow to look for "investment experts" or "financial advisors," or you could toss the name of a stock into Twitter's search engine and follow the people who are discussing it.

But that's all fairly hit and miss. Just because someone is discussing the stock market doesn't mean that what they have to say is worth listening to.

There are also plenty of corporate executives on the site. ExecTweets (www.exectweets.com), for example, lists tweets posted by business leaders such as DK Matai (@dkmatai), Chairman & Founder of mi2g, and Steve Case (@SteveCase), co-founder of AOL. While many of these twitterers are certainly going to be worth following anyway, executives are unlikely to let anything truly valuable about their companies slip on Twitter.

The two most important parts of using Twitter effectively to pick up investment advice are filtering out the bad information and knowing what to do with the good information that you receive.

A better way to find stock information then is to use StockTwits (www.stocktwits.com). Created by a team that includes investment experts, StockTwits tries to make finding information about stocks and following discussions about particular companies easier. Although you might not find breaking financial news directly from the horse's mouth on Twitter, you will find discussions about the news on the site, and StockTwits does an effective job of helping investors to track those opinions.

How to Do It

If all you want to do is find people with good investment advice to follow, then it's just a matter of doing some smart searching. The format for entering stock information on Twitter is to place a dollar sign before the ticker name (so Google is $GOOG and Apple is $AAPL). Entering the stocks you want to follow into Twitter's search engine then, will show you the current discussions.

You can also try looking for the officers of the companies you want to follow.

But StockTwits is still more efficient. The site lets you enter the ticker or company names you want to follow and brings up automatically all of the recent tweets about those firms as well as a graph showing their recent performance. You'll also be able to see which tickers are currently the most discussed and, perhaps more importantly, which twitterers are doing most of the talking.

StockTwits starts you off with 60 recommended financial twitterers, allowing you to read the tweets for a while, filter out those whose tweets are least relevant and add those who are providing the most useful information about the companies in which you've invested.

Tips
for Success

Filter

One of the reasons that StockTwits is so valuable is that it's effectively little more than a filtering tool. Enter the ticker name of a stock that you want to follow, and you'll be filtering out all of the other tweets on the site. It also supplies a number of recommended financial analysts to follow. While you'll still want to filter that initial list down further, it does mean that you're not starting completely fresh with no way to assess the value of what you're reading.

Ask Questions!

Although much of the value of the tweets you'll be reading will be broadcasts—updates posted for anyone to read—remember that Twitter works best as a two-way communication tool.

Don't be afraid to ask an analyst—or even a CEO—questions about their news and opinions. Their answers may yield even more valuable information and could give you a

(continued on next page)

for Success

(continued)

valuable clue to whether their thoughts are worth listening to.

Don't Rely on What You're Reading

Although you should be able to find some valuable advice on Twitter, don't rely on it. Twitter should always be regarded as just one source of financial information and everything you read should be cross-checked before you act on it.

A twitterer might be able to provide you with good suggestions but you can't blame them if you make a bad investment choice—even if it was their idea.

The result should be a stream of valuable information about the firms that matter most to you and the analysts who are providing the most reliable information.

It will then be up to you to decide what to do with that information.

Getting Started

The best way to start is to log in to StockTwits, add the stocks you want to follow and get reading.

Then look through the list of analysts and read their tweets.

Finally, read some more.

The biggest challenge of using the financial information that you can find on Twitter is that there's so much of it. It will be up to you to filter out the bad judgments, uninformed opinions and biased rants from the genuinely knowledgeable and thoughtful stuff. If you're not already familiar with the person doing the tweeting, you'll need to read as many of their tweets as possible, look at their websites and assess for yourself the value of their opinions.

That's going to take some judgment.

A Model to Follow

One of the strange things about following people on Twitter is that sometimes you never know whose tweets you're actually reading. That's true of FaustRoll (@faustroll), one of the most prolific financial tweeters.

FaustRoll doesn't provide a real name or explain where his information is from but he does supply a steady stream of technical and well-thought out predictions. More interestingly, he's also willing to enter into discussions. You can ask him questions (and expect an answer) and you can look at the timelines of the people he's replying to.

Even if you don't want to tweet like him, reading him can certainly be an education.

PROMOTE YOUR ONLINE ART STORE

51

What Are Art Store Promotions on Twitter?

For creative types, creating a storefront to sell goods has never been easier. Online malls such as Zazzle (www.zazzle.com), Cafepress (www.cafepress.com) and Etsy (www.etsy.com) now mean that anyone can put a design on a t-shirt, turn a collection of photographs into calendar or create earrings and make them all available for sale to millions without any of the hassle involved in actually opening a store or attending a craft fair.

For those using Zazzle and Cafepress, they don't even need to see the inventory.

But while the production may be as simple as registering on the site and uploading a design, the selling is difficult. In general, online arts and craft stores leave the marketing to the producers—and few producers know how to market.

Twitter though is one way that sellers on sites like Zazzle and Cafepress have been promoting their goods, and they've been doing it in a number of different ways, some better than others.

How Twitterers Are Promoting Their Online Art Stores

Promoting online stores is one activity which should result in direct sales. The results then are measureable: you should be able to track precisely how many sales a tweet—or series of tweets—produces.

DIFFICULTY

SKILLS REQUIRED

INCOME POTENTIAL

Tips
for Success

Match Your Twitter Timeline to Your Store

Coach Carrie Wilkerson recommends that bloggers with Twitter timelines match the design of their backgrounds to the design of their blogs to create a connection between the two. That principle applies to arts and crafts stores too. Use your logo, your products or something else that connects your timeline to your store so that your followers can easily see that buying from your store is as natural a way to participate in your timeline as replying to and reading your tweets.

But Twitter is not a good place to push sales hard. Readers tend to be looking for information and entertainment rather than sales pitches. Push too hard and you'll push readers away. Don't push at all though, and you won't get sales. Some twitterers understand that the best way to make sales on the site is first to build a community, create loyalty and generate trust and appreciation. Angryrobotwear (@Angryrobotwear), for example, has an active timeline which he uses to talk to followers and friends, only occasionally throwing in references to a new design on Cafepress. It's possible that more links and the odd special offer would bring in more sales—more followers certainly would—but it's important that those notifications appear as typical Twitter news updates rather than hard promotions.

Craig Behrin of BombThreads (@bombthreads) however does the exact opposite. His timeline consists of tweets that say nothing but "Come check out this t-shirt in my Zazzle store" and "I just made this t-shirt on Zazzle," followed by a shortened link. Although he does occasionally answer the odd tweet from one of his followers and send tweets directly to other twitterers, there's little reason that anyone would want to read his timeline.

The principle involved in marketing a store through Twitter is the same as the principle behind a successful website: good content with smart, optimized ads generates sales.

How to Do It

The best way to promote an online store through Twitter then is to focus—initially, at least—not on the sales but on the community. Search Twitter for people who have made a purchase on Cafepress, Zazzle and Etsy, and follow them. Make contact so that they'll follow you and try to bring them into your community.

If they've bought once on one of those sites, there's a good chance that they'll buy again.

And if they have a connection with you, even if it's only a connection created through Twitter, there's a good chance that they'll buy from you rather than from someone else.

In fact, that should be part of your strategy when promoting your store on Twitter. Each of those arts and craft malls is overflowing with talented and creative designers. The choice for buyers is overwhelming. But buyers aren't just looking for good designs; they're also looking for works of art, t-shirts that tell people who they are and items that tell a story and which have a connection with the artist.

Because Twitter is such a powerful community-building tool, it's extremely useful at creating the kind of loyalty that can turn interested browsers into customers . . . and customers into loyal collectors.

Once you've brought in proven buyers, you can also try to attract new buyers by following fashion readers, art connoisseurs and other designers. Again, engage them in conversation to encourage them to follow you, but also to give your timeline interesting content that other people will want to read.

When you come to mention your new products, work them in gently. Talk about the designs you're producing, give readers sneak peeks of items that are about to be released—as Alienation Digital (@alienation_) does with its website designs—to build excitement, and deliver special offers to your followers to make them feel appreciated.

Ask their opinion too. You don't have to follow it, but if you can help your followers feel that they were part of the design process, they'll be more inclined to buy.

Getting Started

Before you can start promoting your art and craft store on Twitter, you first have to create one. The process itself is fairly simple, although if you're using Etsy, you will have to pay for each item you list.

Whichever service you're using though, you'll also need designs to sell and a good idea of which kinds of products you're going to place those designs on. Zazzle, in particular, offers a huge range that includes skateboards and shoes as well as calendars and t-shirts.

Once you've created your store—and that shouldn't take you more than a few minutes—you can then work on building your community.

Tips
for Success

(continued)

Talk, Don't Sell

Followers don't like to be told to go out and buy so don't try to sell on your timeline. Instead, think of your timeline as an information channel through which you tell lovers of the kinds of items that you produce what you're working on and how you're doing it. It's as though you were letting tourists in to watch you in your workshop. Tell them what you're making and point out the souvenir shop, but let your work do the selling.

Make Special Offers

But you can still make the occasional special offer as a reward for following you. Your followers should feel that they belong to a special club . . . and that buying from you is the best way to pay their dues.

A Model to Follow

Etsy is a particularly popular on Twitter and one of the most intriguing Etsy timelines belongs to jewelry Galit Barak (@GalitBarak). Galit has used a catalog page of her products (complete with prices) as her background and her timeline contains a mixture of blog links and special offers. Although she might do even better with some more original content she does bring readers into the design and marketing process with tweets like this: "New blog post, help me decide my Etsy-Versary offers! http://galitbarak.blogspot.com."

The conversation is missing but Galit does provide models of the kinds of bargains, rewards and special offers that can be worked into an arts and craft store timeline.

GEEKPRENEUR

SELL YOUR MUSIC AND WIN DOWNLOADS . . . AND RECORD DEALS

52

What is Music Promotion on Twitter?

The Internet has made it possible for anyone to become a musician. You no longer need to impress an executive at a record company to sell your songs. You don't need to sign a contract handing over most of your album revenues and your certainly don't have to take advice about what you should or shouldn't include in your album from people who have never touched a guitar or put together a verse.

You just have to upload your tracks to a website and make them available for downloading.

But you still have to tell people they're there, and that's where things get a lot more difficult. Producing the music might not be easy but persuading people to buy it—or even listen to it—when there's so much other music available is always going to be difficult.

Twitter though makes it all a little easier. Tra.kz, a URL-shortening service for music-related content, lists almost 1,500 artists and bands as well as a number of important music business contacts, record labels and promoters.

The opportunities for musicians on Twitter then are enormous. Some are using the site to brand themselves and stay in touch with fans. Some are doing it to let people know about their music and their lives. And others are using Twitter to talk to other musicians . . . and make connections with the traditional music industry.

DIFFICULTY

SKILLS REQUIRED

INCOME POTENTIAL

Tips

for Success

Tell People Where You Are

Musicians have the advantage of already having a large source of potential followers. Anyone who listens to your samples, attends your concerts or buys your discs is likely to be interested in following you.

Put a link to Twitter on your website, and include the URL in your disk notes and concert material. You won't just attract fans, you'll engage them too.

Use Tra.kz to Find Connections

Tra.kz might not be the best URL-shortening service (do musicians really need their own URL-shortener?) but its list of musicians, record labels, radio stations, promoters, music publishers and more at tra.kz/v is an invaluable source of contacts. Use it to start following—and building your follower list.

(continued on next page)

How Twitterers Are Promoting their Music

The most famous example of a musician using Twitter to promote her work has to be Britney Spears. With over a million followers, her popularity on the site puts her streets ahead of other celebrities and the way in which she manages her timeline has been both controversial and a model for other stars.

After being criticized for advertising for a ghostwriter to create her tweets, Britney's timeline now consists of posts that are written by her team members, including her manager, and herself. Each writer places their name at the end of the tweet so that readers are clear about who is writing what.

The effect is a timeline that's clearly promotional—it mostly provides information about tours and albums, and links to pictures—but which also contains a certain amount of personal detail provided by Britney herself. What it lacks, though, is interaction. Neither Britney nor her team take the time or effort to bother answering tweets from fans. For them, Twitter is a broadcasting tool rather than a conversation channel.

That might work if you've already sold a few platinum discs and need to keep tight control of your image. Up-and-coming musicians though tend to be a bit more open. Karl Nova (@Karlnova), who describes himself as an "Emcee" uses his tweets to talk to his followers but also to recommend his own music: "Is saying my album is available RIGHT NOW on iTunes and Amazon mp3 it is fly! Cop it now! Or download a tune or 2 or 3 or 4 or 19? LOL."

Folk singer Allie Moss (@alliemoss), uses Twitter in a similar way, answering questions from fans and occasionally, throwing in a little reference to her own releases: "Just booked my west coast CD release at Hotel Cafe. May 27. Yeah-huh. w/ @ianaxel!"

A few musicians are making the most of the presence of music industry executives on the site to touch bases with people like Ron Spaulding (@RonASpaulding), Executive Vice President of Fontana Music Distribution. And finally, some musicians are even shortening links to their music with Tra.kz to make them easy to find and indicate to readers that the link leads to something tuneful.

GEEKPRENEUR

How to Do It

The best way to use Twitter to promote music then is not to assume that your fans will be as patient as Britney's and be willing to be talked to rather than chatted with—not unless you're as big as Britney. Nor is it a good idea to fill your timeline with little more than "thank yous" and greetings, as Bjork (@bjork) does on her timeline.

Instead, take advantage of Twitter's strength and use the site to build a real, human connection with your fans. Follow musicians whose music you appreciate and tell fans on your blog that you're setting up a timeline. That announcement alone should be enough to bring you plenty of followers, ease you through the first weeks of Twitter use and make your timeline instantly dynamic.

Don't overdo it with announcements of track releases and music downloads though.

Fans and followers will listen to your music out of curiosity, because they know and like your approach and because they feel a relationship with you.

Twitter gives you an opportunity to forge and maintain that relationship so not using it means ignoring one of Twitter's biggest marketing strengths.

At the same time, make sure you're following the music business executives on Twitter, ask them questions, reply to their tweets—and get yourself seen by the people who can do your promotional work for you.

Getting Started

The first thing to do, once you've set up your timeline and created your background, is to make sure that everyone knows about it. Tell the fans on your blog that you're now active on Twitter and make a point of answering at least some of the tweets that they send you.

Clearly, the more popular you are, the harder that will be but even answering some of them will show that you're accessible and friendly. Your followers will then be more willing to listen to—and download— your tracks.

for Success

(continued)

Make Business Connections

And don't forget to check out the music business executives on Twitter. Self-publishing might be free but the big money still lies in the studios. Only Twitter gives you the opportunity to make direct contact with some of the industry's most important decision-makers. You can find some of them at tra.kz/v too.

A Model to Follow

Most big musicians on Twitter are doing it wrong. Instead of taking the opportunity to talk to their followers, they're using Twitter to talk at them. Smaller musicians tend to do a better job of creating timelines that include the right mixture of chat and promotion.

One big artist who does have a great timeline though is British singer Billy Bragg (@billybragg). His tweets don't just include responses to questions from fans, he also actively solicits their contributions as well as recommending other singers and saying where he'll be performing.

The result is a timeline that's engaging, interesting and informative. Exactly the sort of thing that's likely to keep people reading—and listening.

GEEKPRENEUR

SELL YOUR PHOTOS WITH TWITTER

What is Photo Selling on Twitter?

DIFFICULTY

SKILLS REQUIRED

INCOME POTENTIAL

For any profession, Twitter should be a great place to meet clients, build a brand, gather a community, foster loyalty and make sales. That's true of photographers too. Twitter contains plenty of photographers, as well as lots of people who are planning their weddings, art buyers and even photo editors who need images for their newspapers and magazines.

Twitter allows photographers to tell their followers that they have new images available. It lets them keep up to date with the latest news from the world of photography, shoot the breeze with other photographers and announce new photo product releases.

Sales though are a lot harder to come by.

It is possible to use Twitter to make money as a photographer. But it isn't going to be easy.

How Photographers Are Selling Their Photos on Twitter

For the most part, photographers aren't selling their images or their services on Twitter. That's not because they aren't on the site. Twellow lists over 16,500 people who have described themselves as a "photographer." Although only a fraction of them will be professionals, these days just about any photographer with a decent camera and talent can sell their images. But few are doing it on Twitter.

Instead, most photographers are using Twitter as a way to talk to other shooters in what can otherwise be a fairly lonely profession.

Tips

for Success

Use TwitPic

Twitter doesn't have the infrastructure to upload images but it does have TwitPic (www.twitpic.com). TwitPic makes uploading images that can be seen by Twitter's users very easy. The image doesn't appear on Twitter itself but can be uploaded to Twitpic, with the caption appearing in your timeline.

Most photographers though, even professionals, use Twitpic to show off their snaps. That means it won't take too much to stand out on the site. Placing a few professional images on Twitpic and linking to them in your timeline will show your followers the images behind your tweets.

(continued on next page)

That's likely to be because photography buyers are relatively hard to find. While Facebook allows photographers to advertise in front of engaged women aged between 20 and 40, and living in a certain catchment area, Twitter has no tool that allows photographers to target a particular demographic.

Perhaps the most common way then that photographers are building sales on Twitter is by talking about their Etsy store. Practical products such as t-shirts, calendars and cards are always easier to sell than framed prints which need dedicated wall space. Twitter is filled with tweets from creative and photographic types announcing new items uploaded to Etsy or Zazzle, or better still, creating curiosity by telling followers about the Etsy products they're working on.

One photographer who does use Twitter to try to drum up business though is wedding photographer Lori Luza. Lori has two timelines: her personal timeline @loriluza is kept private. You have to ask her permission to read her personal tweets. Her professional timeline @asyouwish though is public and filled with tweets about clients (some of whom are on Twitter), her editing work and even updates from weddings themselves. They give potential clients a great insight into how Lori works and the links to clients on Twitter offer implied references too.

And a third way that photographers are selling images on Twitter is by selling them for Twitter. BetterTweetShots (www.bettertweetshots.com) is part of a photography network that matches clients with photographers for a range of online needs, including dating, websites and now Twitter profiles. They're always looking for portrait photographers and accept submissions on their website.

How to Do It

Creating tweets that lead buyers to purchase photo products is a technique in its own right. To be successful, you need to identify potential buyers and use the timeline to make them feel a part of the creative process. Customers are more likely to buy directly from an artist if doing so makes them feel that they've identified something unique and special. Explaining what sort of pictures you're working on, giving your followers unique previews of your images and designs, and asking what they think of different pictures can help to foster loyalty and encourage sales.

For other photographers, landing clients on Twitter will always be a little harder. Wedding photographer Bob LoRusso (@lorussostudios), for example, uses Facebook's technology to tag his images and push them to the profiles of his clients' friends. His ads on Facebook too have won him $40,000 worth of work for just $180 in costs. But he uses Twitter to let down his guard and talk to other photographers because, he says, his clients can't see him there.

Twitter's networking power though can still help photographers. While it might be difficult to identify potential wedding clients on Twitter, the site does have photo editors such as the Daily Tribune's Gerik Parmele (@gerik) and blogger Rob Haggart (@aphotoeditor). Fricafact (@fricafact) highlights images of Africa and could be a channel to showcase some travel photos, while galleries A Gallery Art (@agallerylondon), Tinku Gallery (@tinkugallery) and Glowlab (@glowlab) are just some of the outlets that should be in every art photographer's follow list.

Make sure your website and online portfolio are up to date and looking their best, follow, read and engage them in conversation. That should be enough to get important people looking at your pictures.

Getting Started

The most important first step you can take even before you begin tweeting as a photographer is to make sure that your website contains a good portfolio, and that there's an inviting image on your home page. Anyone who sees your timeline will click the link above your bio to see what sort of pictures you shoot and assess your photographic skills. One mistake that turns up frequently on Twitter is when photographers link to their blog.

Followers can read about you on Twitter. They're clicking because they want to see your pictures. Upload a portfolio that's neatly divided into different sections and includes your personal work too. You'll make it easy for potential clients to make buying decisions.

for Success

(continued)

Use Other Social Media Services

Twitter is fairly limited as a tool for photographers. While Facebook, for example, has been proven to bring in jobs and income, there are few stories of photographers winning commissions directly on Twitter. One strategy then is to use Facebook, LinkedIn and, of course, Flickr for job searching but to use Twitter for chatting to other photographers.

A Model to Follow

Despite the large number of photographers on Twitter there are few good models for photographers who want to use the site to make sales and win jobs. Lori Luza's use of Twitter then stands out for both its creativity and its professionalism. Her professional timeline has an optimized and attractive background, a bio that describes the kinds of images she shoots and a link to her website. Her tweets describe the life of a wedding photographer and create the appearance of a business in demand, and her replies allow for interaction and interest.

And she still manages to use Twitter for fun with her personal—and confidential—timeline.

PICK UP AMAZON REVIEWS ON TWITTER

What Are Amazon Reviews?

Whether you're trying to keep your best-seller at the top of the charts or just hoping to give your ebook a bit of a boost, reviews on Amazon are vital for sellers of information products. According to one estimate, as many as one buyer in five chooses to make a purchase based on the reviews on the site.

Usually though, there's a little authors can do to encourage reviews. Because they can't talk to readers directly, they have no way to persuade them to return to Amazon, share how much they enjoyed the read . . . and prompt other browsers to buy.

Twitter has changed that. Book sellers can now communicate with their readers, urge them to write reviews and promote their books in their timelines.

It's a simple method but one that can do wonders for book sales . . . especially when done correctly.

DIFFICULTY

➡

SKILLS REQUIRED

➡

INCOME POTENTIAL

■ ■ ■ ➡

How Twitterers Are Picking Up Amazon Reviews

Authors are taking two different approaches to encouraging reviews on Amazon.

The most basic is to appeal to anyone who has read the book to head back to Amazon and leave their review. Donna Cutting (@donnacutting), for example, author of "The Celebrity Experience," placed this tweet on her timeline: "Have you read The Celebrity Experience? Would u consider writing a review on Amazon.com? http://tinyurl.com/6bzc2d"

Tips
for Success

Direct Your Requests

Twitter's users are remarkably friendly and helpful. Ask them for a favor or submit a request and as long as it's not too demanding, there's a good chance that they'll agree. Directing your review requests to readers that you've found on Twitter then can be very effective as well as good marketing in its own right.

Put Your Twitter Name in the Book

This might not be suitable for every publication but if you're selling a self-published book or an ebook on Twitter, there's no reason why you couldn't place a request to follow you on one of the pages. You'll have a way to keep readers close to you, you'll be able to ask them for a review when they mention that they've read your book in their own timelines and having bought from you once, there's a good chance that they'll buy from you again.

(continued on next page)

That's a very general appeal. Although it has the advantage of including a link to Donna's Amazon page to make leaving the review easy, it's also easy to ignore. Followers who had read the book may not see the tweet if they're following lots of other people and even if they did see it, they may feel that enough other readers will be leaving reviews so they don't need to bother.

That's why many authors choose to direct their requests specifically at people who they know have read the book. Mark Bell (@Typewriter), for example, asked this of one twitterer who had identified him as the author of "Build a Website for Free": "@voyagerfan5761 would you mind writing a review on Amazon?"

Although that tweet didn't include a link, it was directed at one particular twitterer, a policy that increases the pressure on that individual to actually leave a review. (In this case, it turned out that @voyager fan5761 had helped someone else select the book but in his response indicated that he would certainly have been willing to write a review, indicating that such requests do apply effective pressure.)

How to Do It

If all you want to do is ask all of your followers to leave reviews on Amazon, then you won't have to do any more than place a general request in your timeline. Be sure to include a shortened link in your tweet though and use one of the URL shortening services that allow you to track results, such as Bit.ly or Twurl.

While you should be able to see easily how many new reviews you receive immediately following each tweet, remember that every time you include the link in your timeline, you'll also be advertising your product. You'll want see then how many people click the link and reach your Amazon page so that you can track the effectiveness of those tweets.

That's another reason that it's a good idea to direct your requests. You'll need to track mentions of your book on Twitter and reply to each person, asking them to leave a review. You can also tell them that you hope they enjoyed the book or thank them for the praise if they've recommended it in their own timeline.

Again, your followers will see those tweets, click through to the reader's timeline and read a recommendation for your product.

Those requests then don't only function as encouragement to leave reviews, they also highlight testimonials that people have already placed. (And don't worry too much about looking like a snooper; most readers will be thrilled to find that the author of a book they enjoyed is on Twitter and wants to tweet with them.)

That does mean though that you will need to be tracking keywords, be ready to respond to mentions of your book.

Getting Started

Clearly, before you can start drumming up reviews for your Amazon products, you'll need to have created some. These days though, that's very simple and you don't need to have a contract from Random House to get your book on the world's biggest bookstore.

It's possible to sell self-published books on Amazon as well as ebooks and even Kindle books too. And while you'll struggle to get books that haven't been produced by a major publisher into The New York Times book review pages, with Twitter you can still generate user reviews very easily.

The next stage then will be to track the name of the book and your own name as author too. That will mean keeping Monitter open in your browser or conducting regular searches.

But you should be doing one or both of those things anyway!

A Model to Follow

The best model for authors looking to promote their books on Amazon is probably marketer Joel Comm (@joelcomm). Not only does he place a picture of his cover clearly in his background and mention the book in his bio, he also contacts everyone who mentions his book on Twitter, thanks them for their praise and asks them for a review on Amazon.

Altogether, his book has picked up more than 50 reviews, almost all of them four star and above.

Those frequent mentions in his timeline though don't just generate good reviews, they also act as regular reminders to his 40,000-plus followers that his book is being read—and enjoyed.

SHOW OFF YOUR DESIGN SKILLS WITH TWITTER BACKGROUNDS

DIFFICULTY

SKILLS REQUIRED

INCOME POTENTIAL

What is Demonstrating Your Design Skills on Twitter?

Twitter doesn't give its followers a great deal of room to be creative. While MySpace allows its members to customize their pages with everything from music to image galleries, Twitter only provides space for one background image, much of which is obscured by the timeline.

Twitterers have already discovered how to make the most of that image by placing a picture of themselves or their business logo in the top left corner, and creating an information bar that explains who they are and where followers can go to learn more about them.

Designers too though have also figured out how to make the most of those background images. Some are simply selling them, offering to create bespoke designs for businesses and brands on the site. Others are using free Twitter backgrounds to show off their skills and tempt users to hire them for other kinds of design work.

Either way, the result should be more sales and more income for any talented designer with the right knowledge.

How Designers Are Using Twitter Backgrounds to Promote Themselves

Designers are using a number of models to promote and sell their skills with Twitter backgrounds. The most obvious is probably Hugh Briss's (@hughbriss) TwitterImage.com (www.twitterimage.com).

Hugh sells unique backgrounds for $100 each (or $150 for a choice of two designs). While he tends to stick to the now traditional format of using the left side of the screen as an information bar, he's not afraid to be creative and dominate that space with large pictures of the twitterer behind the timeline too.

MyTweetSpace.com (www.mytweetspace.com) offers a similar service but undercuts Hugh on price, charging just $59 instead of $99. That might win the company some budget clients, but it does yield a higher spot to Hugh who as a more expensive designer creates a better impression too. (Although at $127 per profile, TrifectaBackgrounds.com is even more expensive.)

Hugh also goes cheaper though, offering completely free designs for no-budget twitterers. These backgrounds include his logo, spreading his name across Twitter, and the offer itself is an effective way to bring in more traffic.

Natalie Jost (@natalie) only offers free Twitter backgrounds. The patterns, available at TwitterPatterns.com (www.twitterpatterns.com), can provide an attractive platform on which to add your own information bar and branding information. On the site, Natalie explains that she made the patterns available because she wanted to share, but also notes that some of them are now-outdated commercial designs while others are sketches that were never developed.

There's no doubt though that the availability of high quality free designs can drive traffic to her commercial site at olivemanna.com.

And finally TwitBacks.com (www.twitbacks.com) also offers free backgrounds but uniquely lets twitterers create those patterns themselves. Users can choose from a variety of templates, then complete a series of fields that demand information such as name and company name, "blurb about you," logo, personal photo, and URLs at Facebook, LinkedIn and host of other social networking sites. Those details are then inserted automatically into the background.

At the moment, TwitBacks' backgrounds are free but they do come with the company's logo, which customers can pay $4.99 to remove. For an additional $9.99, TwitBacks will also submit the background to search engines and directories, and supply tracking reports that reveal the number of visitors from each directory. The company also plans to charge for premium features.

Although this model doesn't promote TwitBacks' own backgrounds, it does allow the company to earn from its background templates.

Tips
for Success

Give Your Backgrounds Free to Big Twitterers

Hugh Briss first came to the attention of twitterers when he created free backgrounds for twitterers with large followings, including Darren Rowse (@problogger)and John Chow (@johnchow). He still creates free custom backgrounds for twitterers with more than 10,000 followers, putting his backgrounds in front of thousands of people at a time.

(continued on next page)

for Success

(continued)

Make the Connections

When you're using Twitter backgrounds to show off your skills as a designer—rather than to sell the backgrounds themselves—it's going to be vital to connect the designs with your other services. You'll still need to deliver your backgrounds through a unique site, but link to both of them from your own timeline and describe your real work on the background site. The backgrounds should seem to be free samples derived from your professional work.

How to Do It

The easiest way to use Twitter's backgrounds to promote your own designs is to create a website dedicated to the task. Offer a number of free designs to bring in traffic, and make sure that your logo is clearly visible on each pattern you give away. As your free backgrounds are taken up, you'll benefit from an easy form of viral marketing.

Offering commercial backgrounds will be a little harder if only because the competition is heating up. With prices that range from $59 to $127, choosing the right price point could be tricky too, but around $100 should be about average. Those unwilling to pay can build their own background based on one of your free patterns.

Getting Started

The first steps will be to create a range of backgrounds that show off your skills. For the free patterns that should be simple enough. Natalie Jost has even described her working process on her blog at nataliejost. com/process/ so you can see how she does it.

Try to create patterns that fit different kinds of twitterers though. Twellow's categories ae a good guide to pattern topics.

Creating sample commercial backgrounds that followers will see and which you can show off on your website too will be a little harder. One option though is to give away designs to your own followers and to twitterers with large followings of their own.

Lastly, and most importantly, if you're using the backgrounds to generate interest in your main design business, make sure you mention your other site frequently but without giving them a hard push. Users should feel that they've stumbled onto an opportunity rather than that they're being pushed to buy.

A Model to Follow

Each of the different ways in which designers are offering backgrounds functions as one kind of marketing model. Hugh Briss, TwitterImage and TrifectaBackgrounds primarily focus on selling backgrounds. They offer free backgrounds to twitterers with large followings and provide a range of attractive samples.

Natalie Jost neatly dovetails her free patterns into her commercial work and even her Etsy products, while TwitBacks has created a whole new way of offering designs that requires little further work from designers but could provide a platform for further revenue.

56 COOK UP PROFITS WITH TWITTER-BASED RECIPES

DIFFICULTY

SKILLS REQUIRED

INCOME POTENTIAL

What Are Recipes on Twitter?

One of the most attractive things about Twitter is the creativity of twitterers forced to write in only 140 characters. So you end up reading lots of pithy posts, plenty of short quotes and lots of witty little statements.

Usually when someone wants to pack in more content than can reasonably be expected to fit in one tweet, they put it on a Web page and tweet the headline with a link.

Sometimes though, the twitterer finds a way to include everything in the tweet.

Some twitterers have even managed to write entire recipes in 140 characters. Their timelines are nothing more than recipe books with little or no interaction, but for readers they're a stream of both meal ideas and complete cooking instructions delivered directly to their Twitter page.

That makes for a timeline which delivers the most important benefit that any timeline can deliver: genuinely valuable content. It's that sort of content than can easily build followers—and once you have lots of readers, it's only a small step towards monetizing them, as Twitter's founders would no doubt be willing to tell you.

How Twitterers Are Posting Recipes

Recipes tend to take about half a page to list the ingredients then another half a page at least to describe what to do with them. Squeezing

GEEKPRENEUR

all of that information into 140 characters takes some skill and lots of abbreviations. Maureen Evans (@maureen) uses a systematic shorthand to describe measurements and techniques on her cooking timeline @cookbook. This recipe, for example: "Hot Orange Broccolini: saute4T olvoil/2garlic&shallot/orange's zest/.25t chiliflake&s+p; +500g/lb brocc 1m; cvr3m+orange's juice/T balsamic" would translate as:

"Hot Orange Broccolini.

Saute two cloves of garlic, two shallots and orange zest in four tablespoons of olive oil. Add a quarter of a teaspoon of chili flakes, salt and pepper, then 500 grams of broccoli. Saute for one minute then cover for three minutes. Add orange juice and a tablespoon of balsamic vinegar."

Maureen's timeline consists of nothing but recipes like these and they're remarkably easy to follow. For those who struggle with the shorthand, Maureen's bio also provides a link to an abbreviation table. Her recipes were covered in the New York Times, and are read by around 10,000 followers.

Craig Dugas (@craigdugas) does something similar with his timeline @TinyRecipes. Although this timeline has far fewer followers than Maureen Evans', it also tries to be slightly different. Maureen's recipes are meant to be complex. Part of the attraction of her timeline is the squeezing of long recipes into a short space. Craig's recipes though are meant to be simple. They're often made up of little more than a list of ingredients and some basic cooking instructions: "brown rice—1.5C H2O, 1C rice. High heat, bring both to boil in pot. Upon boiling, cover+reduce heat to simmer 20min. Let sit 10min covered".

Although these simple recipes make for a less valuable timeline than Maureen's, Craig does make better use of them. Maureen links only to a glossary; Craig links to his blog 28may.net/recipes which offers longer and more complex recipes.

For Maureen then the miniaturization of her recipes is the end of the process. Craig's tiny recipes are the tip of a much richer source of information.

What neither has done though is to monetize their mini-recipes. Offering short recipes on Twitter and providing fuller versions on a website as Craig does, should provide a steady stream of traffic. That traffic should be willing to click on ads and affiliate links on blog pages, and even buy a recipe e-book.

Tips for Success

Target a Niche

You'll find it much easier to pick up followers if you create niche cooking timelines. So you could have one for vegetarian cooking, another for Cajun cooking and a third for barbeques. Toss the odd keyword into a recipe title and you should get picked up by followers looking for people tweeting about those topics.

Connect w with Your Personal Timeline

Maureen Evans' timeline contains only recipes and no interaction with her followers. That allows it to read like a recipe book. But your personal timeline should be a place where you interact with followers, answer questions and provide more details if requested. It will depth to your recipe timeline, make it more personal and drive more traffic to your website.

How to Do It

There are two challenges to overcome in posting short recipes on Twitter: you need to have recipes; and you need to be able to squeeze them into 140 characters.

Having recipes will be the harder of the two.

Any recipe you post on Twitter has to be original. You can't cook something from a recipe book and place it on Twitter as your own. While cooks often build on each other's recipes to create new dishes, without the space to provide the proper attribution, that may not be possible on Twitter.

If you're going to post recipes online—and this is true of a blog as well—they really should be your own.

Shortening them will be much easier. You could even use Maureen Evans' glossary as your guide and include a link to it in your bio. Her followers will be used to it, so any of them that follow you will be familiar with the shorthand. Dropping the vowels is always a good way to save space.

There is a third challenge though, and that will be to monetize your timeline. You won't be able to do that easily in the timeline itself, so you'll need to build a website on which you discuss the recipes in more detail, perhaps provide pictures and variations, and offer affiliate links to cooking utensils and cookbooks, as well as pay-per-click ads.

The two channels—the timeline and the website—would then work together to maximize your audience, and your ad revenues.

Getting Started

That means your first move shouldn't be to hit the kitchen and start playing around with recipes. It should be to launch a dedicated cooking blog or website, if you haven't done so already. There are plenty of great example of those on the Web already. Vegandad.blogspot.com for example, is rich with mouthwatering pictures and interesting descriptions. His users even requested that he put his recipes in book format which they can then buy as an ebook or print-on-demand book from Lulu.com.

Begin with a website like that, and you'll have a rich source of mini-recipes that you can create for Twitter.

A Model to Follow

Both Craig Dugas's and Maureen Evans's timelines are good models to copy but neither is perfect. Neither makes use of their traffic to turn it into revenue and neither supports their websites well. Maureen offers more interesting recipes but her timeline stands in isolation. It links to her glossary but she could just as easily have linked from the glossary to the rest of her website.

The power of a recipe timeline lies not just in the recipes themselves, but in what you're able to do with the people who read them.

57 GET PAID FOR YOUR EXPERTISE

What is Getting Paid for Your Expertise

DIFFICULTY

SKILLS REQUIRED

INCOME POTENTIAL

Twitter is rapidly becoming the go-to place for anyone with a question. Want to know how to write a query letter to a literary agent? Look for a literary agent on Twitter and ask her.

Want to know the secret to a successful soufflé? Twitter's full of chefs. Ask one.

Want to know what stocks to buy? There are plenty of people handing out investment advice. You just need to know who to ask . . . and how much to trust the information you receive.

Whatever you want to know, there are now enough people on Twitter with a broad enough diversity of backgrounds to be able to find an answer. But that answer is likely to be brief and shallow. While twitterers are a generous lot, few will have the time and the inclination to talk someone through the fine details of a complex problem—especially when they could be expected to do the same thing for thousands of other people.

They might though if they're being paid for it.

That's the solution that Justin Rockwell (@ThatCssGuy) came up with for his timeline. He provides help with CSS for anyone who needs it and asks in return that they pay him whatever they think the advice is worth.

According to one report, Justin is able to generate around $350 a week by solving the CSS problems of other twitterers.

It's a model that any other expert can easily follow. As Justin himself wrote in one of his tweets: "wish there was an @thatnetworkguy to help @thatcssguy with his down internet!"

How One Twitterer is Being Paid for his Expertise

Justin Rockwell does a number of things that help other twitterers and, no less importantly, make them feel that his advice is worth paying for.

First, he doesn't rely on Twitter. He has a website at www.thatcssguy. com that markets his advice service, explains what he does and provides a way for people with CSS problems to make their payment.

Like Justin's Twitter timeline, that website is friendly and personable. While there are testimonials on the home page, there's no hard sell and there is plenty of fun and friendliness. Clients feel that they're getting help and rewarding a helpmate, not paying for a consultancy service.

His website is likely to bring in some traffic—and business—but Justin also uses Twitter to trawl for people with problems. When Steve Espinosa (@stevemcstud) asked "Can anyone out there help me out with some CSS/Layout issues?" Justin was able to shoot back a response asking what his problem was. He then encouraged Steve to contact him by email or AIM to discuss the problem in more detail.

Sometimes though, Justin solves the problem on Twitter itself. When "Jeannie" (@surferartchick) asked him if he could help with her CSS problem, she sent him the details by direct message and he explained in a series of tweets that there was a problem in her h5 tag. She was then left to surf to his site to make her donation, but Justin was able to show off just exactly how he can help everyone reading his tweets.

And he makes that even clearer by regularly posting little CSS tips: "Remember kids: Use background images on elements instead of image tags for images that are not related to the content." Developers using CSS will follow his timeline just for those words of advice. When they run into a problem, Justin will be the natural place to turn.

How to Do It

Creating a timeline that offers paid help isn't difficult but it does require that a number of separate elements work together.

You'll need to create a website that describes what you're offering and accepts payment. (Justin only takes payment by credit card on his site).

for Success

Produce Visible Results

One reason that Justin's clients are willing to pay for his advice is that they can see the results: a page that didn't work now does. As you're looking for a service to offer, focus on something that generates visible or measureable results. Twitterers then won't feel that they're paying for your advice but for what your advice has done for them.

Help Your Clients Set a Rate

Without a set rate for advice packages, twitterers will struggle to understand how much they should pay for help. Justin gets around this problem by using a slider scale that allows clients to adjust payments but which begins at the position of $55. Raising or lowering the price appears to produce a faster or slower response time. Clients then can see what they should pay and why they should pay it.

(continued on next page)

for Success

(continued)

Keep it Friendly

Twitter is a friendly place—a place where people usually offer help for free. Justin tries to keep that feeling in his timeline by creating the impression that he helps because he wants to … but would really appreciate it if you'd pay him too!

You'll then need to find people with issues related to your field. Again, that isn't difficult but it will take a little time. Search for keywords, follow twitterers posting about your issues and use services like Monitter and TweetBeep (www.tweetbeep.com) to keep track of requests for help as they turn up on Twitter.

Finally, make sure that you post regular tips to keep people following you and show off your knowledge. Justin Rockwell prefaces his tips with the phrase "Remember children" as part of his branding as a CSS super-hero. Creating a similar format for your words of advice will help them to stand out in your timeline.

Getting Started

Your first move will be to create the website and include a system that will allow you to receive payments. Be sure to include your tweets on your website to bring the two platforms together. If you don't have a credit card account, then Paypal should be an easy way to accept payments too.

Then it's just a matter of creating your timeline and building up your followers.

Don't forget that every time you offer help and someone answers you, your name appears in their timeline, spreading word of your services even further.

A Model to Follow

Justin Rockwell's timeline is clearly the one to follow, and there's plenty of room to do so. He himself has put out a plea for help with network issues. There's no reason though that a mechanic couldn't do the same thing, a hardware specialist or any other type of coder.

If you can find a specialty that delivers real, tangible results, following Justin's model should help to bring results for yourself too.

PROMOTE YOUR INFORMATION PRODUCTS

58

What Are Information Products?

Experts have long had a problem. They knew their knowledge was valuable. They knew that people were prepared to pay large sums to know what they know. And they knew they wanted to help them.

The most effective way of delivering knowledge to a market though has always been in book form and putting knowledge into a book has always been difficult. Books cost money to produce, distribute and promote. Publishers have always been very selective about the manuscripts they accept, and the financial returns for authors are generally poor.

Books though deliver more than royalties. They also give the author branding, an image as an expert and an opportunity to spread his or her ideas to people who might not be familiar with them.

Ebooks supply all of those benefits but in a much more democratic—and flexible—form. Anyone can create an ebook and distribute it on the Web, generating both revenue and a market.

They can decide on the length, the images, the cover and, most importantly, the price. While many ebooks are free, others are sold for prices many times that of a conventionally-published book, even though there are no printing or inventory costs.

The disadvantage of creating an ebook though is some loss of prestige. Conventionally published books have a much greater branding power. Ebook publishers too also have to handle their own marketing, finding readers and letting people know that their book is available.

Tips
for Success

Post Tips

Ebook publishers have the advantage of ready access to a large supply of valuable content. Short tips delivered at regular intervals will make a timeline a useful read and a difficult choice to unfollow. They'll also provide free samples indicating the importance of your book's content.

Give Thanks

Gratitude for recommendations and reviews is a very easy and natural way to remind followers about your ebook. Make scanning for references to your publication on Twitter a regular part of your routine.

Twitter is turning out to be one way in which ebook authors are publicizing their products.

How Twitterers Are Selling Information Products

Twitterers are promoting their ebooks in all sorts of different ways. The simplest is just to tell their followers that their new book is available and ready for download. PR professional Stephen Abbott (@nhprman), for example, placed this tweet in his timeline to mark the completion of his ebook. "Just finished a new eBook, 'The American Citizen's Handbook' (go check it out!) http://tr.im/aepach"

An approach like this couldn't be simpler, but it's also going to have limited effect. The tweet will only be seen by the twitterer's followers, and not even by all of them. Because tweeting happens in real time, tweets are often missed and need to be repeated to make the most of the opportunity that Twitter offers.

But the post also looks a little like an ad. That's bad enough once in a timeline but it's not the sort of thing that people want to see regularly.

Announcing that you've just completed an ebook then is not a bad idea. But don't expect it to bring in too many downloads.

The same is true of another strategy but one which looks far less commercial. When Richard M. Krawczyk (@MarketingZap) spotted a reference to his ebook in someone else's timeline, he was quick off the mark with a word of thanks. "@jmancools Thank you for the kind words in regards to my eBook. Greg Reid is a great guy to work with. Good luck with your Documentary. :-)"

Like an announcement, a tweet like this will only be seen once. But it doesn't look like an ad, it lets readers know that the twitter has an ebook available, and it draws the readers' attention to a testimonial for that book.

Once an announcement has been made and the ebook has become known, these kinds of tweets make great follow-ups. Get in the habit of searching for references to your ebook and thanking anyone who made a positive comment about it.

The best approach though is to theme your timeline to the subject of the book. It might even be a good idea to create a unique product-based timeline to do this. Dana Lynn Smith (@BookMarketer), for example, has a timeline dedicated to book marketing. Like any effective timeline, she uses it to contact other people in her specialty, make small personal posts and offer professional advice.

And she also uses it to let her readers know about her books and ebooks.

The overall impression is that Dana's timeline doesn't promote her publications; rather, her publications provide information that her timeline doesn't have the room to contain.

She gets the branding, the following—and it's likely that she's also getting the sales and the downloads too.

How to Do It

Making the most of Twitter's promotional and viral marketing power to sell ebooks will require a little planning. You'll need to create a unique timeline for the topic of the ebook and follow other experts in the field.

You'll then need to post a number of different kinds of tweets.

Replies will make your timeline look active, encourage the people you're following to follow you in return, and invite your followers to bring you into their discussions too.

Tips, possibly taken from the book, will show off your knowledge and expertise.

Announcements of the ebook release, links to reviews and expressions of gratitude will give you excuses to remind followers that your book is out there and available.

And personal touches will bring your followers into your life and develop the kinds of close relationship that leads to sales.

Getting Started

The first step—assuming you already have an ebook—will be to create a unique timeline that covers the subject of the publication. That timeline should have an optimized background and a link in the bio that leads to the ebook's landing page. And that's where the blatant commercialism should stop.

A Model to Follow

George Knight's timeline @MindandBodyYoga contains a good variety of different kinds of tweets, all of them related to the subject of his website. He posts plenty of inspiring quotes, thanks people who compliment the book and refers to it frequently, encouraging people to buy it.

He even reveals that the price will rise soon to create a sense of urgency.

Although George's timeline might not suit every ebook promotion, its non-commercial feel is an important part of successful Twitter marketing.

FIND START-UP FUNDING

59

What is Start-Up Funding on Twitter?

Back in the days of the Internet bubble, it was enough for anyone with a basic knowledge of HTML and an understanding of a keyboard layout to think of a word, add "dotcom" to the end and receive a check for several million dollars from a venture capitalist who could be persuaded that advertising was the solution to every financial problem.

These days, prising money out of the hands of angels and investors takes a little more effort. You need to have a business plan, knowledge of your field and—unless you're Twitter—a monetization strategy too.

You also need to know investors and how to approach them.

That's where Twitter can be helpful. Just as the site has plenty of tech-minded geeks bursting with programming skills and ideas for the next big thing, so it also has a number of investors and angels who are happy to share their advice and, just possibly, their finances too.

How Twitterers Are Looking for Start-Up Funding on Twitter

Most twitterers are looking for start-up funding on Twitter very badly. Spend enough time browsing the site—especially the timelines of hopeful entrepreneurs—and you'll eventually come across a tweet like this: "Searching for $125,000 of start-up funds. We can do it."

That particular tweet came from Higher Hangers (@HIGHER hangers), a timeline created by a student entrepreneur to promote his new design for clothes hangers. As one part of a series of tweets that

DIFFICULTY

SKILLS REQUIRED

INCOME POTENTIAL

for Success

Don't Ask for Money

The most tempting way to find funding on Twitter is simply to ask for it and hope that of all the millions of people on the site, one of them will be kind enough to dip into their pockets and pull out exactly the amount you need. They won't.

Investors don't offer money because they like you. They offer money because they know you and they believe that that money will come back.

Use Twitter to get to know investors and build trust by asking questions and networking. Let the investment come naturally.

Stay Positive

Twitter is often used as a place to say what's on your mind. When you're creating a professional timeline, it needs to be a place where you say the things that have the best effect. Keep your tweets positive and upbeat. You have to show that you believe in yourself if you want others to believe in you too.

(continued on next page)

discuss the young business-builder's attempts to get his company off the ground, the competitions he's entered and the presentations he has to give, it may just deliver results.

But only because it's not the tweet itself that would bring in the cash but the timeline as a whole.

A timeline like Higher Hangers' reads a little like a reality show. It's like watching a candidate on The Apprentice trying to push an idea. Investors may want to learn more about the product but they're almost certain to be impressed by the company's enthusiasm and belief. Reading the tweets already tells them something about the business.

That isn't true of the tweets that read like begging letters.

No investor is ever going to be persuaded by a single tweet to write a check for several million dollars. But a timeline as a whole can function as a platform on which a hopeful entrepreneur can show off his or her talent and drive, and it can also allow small business owners to make the connection and build the knowledge that will allow them to grow.

How to Do It

To find start-up funding on Twitter, you'll need to do a couple of things.

First, you'll need to create a timeline just for your business idea. That doesn't mean you can't have a personal timeline as well, but investors aren't really interested in who you are beyond the extent to which your personality and interests affect your ability to manage the company.

That information you can put across in your professional timeline too but investors will always be more interested in your product idea and what it can do, the extent to which you're tackling problems and building interest than in what you're having for lunch or your discussion with a friend.

Write tweets that describe improvements in your design, the results of research, funding competitions that you've entered or surprises that you've discovered as you were putting together your business plan.

Use that timeline as a showcase for your product rather than for you.

But you also have to build a targeted following for that timeline. While that should include other twitterers in your industry, it's also a good idea to follow people with good advice about start-ups. Martin Zwilling (@StartupPro), for example, is both a start-up mentor and angel investor whose timeline is filled with great advice, offers of help and answers to questions put to him by other entrepreneurs.

He might not be willing to supply the funds himself but he could give you the information you need to win it from other investors.

And asking is the third action step you need to take to find funding through Twitter. While investors aren't going to dip into their pockets just because you asked them to, engaging them in conversation and making yourself known on Twitter is one part of the kind of valuable networking that might just lead to the angel you need.

Getting Started

Begin then by creating a dedicated timeline for your business. Use it to discuss your product, the challenges you're facing, how it's developing and—even more importantly—the positive feedback it's received. Keep the conversation with other twitterers professional rather than personal and ask questions of any venture capitalists and angels that you can find on the site.

Don't ask them for money, just advice. If they think you're an interesting investment they may well ask more questions, and one of them might be how much money you need.

Tips

for Success

(continued)

Make TwitPitches

Not all entrepreneurs use TwitPitches but some do, especially in the build-up to conferences and events to filter out the people they're going to meet. It's not easy to make a complete pitch in 140 characters ... but even if it doesn't generate cash, being able to do it is a great discipline!

A Model to Follow

A good twitterer to follow is Martin Zwilling. That's not just because his tweets are full of useful information, links to thought-provoking articles and interesting answers. It's also because the people who write to him are other entrepreneurs using Twitter to market their businesses. Tracing Martin's replies back to the questioners should provide plenty of models to follow.

But you should also pay attention to Higher Hangers's timeline. The background has been optimized to show off the brand, there's a link to the business's website and the tweets themselves are both professional and exciting. It provides a great example of a business on the rise . . . and letting people know about it.

---

60 RAISE FUNDS FOR NON-PROFITS

DIFFICULTY

SKILLS REQUIRED

INCOME POTENTIAL

What is Fundraising on Twitter?

Much of Twitter's success is a result of its simplicity. Because anyone can write a 140-character text message, anyone can use the site. But sometimes that simplicity can be felt as a limitation. Twitter, for example, has no way to accept funds. That means that selling has to be done indirectly. Twitter might be a great place to make product announcements, cement brands and generate curiosity but followers have to be directed to a website to place their orders and hand over their credit card details.

That's a challenge that has to be overcome too by non-profits.

While Twitter can raise awareness and provide a platform for campaigners to draw attention to their issues, it can't be used to accept donations directly.

But that certainly doesn't mean it's not a useful tool for non-profits. In fact, a great deal of money has already been raised for good causes through Twitter.

How Twitterers Are Raising Funds for Non-Profits

The most famous—and perhaps the most complex—example of Twitter being used for fundraising was the 2009 Twestival organized to collect donations for charity:water (@charitywater), a non-profit that works to supply clean drinking in developing countries.

The promotion was the idea of Amanda Rose (@amanda), an events organizer, who had previously discovered the power of Twitter for charities when she had tweeted a request for donations to a food bank and received hundreds of offers. Twestival though was far more ambitious. Twitterers in 202 cities around the world met for a series of global charity events, raising more than $250,000.

None of that money changed hands on Twitter, of course. Instead, Twitter acted as a means of publicizing the event. Local twitterers around the world took responsibility to organize and hold their own events, and their contact details were listed on the Twestival's website www.twestival.com. The website also provided news and videos, and other fundraising resources such as t-shirt sales and an Ebay auction. Logos of sponsors were also displayed on the website. Amanda continues to provide updates about how the money is being used, tweeting from the first well dug in Ethiopia using Twestival money, and uploading videos to the site.

An easier but perhaps no less ambitious act of fundraising on Twitter was marketer Joel Comm's tweetathon. Instead of organizing events around the world, the tweetathon, which benefited water charity Water Is Life Foundation (www.waterislife.com), attempted to replicate telethons by broadcasting interviews and chat live online from Joel's office.

Although a number of Twitter-based celebrities also joined in, including Wil Wheaton (@wilw) and MC Hammer (@mchammer), this event was much more centralized. It also had a commercial benefit too. The tweetathon was timed to coincide with the launch of Joel's book on Twitter and was sponsored in part by his software and marketing company.

Sometimes, non-profits aren't the only beneficiaries of fundraising.

Most non-profits and fundraisers on Twitter though are taking much simpler approaches to Twitter. Even Amanda Rose has done something as straightforward as tweet for a good cause: "If you do one thing tomorrow, please register as an organ donor and support @holsbattlefront's campaign. http://is.gd/qUxp (pls RT)" and that tends to be the way that charity tweeting usually works.

To Write Love On Her Arms (@TWLOHA), a charity that helps to fight depression, for example, uses its timeline to make announcements that relate to the group's cause. Although there's little interaction with

for Success

Follow the Professionals

The benefits of Twitter don't have to be limited to collecting funds. There are timelines on the site that also hand out support and advice to those involved in charity work. Nonprofit Orgs (@nonprofitorgs) is worth following as a portal for nonprofits, while the Chronicle of Philanthropy (@Philanthropy) provides all sorts of tips and suggestions for more effective fundraising and charity issues.

Make the Appeals Urgent

Appeals tend to work best when donors feel that they're making a difference. Instead of placing appeals on Twitter then to support your work, make sure that any appeals you use relate directly to a single benefit, such as a community in Africa or in the case of one of Amanda Rose's tweets, an organ donor recipient.

(continued on next page)

Tips

for Success

(continued)

**Let Followers See
Behind the Scenes**

And one of the reasons
that donors think twice
about contributing is that
they worry their money
will go to administration
instead of good work. If you
use your timeline talk about
exactly how your group is
helping others, you'll show
that the funds are being put
to good use.

followers, the timeline does do a good job of keeping people aware of depression issues, new blog posts and the group's activities.

How to Do It

To use Twitter as one more platform to keep in touch with supporters and raise funds, you'll need a website that can provide detailed and static information. The link to the website should form part of your profile details so that followers can easily click through.

The tweets themselves should be a mixture of information about the organization's activities and links to Web pages and news reports that concern the group's core issues. Some non-profit frequently re-tweet posts from other charities, and no doubt receive the same favor in return. You can also make the occasional appeal but try not to do it too often.

Followers primarily want to read and be informed. They're more likely to donate if they're moved by the charity's work, and that's easier to make happen on the website. Instead of using Twitter to appeal directly for funds then, use it to bring people to your site and appeal for funds there.

Ideally, you should also make those appeals targeted to a specific benefit rather than allowing them to appear as part of your overall fundraising.

If you're looking to put on an event as large as a twestival though, you'll first need a lot of followers so that you can bring in local organizers, and set up a channel to collect the funds.

Getting Started

The hardest part of creating a Twitter timeline for non-profits will always be finding followers willing to donate. Begin then by telling your group's donors and supporters that you now have a timeline to give yourself a core of followers, retweet posts from other non-profits to get your name in their timeline in return and ask for your own posts to be retweeted.

A Model to Follow

Although there are plenty of non-profits to follow on Twitter, the best model to follow has to be Amanda Rose's timeline. Not only has she proven that it is possible to mobilize thousands of people, her timeline—and off-Twitter organization—reveal exactly how to do it.

Her tweets are a mixture of updates and appeals, as well as replies to followers, and she also describes exactly how the money is being spent, reassuring donors.

The website for the twestival is simple but it's also a very effective support service for the Twitter promotional work, giving sponsors a place to advertise, providing a static source of news and raising more money through sales.

61 MARKET YOUR CONSULTANCY

DIFFICULTY

SKILLS REQUIRED

INCOME POTENTIAL

What is Consultancy on Twitter?

When the dotcom bubble first burst, Silicon Valley was suddenly filled with consultants. Actually, many of them they were laid-off programmers and managers looking for ways to fill their days and earn a little extra cash until the economy picked up again.

But consultancy doesn't have to look like that. A consultant is simply someone with the sort of expert knowledge that other people are prepared to pay for. That advice can take the form of specific strategies to help a company perform better but it can just as easily be a specialist coder employed on a short-term contract to break the back of a particularly tricky project.

That means that anyone can function as a consultant—even if they don't do it full-time—and Twitter, a channel that makes it simple to share nuggets of information is an ideal medium to broadcast knowledge.

Not all of the people on Twitter and swapping expert tips are offering consultancy services, but many of the strategies used by careful twitterers provide good models for consultants to show off their knowledge and bring prospects back to their websites to be converted into clients.

How Twitterers Are Marketing Their Consultancy Skills

The most important tweets on Twitter are usually those sent from one twitterer to another. Those are the messages that build relationships, show that you're active, sociable and approachable, and create follower lists too.

For twitterers who want to use the site to exhibit their knowledge though, it's the tweets surrounding those conversation posts that are at least as vital.

The most common examples are tweets that contain links that can point followers to expert information. "Ottomate" (@ottomate) for example, is the timeline of the editor of AutomatedHome.com. He also does occasional consultancy work and his timeline is filled with sometimes complex information and links either to his own blog or to other specialist sites: "GSM Auto Controls Anything From Anywhere with your Phone 2x 30 amp relays for remote HVAC, lighting, access control etc http://bit.ly/VKLku". Mark Shields (@markemotion), the managing director of a Web marketing firm has a timeline that contains nothing but these types of tweets.

Other tweets though may contain specific hints and suggestions, and occasionally consultants will fire these directly at individual followers. Tweets like these provide multiple benefits: they demonstrate knowledge; they show that you're there to help others; and they deliver valuable information to all of the twitterer's followers making the timeline a must-read for anyone who could potentially become a client. Rob McNealy (@RobMcNealy), a new media consultant, posted this tweet in response to someone who had informed him that he was leaving his bio blank as a way of standing out: "@thizl That doesn't work and it makes you not get found by search engines."

The value of posting tweets that show off the breadth and depth of your specialist knowledge is clear. But it's interesting to note that one commonality that can be found across consultants' timelines on Twitter is their personality.

Making the most of Twitter always means using tweets not just to exhibit your professional skills but to build the relationships that lead followers to want to use those skills. So Rob McNealy might talk about his workshops and offer suggestions that help his followers to do better. But he'll also tweet members of his family and talk about what his doing during the day.

Successful consultancy relies on trust and a close relationship between client and consultant. Frequent, personal tweeting can help to form that relationship so that the information looks reliable and worth taking.

Tips for Success

Use Your Name

The username is a crucial part of a Twitter identity. A name that contains a keyword, for example, will pick up followers just based on the name. Usernames that reflect the name of a business will tell followers that they're following a corporate timeline.

Consultants though rely on the power of their own personality to build the kinds of relationships that inspire clients to hire them—and more importantly, listen to them.

Use your real name in the timeline then, and make your timeline reflect you.

Follow the News

The easiest kinds of consultancy tweets to post are those that link to Web pages where your followers can learn more information about your industry. They benefit your followers—who get content recommended by an expert—and they benefit you by proving that your knowledge is up-to-date.

(continued on next page)

Tips

for Success

(continued)

Don't Worry about the Conversions

It's hard to find any consultants o n Twitter who are openly cruising for business. Wisely, most consultants on the site focus first on relationship-building. A few make occasional references to their workshops and make it known that they still have places available.

Build the relationship, find followers and show off your knowledge and you should find that the increased exposure brings its own business.

How to Do It

Promoting a consultancy on Twitter then will require three kinds of tweets. Firstly, you'll need to post tweets that link to rich sources of information.

These could be on your blog but even telling people about other websites where they can find useful advice will show that you follow the industry news and that the strategies you're supplying are up to date.

Secondly, you should be posting tweets that supply your own information. These could be general tips that you throw in to enrich your timeline or they could be helpful suggestions delivered publicly to individual followers.

And thirdly, you should also be using Twitter for fun. Get people to like you and they'll be more willing to do business with you. It's the standard Twitter mixture.

Getting Started

Promoting a consultancy on Twitter begins by looking for the right kinds of followers. Ideally, you want to find people who need your help. They don't all have to be people who may become your clients. Remember that offering to help to people who need it gives you an opportunity to show off your skills to the small percentage of your followers who could become clients.

It can also win you recommendations and retweets that will reach other prospects.

A Model to Follow

Rob McNealy's timeline is one good model for a consultant on Twitter to follow. Rob uses his real name, his tweets are a mixture of information links, advice to individual followers and posts about his business, and he also includes lots of personal tweets too.

The overall impression is that Rob is an expert in his field, approachable and someone willing to lend a land.

It's that combination that's made him the most popular consultant on Twitter.

GEEKPRENEUR

READ THE WAY THE MARKET'S MOVING

62

What is Tracking the Market on Twitter?

Stock advice has become so popular on Twitter that it's even created own version of a hashtag. Instead of placing "#" in front of words to make them easy to find, investors place a dollar sign in front of the company's stock abbreviation.

The challenge for investors following those trends though is understand how much to trust the advice from someone on Twitter they don't know.

Piqqem (www.piqqem.com) aims to solve that problem by aggregating the recommendations of multiple contributors to display the wisdom of a crowd. The result should be data that reflects real sentiment about the future success of a company, and therefore predicts the way the stock is likely to rise and fall.

The service began operating outside Twitter, but its crowdsourced strategy suits Twitter well. Contributors can use symbols to indicate their prediction and short posts to explain their thinking.

Investors can then examine Piqqem's website to see the aggregated data.

While Piqqem does have a reasonable record, it also has competitors and it's not clear that its predictions are capable of beating a market which could well represent the wisdom (or foolishness) of crowds anyway.

Nonetheless, for twitterers, Piqqem can be a good place to make—and pick up—valuable stock tips.

DIFFICULTY

SKILLS REQUIRED

INCOME POTENTIAL

Tips

for Success

Read the Tweets

Piqqem's most important feature is the graph showing the sentiment of its contributors. But because users have to vote in order to read all of the statistics, it's possible that some of the votes may be worth less than others; some users may vote randomly to gain access to the site's data.

The reasons that the site's users give for their votes then will be crucial. You can find that information in the list of tweets under the graph. You might well find that the same group of twitterers tend to contribute most to predictions about particular companies allowing you to assess the reliability of their votes.

Compare over Time

While you can't judge the reliability of a sentiment prediction in advance, you can judge its historical reliability. Much of your time on Piqqem then should be spent not just looking at the graphs but comparing the sentiment of

(continued on next page)

How Twitterers Are Picking Stocks on Twitter

There's no great trick to picking up stock information with Piqqem on Twitter. Piqqem's own timeline, @piqqem, offers updates, news about top picks and also provides links to Web pages and other relevant information.

The real information though is on the website where you'll be able to browse data about particular companies, view predictions and sentiment, and read the latest tweets related to the business. (Although the automated on-site filters can be a bit haphazard. Tweets about Abercrombie and Fitch, for example, seem to consist mostly of tweets from people who write "anf" instead of "and".)

Clearly, it's impossible to see what people are doing with the information they're picking up from Piqqem. If they're choosing to invest, they don't seem to be sharing the news with other twitterers.

But they are sharing their opinions, pushing sentiment up and down and helping investors to make smart decisions.

How to Do It

The basics of using Piqqem are simpler than they look. You can't see all of the data available on the site until you've registered. Similarly, for Piqqem to read your tweets, you'll need to enter your Twitter username. Then it's just a matter of writing the name of the stock with a dollar sign or hashtag and adding a "piqq" rating: --, -, =, + or ++. Comments about the stock can also be added and appear on the site as a "user take." The tweet must also contain "@piqqem".

So if you wanted to predict that Apple's new iPod model is going to send its stock price through the roof, then you might tweet something like: "@piqqem ++ $aapl. Loving the new iPod. Predict others will too."

That will help you to share your own thoughts about a company, and it will help you to understand what other people are tweeting too. Checking the aggregated data on the site will also provide a general picture of what everyone is thinking.

But having looked at that data, you might want to go further and break it down to understand what the information is based. Piqqem

GEEKPRENEUR

does provide the latest tweets about a company directly beneath the graph but those show every mention of the company on Twitter, even if those tweets don't contain piqq ratings and therefore weren't included in the graph.

Searching on Twitter to see who exactly was providing the ratings will let you form an assessment of the reliability of at least some of those opinions, and perhaps also give you an idea how many people contributed to the sentiment.

Don't be surprised to find that for some esoteric stocks, the wisdom of a crowd turns out to be the thoughts of a handful of twitterers with some stock knowledge.

Getting Started

Begin not on Twitter but at Piqqem's website. Register, play around a little and get used to how the site works. It's not complex but the codes and symbols are new and require some adjustment.

You'll also need to get a feel for the amount of attention to pay to the tweets posted under the graphs and you'll probably want to make some historical comparisons, looking at how stocks have compared in the past in relation to sentiments shown on Piqqem.

Once you've done that, you'll be free to start making your own predictions . . . and investing based on the predictions on the site.

A Model to Follow

Joe Smith (@hedgemeister) is a major contributor to Piqqem. His tweets are great examples of the sorts of messages that most help other Piqqem users. They begin with the name of the stock, his sentiment and then end with a clear a explanation of his vote.

They're perfect models of Piqqem contributors—and worthwhile reading for investors too.

for Success

(continued)

the company's voters with its recent performance. That should give you a good idea of the degree to which you can base decisions on Piqqem's sentiments.

Consider the Bias

Piqqem relies on the wisdom of crowds to create predictions about the future direction of the stock market. When many of the votes are coming from Twitter users, it's important to remember that they're likely to be coming from people who are tech-savvy. That may mean they could be less knowledgeable about manufacturing business and unrealistically optimistic about the future of technology firms.

Or it could equally mean that they're well informed about tech companies and know exactly which way the market is going to go.

63 FIND LOCAL BUYERS

What Are Local Buyers on Twitter?

Twitter is a great place for Internet marketers to generate sales. Bloggers are using it to drive traffic to their monetized websites. Craft sellers are using it generate interest in their online stores. Creators of information products are using to build their personal brands, attract followings and forge the kinds of close connections that lead to sales.

But for owners of local stores, the site can look like overkill.

When all your customers are local, when you transfer the goods over the counter and not by mail and when a lead in Kansas is never going to be a customer, no matter how much he likes your products or how often she answers your tweets, there seems to be little point in marketing your business with Twitter.

In fact, even when you're a local business with local customers serving local needs, you can still benefit from using Twitter. You can benefit by using Twitter to deepen your relationship with existing customers and you can benefit by using Twitter to identify potential new—and local—customers.

How Twitterers Are Looking for Local Buyers

The most obvious way that local businesses are using Twitter is to keep in touch with people who have already visited the outlet. We've already seen, for example, how restaurants are rewarding followers by offering them special discounts on certain days or handing out free meals to people who make quick bookings.

Any timeline that contains interesting, informative tweets though can keep a business on a regular customer's mind, bringing them back more often and to make more purchases.

To find new potential customers to follow those tweets though will take a little more effort. It's not enough for Italian restaurants to search for people who mentioned "pizza" in their timeline or independent bookstores to follow anyone who has ever mentioned a book.

They have to find people who have interest in the kinds of goods they supply and who are also close enough to buy them.

How to Do It

The easiest way to find local customers is with Twitter's own search engine. Helpfully, the Advanced Search feature provides the opportunity to limit searches geographically. That range is useful for local businesses (even if few other twitterers are likely to conduct geographic searching). You know how far people are willing to travel to buy at your store and there may be little to gain from talking on Twitter to people three towns away.

At its most basic, you can simply leave the text field blank and search for all members within buying distance of the store. Unless you live in a particularly small town, you wouldn't want to start following all of them, but even just seeing what local people are discussing may be useful too.

More useful though is the ability to restrict mentions of your business's most important keywords to people within a certain range of your town.

But it's still a pain-staking process. You'd need toss every possible keyword and phrase into the search engine. A local bookstore for example could look for anyone who mentioned "bookstore" within 15 miles of the town in which their store is located. But they could also look for anyone in the same radius who had mentioned one of the thousands of authors whose books they sell.

That could take a while to do comprehensively, although there's no rule that says that your followers have to be comprehensive. Start following some people in your area who you can see have discussed buying the kinds of items you sell and they'll spread your name further

for Success

Look for Products

The biggest challenge of finding potential local customers on Twitter is narrowing down your search. Now that Twitter has become generally popular, there's likely to be a huge number of people in your area who you could follow. Trying to follow all of them might well bring accusations of mass following—the kind of thing that can, in theory, lead to closed accounts—and only a fraction of them would be interested in visiting your store.

Look then for mentions from people in your area of products that you sell and ask them what they thought of them. Don't make a sales pitch. Just make a connection. You might well find that that link is enough to bring them to your store next time they want to make a similar purchase.

(continued on next page)

for Success

(continued)

Look for Place Names

While geographic searching can be helpful, not everyone includes their geographic data on their profile and it's not always accurate. Students and people who travel frequently may not turn up in results.

Looking for place names in tweets will help you to identify people who are familiar with your area and may be around frequently enough to buy from you.

Make Local References

You won't be the only person searching for local twitterers. Those local twitterers may be doing some searching too. Make sure that you've indicated where you're located and mention place names in your own tweets so that other people can find you easily.

while communicating with at least one potential new customer even if you're not talking to all of them.

An alternative approach is to look for people who have mentioned certain local place names in their tweets. That can have unexpected results though. At least one twitterer who looked for mentions of areas that were particularly expensive found himself following plenty of lawyers.

For a real estate agent though, looking for places rather than people on Twitter could turn out be very useful indeed.

Getting Started

Finding local potential customers isn't particularly difficult. Giving them a reason to follow you—and to continue reading your tweets—might be though.

Before you start searching for local buyers then, it's a good idea to create the kind of timeline that those potential customers might actually want to read.

Spend some time looking at what people in your area are discussing. Include links to stories in local newspapers and make references to issues that are of local interest.

Make it easy for other local people to find you too.

Once you have a number of tweets in your timeline that are of local interest as well as referring to your products, start following and join the conversation.

A Model to Follow

The Big Peach Running Company (@PeachyRuns) is a chain of four running stores in Georgia, Atlanta. The company's timeline has used its background to list the addresses of its stores, its bio mentions its location and its tweets make frequent mentions of local events—especially runs.

While it's difficult to say what percentage of its followers are local, the timeline does do a great job of appealing to those within buying distance and makes itself a node for local runners.

GEEKPRENEUR

BECOME A TWITTER TRANSLATION AGENCY

What is a Twitter Translation Agency?

Twitter has made the world a smaller place. It's a process that was happening anyway. Telephones and air travel might have really got things rolling, and email and instant messaging have given it a giant push, but Twitter's ability to bring people together who would otherwise never have met is unique.

But it doesn't solve one problem: two people on different sides of the planet, speaking different languages, aren't going to be able to understand each other.

The distance might have been bridged but without a working knowledge of a common tongue—and the abbreviations used on Twitter make English hard even for native speakers to understand—the language barrier is still in the way.

Where there's a problem though, there's always an opportunity. Some companies are offering to stand between twitterers, translating their tweets to bring the two sides a little closer.

How Twitterers Are Offering Translation Services

Twitrans (@twitrans) is an offshoot of OneHourTranslation (www. onehourtranslation.com), a translation agency that offers translations and proofreading in more than 30 languages. With 8,000 translators around the world, it aims to offer a fast turnaround and prices as five cents per word. Translators are paid three cents a word.

DIFFICULTY

SKILLS REQUIRED

INCOME POTENTIAL

Tips
for Success

Ask for Credit

Marketing the service will also be difficult so don't waste the chance to use Twitter's viral power. At least when you begin, ask your clients to provide you with credit by including your translation username when they pass the tweet on. The more your name is seen on other timelines and by other twitterers, the more business you'll bring in.

Get Referrals

OneHourTranslations uses Twitter as a way of promoting its translation service. Understandably, the company assumes that someone who wants the odd phrase translated will also need documents translated.

While you could offer that sort of service yourself too, you can also win commissions for sending clients to translation companies for their larger projects. OneHourTranslations, for example, pays 50 percent of their commissions for a year.

(continued on next page)

Twitrans allows customers to submit tweets in one language and receive them back in another, ready to be forwarded to a contact on Twitter. Not all of the languages offered by OneHourTranslation are available on Twitter but the service does provide translations to and from Arabic, Chinese, Dutch, English, French, German, Greek, Hebrew, Hindi, Italian, Japanese, Portuguese, Russian and Spanish. To receive a translation all a twitterer has to do is send a tweet to @twitrans with the the phrase "en2" followed by the language code and the text. So tweeting "@twitrans en2fr What's the secret of a good croissant?" would produce a return tweet containing the sentence in French. (Actually, it would first produce an automated response that says "Human translation started. You'll receive the translation here in a few minutes. Thank you!" The translation itself will appear within an hour and sometimes within a few minutes.)

Unlike OneHourTranslation, which uses its network of translators to power the service, Twitrans is free. That means it's limited. Qian Chenchuan (@qiancc), a twitterer with no followers and following no one on the site, broke a long Chinese document into tweets to receive a free translation. He got through around 50 tweets before Twitrans finally gave up and tweeted "Twitrans was not developed for this purposes. Please don't use it any more." It's unlikely that the service would be willing to wait so long before supplying a Twitter-based document translation service again, and when Qian Chenchuan apparently started a new timeline at @qcc228, his tweets were left untranslated.

But that also means that Twitrans isn't intended to make money. It's meant to publicize the work of the translation company by allowing twitterers to receive translations of the sorts of small phrases that aren't worth buying normally.

That represents an opportunity for other bi-lingual twitterers.

How to Do It

Receiving the original text and sending back the translation will be simple enough. You can set up a timeline dedicated to offering translations and use Twitrans language shorthand to indicate the target language—if you're offering more than one.

Much harder will be limiting use of the service to keep it reasonable, ensuring a fast-enough turnaround to make it worthwhile, and—hardest of all—getting paid for it.

A simple method would be to copy the model used by Justin Rockwell of @ThatCssGuy. Offering to translate for free but suggesting payment by way of goodwill would free you of any obligations. If someone sends in a tweet while you're away from the computer, or if your dictionary breaks down over a word you don't recognize, they're unlikely to complain. Your website would suggest a rate for each tweet—a dollar, say—and allow twitterers to pay more or less depending on the turnaround time.

If you really wanted to turn Twitter translation into professional service though, you could put together a team of translators, use Hoot-Suite to allow them all to receive original text and send in their translations. Maintaining a network of translators means that you should be able ensure a fast turnaround 24 hours a day.

To receive payment, the best model is likely to be subscription-based. Twitterers would be able to purchase a set number of words to be translated each month, and pay a regular fee.

You'd get a steady income while still preventing people like Qian Chenchuan from abusing the system.

Getting Started

Start small. Begin by creating a timeline that offers occasional translations into your mother tongue on a tip-supported basis. Creating a network of translators will take time and effort, and that's work you don't want to do until you're certain there's enough demand for the languages you want to offer.

Once you can see that requests are coming in steadily, that there's more work than you can handle and that people are asking you about other languages then consider expanding and making the service more professional.

A Model to Follow

Twitrans' timeline is the model to follow but do bear in mind that the translation company that runs it has not yet decided to monetize the service. Justin Rockwell though has shown how it's possible to provide a valuable service on Twitter and still receive payment so the best approach might be to combine the two models and get paid for supplying help.

Alternatively, you could use Twitter as a promotion for your off-Twitter translation agency.

GIVE RECOMMENDATIONS, WIN TESTIMONIALS

65

What Are Testimonials on Twitter?

DIFFICULTY

SKILLS REQUIRED

INCOME POTENTIAL

The key to landing deals for any business is always to build trust. As soon as leads understand that you will deliver the goods or services they need, that they will be at the quality they demand and that they can rely on you to fulfill your side of the bargain, they'll become customers.

Often, that trust is built by overcoming objections.

More powerfully though, it's created through reputation. Customers trust sellers they've heard of, especially if they've heard of them through other people they trust.

Twitter provides a way for businesses to recommend customers to each other, transferring testimonials—and trust—across the Twitter-verse.

How Twitterers Are Swapping Testimonials

The simplest form of testimonial exchange takes place on Twitter at the end of every week. FollowFriday is a convention that allows twitterers to recommend people that other twitterers should follow. The recommendations are made by typing "#followfriday" followed by the names of the people you want to recommend. While there's no limit to the number of people you can suggest—and some twitterers are known to produce long series of FollowFriday tweets—the more people that follow the hashtag, the weaker the recommendation appears. Three or four each Friday is usually a fair number and may leave a little room too to explain why you're recommending them.

Tips

for Success

Make Recommendations

You can't ask for testimonials on Twitter, so to receive them, you first have to give them. While waiting for an opportunity to do that might be natural, it's a slow process and one that may never actually happen.

Instead of waiting, take action. Look for someone who needs the services of someone you know and make your recommendation

Make the Recommendations Count

But only give testimonials that you believe in and which can deliver results. Telling someone on the other side of the country that you know a great wedding photographer is not going to help anyone if that photographer never travels. And telling someone to hire a copywriter who can barely spell his name will make life difficult for both the client and the writer—and damage your own reputation too.

(continued on next page)

FollowFriday is simple and conventional but it's also probably the weakest kind of testimonial you can receive on Twitter. It tells other twitterers that they should read your tweets but it doesn't necessarily recommend your professional services. Nor do you have to wait until Friday to do that. In fact, making a unique recommendation may be a lot more powerful. When Twitter co-founder Biz Stone, for example, posted a tweet recommending that his 350,000-plus followers follow Mark Malkoff (@mmalkoff), the comedian and filmmaker picked up 350 new followers in the space of just two hours.

But professional recommendations are happening on Twitter too and they're much more powerful. This tweet from Aaron Abber (@aaronabber), for example, is just one of many that turn up frequently on Twitter suggesting that the personal recommendations are being passed back and forth on Twitter and winning jobs: "@amp529 Hi, I was looking for a WP Theme guru to help me do a few final tweaks, r u available? @redyelllow recommended you to me".

How to Do It

Testimonials on Twitter don't quite work in the same way as the kind of recommendations that appear on sales sites and book covers. To win those testimonials, there's nothing wrong with asking a client directly or even running competitions to persuade customers to send in their success stories.

On Twitter though, you can't ask a client to recommend you for a job to someone else on the site.

Instead, like the formula on FollowFriday, you have to earn the testimonial by delivering services that people appreciate—and build up credit by recommending others and telling them.

Evan Thor (@evan_thor), for example, recommended a twitterer he knew for a job, and made the point of telling him: "@benjaminkendall I just recommended you for a 'small graphic design job' to @ryanchenwing. Good friend of mine and is looking for a local." Claire Copeland (@SimpleWeddings), sent this tweet to a vacation resort letting them know that she's giving them business, and presumably hoping that they'll return the favor: "@TWResorts Thanks for following us! We offer beach wedding packages and photography, and I just recommended you to a client earlier today!"

Clearly, there's no guarantee that having given a business a recommendation they'll be willing to do the same for you. But on the whole Twitter's users tend to be a generous sort and once you've recommended they will feel the obligation to do the same . . . even if they don't do it right away.

Getting Started

Starting the process may well be the hardest part of winning a recommendation. To recommend someone else's timeline is simple enough and can be done immediately, even if it isn't Friday.

But to put yourself in the position of being able to win a testimonial from someone else, you first have to deliver a recommendation of your own—and that means finding someone to deliver it to.

One option is to wait until someone asks if you know of a designer, a photographer or whoever you're hoping to recommend you, then send out your testimonial. But a more pro-active choice could be to search Twitter for someone "looking for" those services. Tweet them back saying that you know someone who fits the bill, then let that person know.

You'd cut down the time you'd have to build up credit—but you'd still have to wait for their opportunity to repay you.

A Model to Follow

Biz Stone's recommendation of Mark Malkoff was very nicely done. Instead of telling his followers that they should all be following Mark, he hedged his bets: "I'm following @mmalkoff and maybe you should too—but that is your decision to make." The effect was to make his followers feel that Biz wasn't pushing them to do something they didn't want to do but that he was making a suggestion because he was enjoying Mark's tweets and felt that they would enjoy them too. That kind of easy suggestion is more likely to be effective on Twitter than a hard push.

For professional recommendations though, the tweets themselves don't have to be at all complex. Dominic Sicotte

(continued on next page)

A Model to Follow *(continued)*

(@Dominic_Sicotte) recommended a public relations source with this tweet to help out a twitterer: "@ChicagoDesign You should contact @nadinet, she will help you out with this she is at Canada News Wire biggest NewsWire in Canada. Cheers!" That won him the thanks of the recipient and he quickly followed it up with a second referral. The tweet itself told the recipient where to turn and why, and should have been enough to win him the gratitude of both @nadinet and @ChicagoDesign.

FIND NEW TUTORIAL STUDENTS

What Can Twitter Do for Teachers and Tutors?

Twitter can do a surprising amount for teachers. Steve Wheeler (@timbuckteeth), an education lecturer at the UK's University of Plymouth, has listed ten ways in which teachers can use Twitter. These range from using the site as a noticeboard to announce changes to schedules, classrooms or content and sharing links to helpful content, to encouraging students to tweet as historical characters or tweeting in foreign languages.

Certainly, the site seems to have been taken up by a number of teachers. Elizabeth Davis (@lizbdavis) has created a giant spreadsheet of teachers on the site, organized by location and subject. (Adding your own name to the table is one way to pick up new contacts.)

But while Twitter may be used by some tech-savvy teachers as a pedagogic tool, it's not going to make them any money. Teachers are paid by their institution so they won't be using the site as a marketing tool.

That though is being done by independent tutors, and it's leading to a number of informative and creative tweets.

How Teachers and Tutors Are Using Twitter

While there might be a huge range of different ways that teachers can use Twitter to pass on information, most of the teachers on the site are using to chat to other teachers. Even Steven Wheeler's timeline tends to consist of information about TV shows and articles in production, with just about nothing aimed at his students.

Tips
for Success

Take Part in #educhat

#Educhat is an education chat that takes place regularly o n Twitter. The issues to be discussed can be found at @Educhat, and anyone can take part by tweeting and adding the hashtag #educhat to their posts. It might not be a good way to meet potential clients but it may keep you up to date on what other teachers are discussing and give you some useful contacts.

Use Twitter to Prove Results

Tutoring is a profession with measurable results. Clients are rarely paying you to teach their offspring how to do calculus or scan Catullus. They're paying you to improve their kids' grades. If you've got the numbers that show you can do that, work them into your tweets and prove that you can do the job.

Not surprisingly, it's the tutors who are putting in the real effort at using Twitter to win clients and transmit information.

The form in which that's most clear is the names that tutors on Twitter choose for their timelines. "Anthony," a tutor in Los Angeles, has chosen @HomeSchoolTutor for his Twitter identity. Linda Edgar is known on the site as @SATteacher, and Juan Castenada is @mathguide.

Those are all smart decisions. A Twitter name might look like a simple choice but in choosing your name, you also define your identity on the site. Taking a name that describes your work—as opposed to your real name or your favorite sports team—reveals the most important thing that followers need to know about you. It also makes it much easier to build followers; a keyworded name alone can sometimes be enough to bring in followers.

The bios tutors use too can be very revealing. @HomeSchoolTutor's bio—"I tutor in Los Angeles and offer help to homeschoolers everywhere by phone, fax, email, whiteboard. Lots of free info on my blog, including Cheat Sheets."—describes exactly what he does and even gives followers a reason to visit his website, a neat marketing device. Linda Edgar goes for the much simpler: "I teach SAT and ACT prep courses and tutor Reading,Math, Writing grades K-12."

That might look like a lost opportunity but Linda appears to prefer her clients to contact her directly. Her tweets then contain a variety of personal updates—about her daughter, her dancing classes and the odd wardrobe issue—but they also provide plenty of solid, professional information too. She explains which scholarship sites she found useful, and most importantly, reveals the results of her classes and adds her contact details: "Just finished up the last SAT class! Most students went up 200 points! ledgar@cox.net 602-795-6312".

Tweeting your results is certainly one way of showing off your skills and proving that you're worth hiring. Juan Castaneda takes a slightly different approach by inserting specialist bits of trivia into his timeline: "Take a fraction a/b, and form a new fraction with new numerator = a+2b; and new denominator = a+b. Repeating this approximates square root 2".

Tweets like these might not make for the most exciting timelines on Twitter but they are good marketing.

How to Do It

For teachers looking to use Twitter as a tool to educate students, the best advice might be not to do it. EdModo (www.edmodo.com) is a microblogging platform dedicated to teachers and students, and is likely to create better results. Twitter, after all, is a mass communications tool. A teacher doesn't need tens of thousands of followers when he or she is only trying to teach a class of 20 or 30 students.

For tutors though, Twitter can be very useful, but they'll need to do two things. First, they'll need to find the right followers. That might seem difficult; Twitter's search is still a little clumsy and without demographic data, finding potential clients won't be straightforward. No one lists themselves on Twellow as "High school math struggler." But it's rarely high school students themselves who make the decision to hire a tutor, and Twitter biggest demographic is actually aged 35 or older—precisely the sort of people who pay the tutor, even if they don't use one themselves.

Use LocalTweeps (www.localtweeps.com), a local directory of Twitter users, to find twitterers within your working distance, and follow any who mention children at roughly the ages you tutor.

That should start to put you in touch with potential clients, and if you're lucky and show off your skills well, they should pass your name along. That will only happen though if you post the right tweets, and that's the second thing you should be doing. Make sure that you post tweets that describe the classes you've been giving, that offer tips about the exams for which you coach, and ideally, which mention the grade rises you're tutoring has created.

Getting Started

Begin by reading through the timelines of local twitterers to identify which might make potential clients. That isn't going to be easy. Use LocalTweeps to draw up a rough list, then toss their names into Twitter's search engine with the keywords "son" or "daughter" to discover which are parents. Those should be the first people you follow.

A Model to Follow

Juan Casteneda's timeline contains some fascinating tweets. Filled math trivia and problem-solving tips, followers are likely to actually enjoy seeing his posts on their pages. Tweets like "Today I was flipping a coin for a living. Not gambling but helping a student figuring out his probability homework, an interesting problem" and "@mathheadinc Yes, I sure had a lot of fun that day tutoring all those math topics. I love discovering how my students look at math problems" reveal his passion for the subject, and suggest that that passion might even wear off on the students too.

Juan even sometimes replies to questions from students, recommending online tutoring to one twitterer in Canada.

The overall effect is that Juan is someone who loves his subject, understands and can pass on that knowledge to others who need it.

LAND
NEW LAW
CLIENTS

What Are the Benefits of Twitter for Lawyers?

Twitter really became famous when one lawyer used it to describe his days. Barack Obama soon became the most popular twitterer on the site. Candidate Obama wasn't exactly using Twitter to promote his legal work but politicians aside there are plenty of lawyers and legal resources on Twitter that can keep law professionals informed, in touch and in their markets.

While Twitter is never going to be a replacement for the more traditional ways of landing clients for legal firms, it can be a very useful supplement for them. Individual lawyers too have been known to win higher profiles, consultancy work and even speaking jobs as a direct result of keeping an active timeline and using it to connect with other professionals.

How Lawyers are Using Twitter

The most obvious way that lawyers are using Twitter is the same way that many other professions are using the site: as an adjunct to their blogs, websites and information products. Green Build Law Update (www.greenbuildinglawupdate.com), a blog run by construction lawyer Chris Cheatham (@chrischeatham), for example, was spotted by King County Executive Ron Sims (@simsron) who recommended it on his timeline. The result was a great deal more exposure for the Chris's

DIFFICULTY

SKILLS REQUIRED

INCOME POTENTIAL

for Success

Talk to PR People

Kevin O'Keefe (@ kevinokeefe) has noted on his blog kevin.lexblog.com, that Twitter has allowed him to form a connection with a "high profile PR person" that led to a speaking engagement at a major

(continued on next page)

Tips
for Success

(continued)

blogging and new media conference.

That may not be the direction in which you want to move your career, but landing speaking gigs can certainly help your profile—and tweeting with PR professionals may well give you some advice about giving your law firm the right public profile.

Think about Your Site, not Clients

Finding lawyers to chat with on Twitter is simple enough. Finding potential clients on Twitter is always going to be a lot harder. Twitterers tend not to list themselves o n Twellow under "criminals," there's currently no way to advertise legal services—or to focus your ads on a target demographic—and even searching for people discussing "divorce" in your area and offering your services would be bad form. (Although you might just get away with offering professional advice, especially if they've asked a question.)

(continued on next page)

website and for his own expertise. Carolyn Elefant (@carolynelefant), an expert in cases involving the Federal Energy Regulatory Commission, uses Twitter to promote her own website (www.fercfights.com) as well as her blog MyShingle (www.myshingle.com), and even manages to throw a few references into her tweets to her ebook.

It is notable though that even though even for these twitterers, most of their tweets relate not to their own content but are conversations with other lawyers. Legal professionals on Twitter tend to be fairly collegial.

Those connections allow them to keep in touch with the latest developments in their field while reading the tweets posted by reporters such as Ron Sylvester (@rsylvester) who uses Twitter to provide live coverage court trials can be helpful too.

How to Do It

Tweeting as a lawyer can be simple. You can do nothing more than sign up, tweet, pick a few followers and use the site to connect and chat. But the best timelines specialize and show what their lawyers specialize in. Jay Fleischman (@JayFleischman), for example, is a bankruptcy lawyer who also helps other lawyers market their practices. His background has been optimized to show who he is and where followers can go to learn more about him and while some of his tweets are friendly replies to followers, many of them focus on his topic and include links to tips and articles.

That's a formula that's pretty easy to copy with a well-designed background and a good list of favorite websites, or even better, your own active blog.

TwitterFeed can be one very simple way of automatically informing your followers about new posts and content. Retweeting too is popular among lawyers on Twitter and a good way to send content viral, win favors and improve the value of your own timeline with no extra effort.

Perhaps the most important action that a lawyer can take on his or her timeline though—beyond identifying what they do—is to make their replies smart and helpful. Carolyn Elefant posted this tweet in response to a discussion about how lawyers should deal with criticism. "@ScottGreenfield criticism can be subjective. E.g. client gripes re: attny's brusque attitude but attny delivered. Shouldn't attny explain?"

The effect is to make the overall timeline look professional and valuable. Even if clients don't see that, winning the respect of your peers is always going to be important too.

But that can only happen if lots of other lawyers see your tweets. To make sure that happens, you're going to need to use the usual Twitter technique of following, reading and replying.

Getting Started

Start following lawyers on Twitter and you'll soon find that the same names keep cropping up in timelines again and again. Lawyers on the site tend to be very friendly and are happy to swap tips and advice, answer questions and enter into discussions about various aspects of the law.

A quick way to get started with a long list of followers is to take a short cut. Instead of searching on Twitter for "lawyers" or browsing on Twellow for the right professional category, you can find a long list of lawyers at: http://scoop.jdsupra.com/2008/09/articles/law-firm-marketing/145-lawyers-and-legal-professionals-to-follow-on-twitter/.

A Model to Follow

There are plenty of lawyers on Twitter with attractive timelines, but Jay Fleischman's profile stands out. His background has been professionally designed (by CustomTwitterBackground. com) to show who he is and how they can contact him. His bio "Bankruptcy lawyer who helps other lawyers market their practices" describes clearly what he does and comes under the link to his website. But it's really his tweets that provide such a great example.

Mostly they consist of tempting headlines that lead to interesting articles. That's not difficult to do but the articles are well-chosen enough to make his tweets worth reading. Scattered between those tweets are replies to other twitterers, making his timeline feel dynamic and personal, and comments about his work.

It all comes together to create an on-Twitter presence that's professional, personal and personable too.

Tips

for Success

(continued)

Instead of looking for clients on Twitter then, focus on raising the profile of your blog or website. As your site picks up more traffic from other lawyers, and other legal bloggers, it's likely to pick up links and references, improving your search engine rankings and bringing in new traffic—and with that traffic, perhaps new clients too.

Join the Community

There is one benefit for lawyers that's hugely valuable on Twitter and that's the feedback from the rest of the legal community on the site. It's true that other professions also club together on Twitter and hold discussions in organized "chats" such as #educhat and #editorchat, but lawyers—perhaps because of the nature of their profession—tend to be very active in discussions and arguments, especially about legal ethics. Join the conversation and it won't be too long before opportunities and interest start building.

68 GET PAID TO TWEET WHILE YOU TRAVEL

What is Twitter for Travelers?

The idea of traveling the world—and being paid for it—sounds like a dream job. You could hitchhike across Kazakhstan, ride a camel train through the Maghreb and eat curry in the Hindu Kush knowing all the time that it's your tweets that are paying for your bed, board and local beer.

If only. The bad news is that Twitter won't give you the funds to pay for your round-the-world ticket no matter how regularly you use it or how good your tweets. But the good news is that travelers—professional and enthusiast—have found ways to make the most of microblogging.

Sometimes that means using the site to build a community and drive users to a site that's easier to monetize. Sometimes it means tweeting to promote a travel guide—or series of travel guides. And sometimes it can mean looking for bargains, cost-saving travel tips and even long-distance companions to chat with while you're on the road.

None of these strategies are likely to make someone a millionaire or land them a free first class ticket on Virgin Atlantic. But they can make traveling a little easier, and maybe a little cheaper too.

How Travelers are Using Twitter

Perhaps the most profitable way that people with an interest in travel are using Twitter is as a channel to promote their travel-related businesses. "Michel Travel Notes" (@TravelTweet) sends out posts from his trips around the world and refers frequently to his ad-supported website, Travel Notes (www.travelnotes.org). Julie Blakley (@WhyGoFrance) does something similar, linking to blog posts on her website FranceTravelGuide (www.francetravelguide.com) but she does go a little further. Her timeline is actually published by travel company, BootsnAll (www.bootsnall.com), and occasionally Julie will toss in a link to a special offer on the firm's website: "Don't forget, folks, there are only 5 days left to get 20% off select @BootsnAll adventure trips! http://bit.ly/MjND."

Travel writers too are using Twitter to promote their books, their expertise and their brands as specialists on their topics. Beth Whitman (@Wanderluster) is the author of a series of guides for women travelers. Her timeline is filled with references to her blog but also provides plenty of travel information and the occasional request for information about places she's visiting. While that might sound demanding, it does show that Beth is as much a traveler as her readers and it makes her book look grounded.

Twitter also contains plenty of companies that are using the site to promote their packages, deals and special offers. Airline companies such as JetBlue (@JetBlue) and Southwest (@SouthwestAir) have long been on Twitter, and even hotels such as the Marriott chain (@MarriottIntl) and small bread and breakfasts like Pennsylvania's Artist's Inn (@ArtistInn) are promoting themselves—and letting potential clients know about bargains—on Twitter. You can find a fairly long list of travel companies on Twitter at travel-write.com.

But perhaps the simplest benefit that Twitter offers travelers isn't website referrals, savings or even tips from people who have been there, done that and know where to find the tastiest, cheapest food in Burkina Faso. It's the companionship. Gary Arndt (@EverywhereTrip), for example, says that he has tweeted from over 60 countries and territories since 1997 as part of his endless round the world tour. Most of his timeline consists of chats with other twitterers, an easy way to beat the occasional loneliness of solo travel. He's even mentioned that he's looking for a travel companion for phase two of his trip.

Tips
for Success

Use TwitPic

TwitPic might be a pretty blunt tool with few features and lots of downtime, but it's perfect for on-the-road picture uploading. The fact that your followers can see exactly what you can see as you're seeing it goes a long way towards helping them feel that they're standing right there with you.

Write a Blog

Microblogging is dynamic, friendly and communal but it's very difficult to monetize directly and it doesn't allow you to go into detail. When you're looking to make money from Web while you're traveling—or even if you just want to offer a little more information than you can squeeze into 140 characters—then you will need a real website.

Blogger.com and Wordpress.com both offer free services but paying for your own domain and hosting won't cost you too much and will help to give a more unique look.

(continued on next page)

for Success

(continued)

Ask for Advice

Income might be what you're really hoping for when you're tweeting from the road but advice can be valuable too. When someone is a few miles ahead of you, then their tips on where to stay, where to eat and how to buy a genuine antique in the market for less than a dollar can be worth much more than a few clicks on a Web page ad.

How to Do It

A good traveler's timeline should consist of a mixture of different kinds of tweets. They should describe what you're doing, eating, seeing and visiting so that readers can get an idea of what you're experiencing. You should also be prepared to answer questions—and once you have a long list of followers, there should be plenty of those—and to ask them too. Twitter is a huge resource of good advice and top tips for people heading to places they've never been before. When Gary Arndt mentioned that he was staying at Momo's Hostel in Tel Aviv, for example, it didn't take long for someone to post a reply recommending a better place nearby.

Even the best travelers' timelines though only really fulfill their potential as a dynamic adjunct to a full-sized blog. Just about all of the travelers on Twitter also write longer posts about their experiences, linking to them from their tweets.

Twitter works as a great place to be able to exchange views with other travelers, with people in the areas you want to visit and with companies in the travel industry. It can provide tips, advice and companionship. But if you want to do something with the community you build around your tweets—and in particular, if you want to monetize them to help pay for at least part of your trip—you'll need to direct them away from Twitter to a site with a revenue stream.

Getting Started

To get started with a timeline dedicated to travel, you'll need to join the community. Elliot.org has a list of "50 travel twitterers you must follow" at www.elliott.org/blog/50-travel-twitterers-you-must-follow. Although that list clearly isn't exhaustive, it is a good place to begin.

Start by following those twitterers, read their posts and ask them questions. As replies come in—and as you start tweeting and blogging about your own trip—you'll find that you're asked questions too.

Hopefully, the traffic will also start flowing into your website soon as well, giving you a few extra dollars to spend on the road.

A Model to Follow

"Michel Travel Notes'" timeline is probably the best model to follow when you're looking for a monetization strategy. The website is packed with ads, affiliate links and information. While it might not be the most attractive site in the world it's hard to leave without clicking on at least one ad somewhere. The site's URL is mentioned several times in the background and bio, the picture is of the person behind the site, keeping the tweets personal, and most importantly, the tweets themselves contain a mixture of chat, advice and on-the-road adventure.

For real traveling notes though, you can't beat the tweets posted by @soultravelers3, a family of three on their third year of open-ended travel. They're unlikely to be monetized but it's a fascinating read—and that's always a good model to follow.

69 SELL YOUR ARTWORK AND LAND GALLERY DEALS

What is Art-Selling on Twitter?

DIFFICULTY

SKILLS REQUIRED

INCOME POTENTIAL

You can find all kinds of artists on Twitter. You can find sculptors and painters, actors and dancers, performers and writers . . . and all sorts of people who once produced a pretty good doodle while they were on the phone.

Being an artist is easy. It doesn't require anything more than a pad, a pencil and the willingness to give yourself the label.

Selling your art though is a whole other business. That requires persistence, a knowledge of the industry and a sellable style.

It also requires talent—and connections too.

Twitter can't provide artists with the ability to produce works that other people might want to buy. But it can put artists in touch with buyers, galleries and other artists, and give them a platform from which they can discuss their works and build the kind of following that could lead to sales.

How Twitterers Are Marketing Their Works of Art

We've already seen how craftmakers are using Etsy to sell their goods, and Twitter to promote their Etsy stores. Selling artworks however is a little more difficult. Works of art tend to be more expensive than the jewelry and accessories offered on Etsy, they're more collectible, which makes repeat sales easier to land, and they often require intermediaries such as galleries to sell them and market knowledge to understand the sorts of works that are selling now.

Twitter helps artists to find all of these things.

Mike Brenner (@MikeBrenner), for example, is an art writer, curator and co-founder of a gallery. Around half of his tweets are conversational and form discussions with other people in the art industry about art and design. He also posts pictures of objects that have caught his eye. Following his timeline lets readers feel that they have their finger on the pulse of the art world and can see what critics are now considering good works of art.

It's no wonder that among his thousands of followers are many artists keen to now what's happening in the art world.

Following art critics isn't the only way that artists can pick up valuable information on Twitter. The site also contains plenty of galleries that tweet about their exhibitions and report on sales.

For artists, galleries often represent the ultimate goal. Gallery owners, who rely on art sales to pay the bills, have direct connections to collectors, need to be selective about the images they display (delivering plenty of bragging rights with every exhibition), and charge high prices for the works they offer (even if they do take around half the sales price as commission.)

A Gallery Art (@agallerylondon), for example, a contemporary art gallery in London, uses its timeline to tell the world about the artworks it's selling. For the gallery, those announcements act as straight marketing. They tell collectors that they're bringing in the kinds of artists whose works are taking off. They also help the gallery to recruit sales staff. Because they're only paid on commission, seeing that the gallery is selling items for thousands of pounds tells potential sellers that they should be able to make some money.

But artists who follow the timeline can also see exactly which types of art are selling and how much they're selling for.

And of course, artists are tweeting themselves. Jaime Lyerly (@jaimelyerly), for example, describes herself in her bio as an "emerging artist." Her timeline is filled with tips for other artists about marketing their work, chats with friends and nuggets of information about the works she's creating: "Beeswax and #encaustic #sculpture pictures coming soon. Promise! Sorry I neglected you all. Do I get karma points for helping others?"

Tips
for Success

Follow the Sellers

Twitterers tend not to identify themselves as "art collectors" on the site so finding potential buyers for your art will always be difficult. Galleries though are much easier to find. They may be the closest you'll get to putting your work directly in front of buyers o n Twitter.

Pay Attention to the Bio

Your bio is going to be a crucial part of marking yourself out from all of the other creative types on Twitter. Many artists tend to offer a combination of one-word descriptions and categories that generate curiosity, such as Jaime Lyerly's "Emerging Emerging Artist, blogger, SDSU student, mom, workshop instructor, healer, creative, mixed media, visionary, drum circle, sculpture, encaustic painter & scul."

(continued on next page)

Tips

for Success

(continued)

Make Buyers Part of the Process

Like Etsy sellers, the more you can make buyers feel that they're part of the creative process, the more they're likely to buy. Tell people what you're making and how you're making it, and they'll want to know what the final result will look like.

How to Do It

Using Twitter to land art sales will require a combination of different techniques. The wealth of information available on industry timelines make them invaluable reading. Interacting with those twitterers too will bring industry experts to look at your online portfolio. That's always going to be critical when you'll struggle to find individual art buyers on Twitter.

That makes the bio and your link crucial.

The bios of artists on Twitter are often pretty rich and eclectic. Heather Francell (@heatherartworks) for example, says that she is an "artist. writer. partner in crime/love. meat popsicle. bunnyfly wrangler. massage therapist. helper. that is all." Those sorts of bios hide as much as they reveal, prompting readers to click the website link to learn more.

And it will also prompt them to start reading the tweets themselves, where the artist should be posting the sorts of messages that give readers hints about their work, how they're being created and where they're being shown and sold.

Getting Started

Making the most of Twitter as an artist then begins not with Twitter itself but with the creation of a good website where potential buyers, critics and gallery owners can browse your works and offer comments.

Once that's ready, you can create your timeline and begin following galleries, art writers and other artists too.

A Model to Follow

Jaime Lyerly's timeline contains a good combination of the various elements that together make up an excellent timeline for artists. Her bio is interesting enough to stand out. Her tweets show that she's active in the art community, and she's willing to talk too about the kind of work she's doing.

Jaime does tend only to post images of her work on her website rather than on TwitPic, but her tweets and the success of her timeline make it a good model to follow.

BUILD YOUR BLOG WITH MICRO-BLOGGING

70

What Does Twitter Offer Bloggers?

For bloggers, Twitter's arrival might well have looked like a threat. Here was a service that cost nothing to use, whose pages took very little time to personalize and whose posts took just seconds to write.

While bloggers were sweating over 500 and 1,000-word posts, micro-bloggers were churning out dozens of tiny updates every week and building a solid community around their activities. It just wasn't fair.

As Twitter took off though, it became clear that the site wasn't a threat to blogging—after all, the site's founders were also the creators of Blogger (www.blogger)—but a powerful adjunct to blogging that can generate additional traffic and build an even more loyal following.

Blogs demand an investment from their users. They demand that users visit their pages or click the link in their RSS readers. And they require them to read long posts that take some time to complete.

Twitter's posts though are delivered directly to a follower's home page. They're absorbed with a glance and require no further clicking or scrolling.

But that shortness also means that they spark an appetite. Tweets create the kind of curiosity that can only be satisfied by visiting a full-length Web page.

For bloggers then, Twitter's posts can remind users to re-visit their content and let new readers know where to find them. Perhaps most powerfully though, they can also draw users into the life of the blogger, returning the personal connection between blogger and reader and writer that online Web blogs were originally intended to create.

DIFFICULTY

SKILLS REQUIRED

INCOME POTENTIAL

for Success

Keep Your Timeline Active

Although bloggers are using their timelines in different ways, in general, the more active and personal a timeline, the more effective it's likely to be at building and holding followers, and sending them to the blog's pages.

The biggest bloggers can get away with timelines that consist of little more than headlines and links. But most bloggers will find that followers want to know about them as much as their blog.

Track the Clicks

While a timeline for a blog will have branding value, the real benefits are measurable: you can see how many followers click the links and read your content.

Make sure that when you include a link to your blog post, you use a shortening service that allows for link tracking, or that you note the source of your traffic in your own data analytics.

(continued on next page)

How Bloggers Are Using Twitter

There are huge numbers of bloggers on Twitter and they're using the service to promote their blogs in any number of different ways.

The most basic is to turn the timeline into a kind of RSS reader. Services like TwitterFeed (www.twitterfeed.com) can automatically post the title of a new blog post, together with a shortened link to a twitterer's timeline. "Steven" (@denouncer), the editor of a blog about XBox gaming, is one of over 250,000 twitterers feeding news of updates from his blog to his timeline.

That's simple enough and when that's all the timeline is used for, it turns it into a kind of unique, online RSS reader.

In practice though, most bloggers are grappling with a dilemma: how much should their timeline be about them, and how much should it be about their blog?

Pete Cashmore (@mashable), the founder of social media blog Mashable (www.mashable.com), used to run two timelines: a personal timeline for himself and a blog timeline for his site. It didn't take long though, before he abandoned his personal timeline to post about solely about the site. While the Mashable timeline has been personalized with Pete's own name and picture, most of the tweets on the Mashable timeline are about the blog, so that it largely looks like any Twitterfed stream. Only occasionally does he bring the timeline to life by tweeting directly to a follower or by discussing himself.

Lisa Lynch (@alrighttit) on the other hand, has placed the emphasis in her timeline on her life rather than her blog, alrighttit.blogspot.com, which describes her battle with breast cancer. While she'll notify her followers whenever a new post goes up, her tweets tend to act like short blog posts. They let followers into her life, allow her to chat with her friends and followers, and in the process, they build a loyal community based around her personality.

There doesn't appear to be a perfect solution to this dilemma. Much depends on the personality of the blogger and the extent to which the blog reflects the person behind it. Lisa Lynch's blog is entirely about her; Pete Cashmore's blog is about an industry and most of the posts aren't written by him.

In general, the more interactive and personal a timeline, the more it will succeed and the closer the sense of community the tweets will generate. But for bloggers, it is possible to drive followers to a new post without doing anything more than telling them the site has just been updated.

How to Do It

Twitterfeeding your blog simply requires you to register at Twitterfeed. com and enter the blog's URL. Any updates will then be fed automatically to your timeline.

Creating a timeline for your blog though will be much harder work. It should be fun, but it will take time and effort. As always, it begins with attracting followers. One simple way to speed up that process is to add a badge to your blog that tells your readers you're on Twitter or, even better, a widget that posts your tweets to your blog page. Twitter's own widgets at Twitter.com/widgets make that very simple, and it means that many of your blog's readers will quickly become your Twitter followers.

Getting Started

Adding a widget then should be the first thing you do after creating your timeline. You should find that it won't take too long before readers start following your timeline as well, allowing you to engage them directly and inform them of new posts.

You'll also be able to pick up new followers and readers, and benefit from Twitter's viral marketing.

A Model to Follow

Which model you follow will depend on how you want your blog's timeline to operate—and that depends on your personality and the nature of your blog. For blogs created by multiple writers, a dedicated Twitterfed timeline like @digitalps might do the trick.

Blogs that rely entirely on the personality of the person behind them can look at the dynamism and interaction of Lisa Lynch's @alrightit. And bloggers whose identities are an important part of their site—even if the site doesn't depend on them—can look at how Pete Cashmore blends his personal brand with his blog at @mashable.

71 DOUBLE YOUR MARKETING POWER WITH TEAM-TWEETING

What is Team-Tweeting?

Tweeting might be a communal activity, one in which you can make new friends and chat with people from all walks of life anywhere in the world, but it's also a lonely one. Some corporate timelines—such Britney Spears' account—are operated in teams but most twitterers tweet alone.

It's up to each twitterer to build their own following, introduce themselves, entertain and inform their followers and create the connections that can lead to increased sales, deeper branding and useful contacts.

But stepping into Twitter alone is a bit like turning up to a party by yourself. It's possible and people do it all the time. But going as part of a group can often make things a lot easier. Not only will you start with at least one follower but you'll always have someone to talk to.

That's important because while joining a conversation on Twitter is as easy as hitting the Reply button, shyness exists on Twitter too. There's a good chance that many of your replies—especially to popular twitterers—will be ignored, and everything you write can be seen by thousands of people. Making those posts to someone you know can make the chats a great deal easier.

And, of course, when you have a close friend or colleague on Twitter, you end up sharing your followers. Your name will appear frequently in their timeline and vice versa. Inevitably, followers will flow across the timeline in both directions.

The result should be a more interesting timeline, easier tweeting, a larger follower list and perhaps too, the kind of loyalty that makes it more likely that your followers will click your links.

How Twitterers are Tweeting in Teams

The most famous tweeting pair is Ashton Kutcher (@aplusk) and Demi Moore (@mrskutcher). Although they both tweet independently, talking to their own fans and discussing issues that interest them, they also refer frequently to each other and post pictures of each other to TwitPic. Demi Moore's frequent posts to her half-million-plus audience about Ashton Kutcher's race to a million followers with CNN went some way towards helping him to win.

Their connection gives them something to talk about and while each timeline certainly stands alone, there's no question that each side benefits from the other's presence on Twitter.

Demi Moore and Ashton Kutcher though are a couple, both of whom are well-known. Kathleen Hessert (@kathleenhessert), a celebrity branding expert, is not well-known outside sporting circles but she benefits from the presence of one of her clients on Twitter. Shaquille O'Neal (@THE_REAL_SHAQ) occasionally replies to her and her replies to him are answered.

While Shaquille—and other celebrities—might post the occasional tweet to a fan, few followers get more than one reply. Conversing with Shaquille O'Neal helps Kathleen Hessert to stand out and shows that she mixes in celebrity circles.

It's unlikely that Shaquille O'Neal benefits much from this relationship but it does show one way in which a business can benefit from attachment to a bigger personality on Twitter.

The relationship between Shaquille O'Neal and Kathleen Hessert is professional, and business relationships are probably the easiest form of team-tweeting, especially when it occurs between people working in the same company or on the same projects. Twitter's own Biz Stone (@biz), Evan Williams (@ev) and Jack Dorsey (@jack) are all on Twitter, of course, and occasionally mention each other in their tweets to give a view of what's happening in the company. Sheri Salata (@SheriSalata) too, the Executive Producer for "Oprah" benefits from her relationship with Oprah Winfrey (@oprah) and the effect for the firm as a whole is more views on the same company and a stronger link to the brand.

That's a model that's very easy for any business with employees to follow.

for Success

Keep Your Timeline Independent

Having friends on Twitter and becoming a part of each other's timelines can bring all sorts of benefits. But you're still on your own. Your timeline has to be strong enough to stand by itself. It has to describe your life, your actions and your interests.

Some of those interests will, of course, be the people you know so replying to them and referring to them should be a natural part of your tweeting. But your timeline is always about you.

Follow Your Partner's Followers

One of the benefits of team-tweeting is that your partner's followers will see references to you in your partner's timeline and visit your tweets. Many of them will then become your followers. And of course, followers will flow in the opposite direction too.

But you can speed the process up by following people who are reading your partner's posts. If

(continued on next page)

Tips

for Success

(continued)

someone is interested in your friend or business associate, there's a good chance they'll be interested in you too. There's no harm in bringing yourself to their attention.

How to Do It

Team tweeting doesn't mean planning your posts together and co-ordinating what you plan to say; Twitter usually works best when it's spontaneous. It does mean referring frequently to people on Twitter who you know outside the site too.

Those tweets can be about anything. While they may give a unique view into your company or on the project you're both working on, the most important aspect of this strategy is the regular spreading of each team member's name across the team's timelines. Followers should feel that in following each member, they're on the edge of a friendly, interesting social circle.

Getting Started

Begin by looking for people on Twitter that you already know. Twitter's "Find People" feature lets you search your email contact list for people you know on Twitter and you can also send an email to friends and suggest they sign up. While that might be effective, writing your own email and talking to them about it will probably be more persuasive!

Once you've found someone you know, it's just a matter of replying to their tweets and communicating with them often.

A Model to Follow

The model you should follow will depend on the nature of your relationship to your Twitter partner. Friends and relations can look at the way Demi Moore and Ashton Kutcher have built independent timelines but whose frequent references, and Twitpic-posted images lend each other plenty of support.

Businesses with prominent clients can look at the way Kathleen Hessert sometimes answers Shaquille O'Neal—and his willingness to reply to her—as a model of a way to benefit from strong professional relationships.

And Twitter's own staff reveal how personal posts from executives dedicated to a business can help to brand a company as friendly, personable, smart and fun.

WIN POWERFUL REFERRALS

What Are Powerful Referrals?

There are few marketing techniques more powerful than a trusted friend recommending a product. A friend will know exactly what the potential buyer wants, will be able to describe the product in a way that's most likely to persuade the buyer, and their trust is transferred directly to the product, making it look like a safe buy.

On Twitter, the power of those recommendations is massively multiplied. When a follower with several thousand followers—and in particular, when that twitterer is a celebrity—the suggestion to buy is spread widely. And retweets can spread it even further.

The result, when it happens, is that an online seller can win so much interest that their site crashes.

But while word-of-mouth recommendations can be hugely effective, for marketers they're also hard to achieve. Because the risk is high and the rewards low, friends will only recommend products that they completely believe in and enjoy. If the product is as good as they suggest, then the best they can win is gratitude. Recommend a product that their friends don't like though and they can lose trust and respect.

Winning a powerful referral then—whether it's to a website or for a product can have a huge effect—but it's not an easy task to achieve.

DIFFICULTY

SKILLS REQUIRED

INCOME POTENTIAL

for Success

Make Your Referrer Match the Product

People are only going to recommend products that they genuinely like, and which they feel that their followers might like too. Before you offer your product to someone with a large following on Twitter then, make sure that they have talked about similar products in the past.

There's little point in pitching your item—or your blog—to someone with little interest in your topic just because they have a large number of readers.

Be Charitable

People with large followings understand the power of their recommendations and they don't hand them out lightly.

But they are usually willing to hand them out if it's going to help a good cause.

That could be something as simple as being willing to donate a percentage of your profits to charity for a certain period of

(continued on next page)

How Sellers are Winning Powerful Referrals on Twitter

In February 2009, Stephen Fry, tweeted that he was thinking of "stopping by a kitchen shop and getting one of those hand pump travel espresso doodads." His followers, who then numbered around 50,000, asked what he was talking about. Stephen responded by posting a link to the company's website.

And the company's website responded by crashing under the weight of the extra traffic.

That recommendation came unrequested. But Lisa Lynch (@alrighttit), a blogger and cancer sufferer, asked Stephen Fry what he thought of her blog alrighttit.blogspot.com. Stephen suggested that his followers read it, and the result, predictably, was a giant spike in followers and hits . . . as well as media interviews from around the world.

Stephen Fry's recommendations, in fact, have been so effective that he became inundated with requests for attention and had to write a blog post describing the conditions under which he would post a link to a website on request: he would do it only once a week, and the requests had to be made containing a #fryretweet hashtag.

They also have to be charitable. Stephen makes clear that his rules do not apply to anything commercial. While he is known for his appreciation of Apple products and is happy to recommend gadgets which he likes, those recommendations aren't made at the request of the companies who produce them.

That seems to be generally the case on Twitter. Companies aren't getting referrals on request; they're getting them either because the recommendation supports a charity or because the twitterer happens to have used the product enjoyed it and wants to mention it in their timeline.

How to Do It

There is no one formula that can win a business a recommended product placement in a celebrity's timeline. Stephen Fry's hashtags come closest but his system is aimed at charities rather than businesses.

It is notable though that when marketer Joel Comm offered to send his book on Twitter to Ashton Kutcher, he didn't receive a response—

or at least not a public one. But when he wrote a blog post praising the dynamism of Ashton's timeline, he did receive a reference (if not exactly a recommendation) from Demi Moore.

Asking for a recommendation then isn't likely to work unless you're promoting a charity. But give the celebrity a reason to mention you—by discussing a topic on your blog that interests them, for example—and you might get something close to the same effect.

Getting Started

The best way to begin is to follow a number of people with large followings. Celebrities can certainly be one source, and you can find a list of them at www.celebritytweet.com, but anyone with a following of more than 50,000 or so should have the power to drive enough people to look at your product.

In fact, you might even be better off targeting a twitterer with a medium-sized following than a very large one. While the result might be smaller, there's a greater chance that your tweet will be noticed.

But don't ask directly for a plug. Offer to send them a sample of your product or send them a link to a page that describes your product ask them what they think.

A Model to Follow

Lisa Lynch's request to Stephen Fry was one good example of winning over a major influence on Twitter but it was for a charitable cause, and it was remarkable for its rarity. There's no real model to follow win a powerful recommendation on Twitter. You'll just have to interact naturally with big twitterers and hope that you set an example for others to follow.

Tips

for Success

(continued)

time. Or it could be a charity event which also promotes your company. Joel Comm's Tweetathon, for example, won plenty of recommendations around the Web, but it also promoted himself and his book.

Don't Rely On It

There are likely to be few strategies harder than willing a solicited recommendation on Twitter from someone with a large following. With thousands of replies flying past them every day, there's a good chance that your request will be lost in the flow.

Even if they're interested in the product, they may not be interested in supplying a recommendation.

And if they are willing to mention it in their timeline, there's always the risk that they won't like it, and you'll end up with a bad review.

The best solution is to interact on Twitter with key influencers in your field and hope that they become interested in what you're doing and mention it naturally.

73 GIVE YOUR VIRAL TWITTER MARKETING AN EASY BOOST

What is Viral Twitter Marketing?

DIFFICULTY

SKILLS REQUIRED

INCOME POTENTIAL

One of Twitter's greatest benefits is its ability to spread marketing messages virally. One program makes that even easier to achieve. ViralTweets is a software program available from ViralTweets.com (www.viraltweets.com). The program allows you to place a box on your website on which users can enter their Twitter username and password, and send a pre-written tweet to their followers. You supply the copy, and your users choose to spread your message to their readers.

It's a very simple program and for websites with plenty of the kind of tech-minded visitors who have Twitter accounts—and who make the most of the system—it can be a very powerful traffic generation tool.

How Marketers are Boosting Their Viral Marketing Power

The challenge with ViralTweets is motivating visitors to use it. Lance Tamashiro (@lancetamashiro) simply asks. He's placed the ViralTweets box at the bottom of one of his posts on his blog, www.lancetamashiro. com/blog/, and written: "Leave your comment below and don't forget to tell your Tweeps about this post!"

SillySticker.com (www.sillysticker.com), a system that offers tags that can be used to find lost property, doesn't even do that. The site simply places two of the boxes in different places on the page and hopes that users will be impressed enough to send out the tweet.

Many publishers are going a little further. They're bribing their users to tell their followers about them. Mike Corso (@cnotes) of

CoolSiteoftheDay.com offers a series of prizes just for filling in the form and sending a tweet that says: "I just entered to win some cool prizes from Cool Site of the Day! You can too, just follow @cnotes and retweet http://budurl.com/twitterprize."

And Swedish singer Sofia Talvik, urges her users to send out a tweet that says "RT I just downloaded a full remix album from Swedish artist Sofia Talvik with one tweet . . . http://www.sofiatalvik.com."

How to Do It

ViralTweets comes in two versions. A paid version, costing $49 allows you to place the code on as many domains as you want, earn as an affiliate and includes an auto-follow feature. The free version though is fine, especially if you're only planning to use it on one site.

There is a price to be paid even for the free version though. In order to be taken to the Web page that contains a downloadable link to the program's zip file, you'll first have to complete a ViralTweets form that sends out this message about creator Ryan Wade (@ryanwade) to your own followers: "RT Here's The Software @ryanwade Used To Make Over $4000 With One Tweet . . . http://www.viraltweets.com."

Sending your followers a marketing message as blatant as that might not be something you'd want to do. But there's nothing to stop you from creating a new Twitter account and posting the message on a timeline with no followers.

If you want to reward Ryan for the software, then you can certainly write a tweet recommending ViralTweets yourself. But his own message looks far too much like a hard sell to sit comfortably in most timelines.

You'll then be able to download the file, extract it, upload it to your ftp server and enter the message that your users' followers will see. You'll also be able to ask the users to follow you, requiring them to uncheck the box if they don't want to. There's a good chance that a user who likes your site will be willing to follow you, so that's an option worth taking.

Finally, you'll just need to place the box somewhere visible and close to the product that you're offering as a giveaway.

Tips
for Success

Make the Message Persuasive

Success with ViralTweet depends on two factors. One of those factors is the message that your users will be sending to their followers. Ryan Wade's own message is a good example of how to get that wrong. His tweet reads like an ad, which never sits well in a timeline. Sofia Talvik's message however, reads like a service. It tells people where they can pick up an entire album for free. Even if they're not interested in Sofia Talvik's music, followers won't mind being told where they can find free albums.

The message has to be valuable to the recipient as well as useful to you.

Make the Bribe Big

And one way to make it valuable is to ensure that the giveaway is high quality. Telling people that there's a good blog post available will only have limited appeal. Telling them that they can download two chapters of a book, a free collection of songs or a white paper is going to be much more powerful.

(continued on next page)

 GEEKPRENEUR

for Success

(continued)

Those are the kinds of tweets that do tend to get passed around on Twitter and take on a re-tweeting life of their own.

Put the Box on the Right

You'll also need to make sure that ViralTweets box can be easily seen. Some publishers have placed it at the bottom of the blog post, but that creates the impression that the valuable item on offer is nothing more than a blog post.

Place the box in the right sidebar, near an image of the giveaway itself, and you'll take it of the main content flow and make the reward look much more special.

Getting Started

There are number of things you have to do before you can download and install ViralTweet.

First, you'll need a giveaway. Although you can simply ask people to retweet on your behalf, as some bloggers are doing, offering a reward—and using the message to tell other people where they can pick up that reward—will massively increase your viral marketing power.

Every website has free content; only this page is giving away this free download. That makes the content of your message much more valuable.

And you'll also need to set up a new Twitter account so that you don't spam your own followers with Ryan Wade's marketing message.

A Model to Follow

Sofia Talvik's use of ViralTweets was particularly clever. She did a number of things that helped her ViralTweets box to stand out.

First, she made the reward valuable. Rather than just offering a single track, she gave away an entire album. It takes a lot of free to get Internet users excited, but a free album is strong enough to do it.

Second, she wrote a message that matched Twitter's style. By using the first person and the past tense, the tweet was both honest and personal. A tweet like that is unlikely to look out of place in anyone's timeline.

She also optimized the ViralTweets box, placing her own artwork inside it and pasting it onto the page beneath her jukebox.

And finally, she didn't keep it up forever. The giveaway lasted just long enough to attract attention but by keeping it short, she made sure that she wasn't completely destroying the value of her album.

That's a winning combination of persuasion and placement that can make for a successful viral marketing campaign.

GIVE YOUR SITE THE DIGG EFFECT WITH TWITTER

What is Digg?

Digg.com (www.digg.com) is a social news network which allows Internet users to recommend Web pages. Users can vote for content in a number of different categories, explain why the content is worth reading and comment on it.

They can also vote pages down, dropping them through the listings.

The most popular Web pages appear on Digg's front page, a prize that can have dramatic effects on traffic flows to the website.

In fact, "the Digg effect" is so dramatic and bring in so many new visitors that even medium-sized websites have been known to collapse under the strain of serving so many views.

Few methods though can be so effective at making a website visible. Although Digg's users are notoriously shy of clicking on ads, some of them will stick around, giving a website a host of new readers and RSS subscribers.

And because Digg is social, there are strategies that publishers can use to encourage votes for their content, putting their pages in prominent positions. Those strategies now include trawling for votes on Twitter.

How Twitterers Are Getting Dugg

Some publishers are taking the simplest approach to trawling for Digg votes on Twitter: they're asking for it. Bob Pease (@bobbo0521), for example, asked his followers to push his article about spammers on

DIFFICULTY

SKILLS REQUIRED

INCOME POTENTIAL

for Success

Be Persistent

The Digg Effect can be so huge that it's worth putting some real effort into reaching Digg's home page. A single tweet is unlikely to be enough. Make it clear that your goal is to get your article on Digg's home page and make it your followers' goal too.

Update them with your progress up the chart, look for people on Twitter discussing related topics and tell them about the article, and make repeat requests to ensure that your first requests aren't missed.

You can also try looking for Diggers on Digg.com, follow them on Twitter and ask them to vote for you. Because Digg is social, some Diggers' recommendations can bring in many more votes from their own network.

Be Polite

And when you're asking for a favor, it pays to be polite! There's a good reason that the word "please" turns up more often in requests for retweet.

Twitter up the Digg charts with this tweet: "Digg me: http://tinyurl.com/cqnrps (expand)."

That wasn't very effective. Four days after asking his 640-plus followers to Digg him, his post had received three votes.

That might have been because the article just wasn't very interesting, but it could also have been because the request itself wasn't very clear. Followers had no reason to even click the link and read the article, let alone urge other people to read it.

Steve Richardson (@SteveRichardson) added a little more detail to his request for Diggs. He wrote: "do you hate all that pesky junk mail?! . . . Digg me up! (please) http://www.digg.com/d1p9qy—please RT If you like! :-)"

That tweet contained a number of elements that increased the chances that someone would give him their vote.

It began with an intriguing headline that told readers what the post was about. Bob Pease was relying on the loyalty of his followers to read his post and Digg it; Steve Richardson looked to the topic of his post.

It was polite, which is always a good idea.

And it asked for retweets. Followers generous enough to provide the favor of a Digg vote would have another pain-free way to help by posting the tweet in their own timeline, spreading it across Twitter.

The only thing that Steve got wrong—a mistake made by Bob Pease too—was to link to the Digg page instead his own Web page. Again, that turns the request into a favor to the twitterer instead of something that the reader wants to do because the publisher deserves it. It is possible to place a Digg button at the bottom of a post, so a more effective approach might be to urge people to read a post, link to it, then suggest that they Digg if they like it—and retweet too.

And finally, some twitterers are giving their followers an added incentive to vote for them by thanking them publicly in their timelines. Edward Lewis (@pageoneresults) wrote this tweet to thank a follower who had voted for him on Digg: "#SuperTweet Looks like @notifyneal Dugg me, THANK YOU! http://tinyurl.com/d75oen."

Place a few tweets like that in your timeline and you can expect to receive more votes—and tweets from followers telling you they voted for you.

How to Do It

Writing tweets that urge followers to Digg posts isn't difficult—although it does appear to be difficult to get right. The tweet should contain:

The title of the post;

A short link to the post, not to the Digg page;

A request to retweet;

And good manners.

You might need to make the request more than once to get the full effect!

Getting Started

Using Twitter to benefit from Digg begins with creating the kind of article that Diggers like.

Unless you have tens of thousands of followers, many of whom are loyal enough to vote for you, Twitter will only give you enough traction to get started on Digg and attract the attention of other Digg users. To get to the front page, you'll need their votes too and they like particular types of posts.

Spend some time then browsing Digg and looking at the topics on the front page. You should find that many of them are tech-related, lighthearted or list posts.

A Model to Follow

Steve Richardson's request to his followers to Digg his article provides one good model to follow, even if it did link to the Digg page rather than to his site. But it would be a good idea to repeat it and turn the request into a campaign.

A Digg campaign doesn't have to last long but if it is successful, it should have a fantastic effect.

75

INCREASE YOUR REACH WITH FACEBOOK

DIFFICULTY

SKILLS REQUIRED

INCOME POTENTIAL

What is Tweeting on Facebook?

Facebook blinked. When the site received a facelift at the beginning of 2009, it chose to copy Twitter. Log in to a Facebook account now and the feature that dominates the member's page isn't contacts, games or news updates. It's what used to be called status updates—short messages that members use to tell each other what they're doing now.

Or to put another way, tweets.

The tweets—or updates—on Facebook aren't quite the same as those on Twitter. There's no character limit, for one. That should make them more flexible but in practice, most of the updates that people post on Facebook tend to be short and to the point. Twitter's 140-character limit isn't as restrictive as it looks.

More importantly, the updates are aimed at a different crowd and can receive different kinds of responses.

The biggest attraction of Twitter is that it's possible to communicate with anyone on the site. That makes it an incredibly powerful networking tool. Authors can chat with agents, entrepreneurs with investors, and businesses with potential clients. On Facebook, those connections are limited. To connect with someone on Facebook, you have to ask their permission first. To find them, it helps to be a part of their network.

Although businesses do use Facebook—and they're seeing results from that use —networks on the site tend to be largely friendly and less professional. Twitter's networks are often more professional than friendly.

GEEKPRENEUR

If that's a drawback, another is that Facebook limits friends to just 5,000.

There is an advantage though. Just as the posts can be bigger, the responses can be bigger too. A tweet might generate a reply and a #chat can generate a long and complex discussion, but conversations on Twitter tend to be short and consist of just a few exchanges. Facebook's discussions are generally more detailed and because everyone can see what everyone else is posting, even if they're not on their friend list, the conversations are often more comprehensive too.

A good strategy for any business using social media is to use a number of different sites. That increases your reach, but it does give you a fragmented audience. With Twitter though—and an app that feeds your tweets to your Facebook—it is possible to spread the conversation and Twitter's marketing power over different platforms.

How Twitterers Are Using Facebook

Facebook's Twitter app leaves very little flexibility in its use once you've chosen to use it. Post a tweet on Twitter and it will appear in your Facebook profile.

That's about it.

Reply tweets won't appear on Facebook and neither will tweets that begin with a Twitter username or a hashtag.

All of your other tweets though will appear on Facebook. You can't filter them so that only personal tweets turn up on Facebook and business tweets on Twitter, nor can you direct your tweets to the different locations by keyword.

Most of the people who use Facebook's Twitter app then simply use it to spread their tweets further. Tweets appear in both places and the result is usually a more detailed discussion on Facebook than the kind of responses you can find on Twitter. While you might receive fewer responses on Facebook—which has a tighter limit on the size of the network and where people check in less frequently than they do on Twitter—those responses are more likely to contain examples and longer opinions.

Some businesses though are posting to both Twitter and Facebook, and they're doing it in different ways. Those different kinds of tweets

Tips
for Success

Don't Overdo It

In general, Facebook members don't place updates more than once a day and they don't do it every day. Twitterers though update several times a day. That means a Facebook friend might discover that you're dominating their homepage. That's not just rude, it also means that they might do something that twitterers can't do: choose not to display your messages while still remaining in your network. If you post to Twitter frequently you could find that you're no longer visible to your Facebook friends.

Check Facebook Frequently

The benefit of posting your tweets on Facebook is that you get a different kind of response. To make the most of those responses though, you'll need to log in to Facebook frequently and answer those responses. The activity that builds a community on Twitter, builds a community on Facebook too.

reveal a great deal about the strengths and weaknesses of each platform—and how to make the most of them.

CNN, for example, maintains multiple Twitter accounts but its most popular timeline is CNN Breaking News (@cnnbrk), which was also one of the first timelines to pick up more than a million followers. CNN also has a commercial Facebook account which has fewer than 400,000 "fans."

CNN takes advantage of Facebook's larger updates to place more information in its Facebook posts than it does on its Twitter timeline. So while the Twitter Breaking News timeline says: "U.S. ship captain held by pirates off Somalia has been freed, senior U.S. official says. Three of four pirates killed" the Facebook update says: "CNN invites you to watch President Obama's administration respond to questions about gun control and the pirate hijacking during today's White House press briefing. See LIVE streaming video of the briefing here: http://bit.ly/XHMsp". That Facebook post generated 145 comments and received 384 votes of approval.

While it would have been a great deal easier for CNN simply to have fed its Twitter updates into Facebook—as many individuals do—it wouldn't have been able to include that much detail.

How to Do It

To place your Tweets automatically in your Facebook profile, you won't need to do anything more than surf to www.facebook.com/apps/application.php?id=2231777543 and choose to use the Facebook Twitter app.

You'll then be able to place tweets from Facebook in Twitter but to continue doing that, you'll need to work directly from an application page that looks exactly like Twitter. It will be easier to tweet from Twitter directly.

Getting Started

Begin by installing the Twitter app and writing a tweet. But don't stop there. You now have to make sure that you check your Facebook account regularly to review the responses. Being able to see everyone responses in one place—and in a way that lets everyone else see them easily too—means that you can expect a lively discussion with your followers, powered by your activity on Twitter.

A Model to Follow

CNN provides one model to follow if only because the news company clearly understands the differences between the two sites. Its posts on Facebook are longer than its tweets and it also includes rich media posts and "fan notes" to make the most of Facebook's flexibility.

On Twitter though, it uses broadcast tweets to insert its headlines neatly into its followers' timelines.

76 BOOST YOUR IMAGE AS A TWITTER-BASED EXPERT

DIFFICULTY

SKILLS REQUIRED

INCOME.POTENTIAL

What Are Twitter-Based Experts?

Twitter is free. All of the tweets, all of the connections, all of the advice that's provided by professionals, experts and specialists is all delivered completely free of charge. Some of that information can be very valuable. Investment experts are handing out stock advice to anyone who wants it (and to show off their own expertise), computer specialists are answering questions from twitterers about server problems, software glitches and hardware installation. Literary agents are explaining to writers how to get their books published.

All of that knowledge can help people to make money, and all of it is available on Twitter for free.

But "free" always has a price, and on Twitter that price is a lack of exclusivity. Ask an expert a question on Twitter and there's no guarantee that you'll get an answer. For really popular experts who like to spread their replies around there's little chance that you won't get a second answer.

TwittExperts (www.twittexperts.com) is a service that allows specialists to create exclusive timelines. The timelines are kept private and can only be accessed on request and for a fee. In return, TwittExperts promise . . . well, nothing. The experts who sign up at TwittExperts. com don't guarantee a set number of posts or even to answer questions put to them from their subscribers. But with a share of subscription-based revenue on offer, they do at least have a strong incentive to do so.

ⓖ GEEKPRENEUR

How Twitterers Are Marketing Themselves as Experts

Becoming a TwittExpert is simple enough. Simply hit the "Contact Us" link at TwittExperts.com and ask to be added to their list of specialists. At the moment, that list includes a handful of computer and Internet experts, a pest control specialist, a "fashion, style and runway trends" experts (who is also a "web researcher, blogger and fashion designer), a few others. The service, like many of the revenue-based services that have sprung up around Twitter, is fairly new so it's difficult to assess how effective it will be at bringing in subscribers and generating revenue.

At the moment, few of the experts who have signed up at TwittExpert appear to have large numbers of followers. Almost two months after signing up, Jessica Hayes (@TheVogueTrotter), TwittExperts' fashion specialist had just two followers and it's possible that they weren't paying. (TwittExperts allows five days of free access before charging in ten-day increments.

How to Do It

TwittExperts does solve a problem. Twitter is an excellent networking tool. But its open access nature means that twitterers are always competing for the attention of the most important specialists. That does create an opportunity for those willing to charge for special attention—and those willing to pay for it.

It turns Twitter into a an effortless consultancy platform.

But beyond listing them on its site, TwittExperts does nothing to promote the services of the experts it offers. That means the experts who succeed at earning from subscribers will be those who offer good content, plenty of attention—and who market themselves too.

TwittExperts might not guarantee a set number of tweets but you should be posting good information regularly and ideally it should be information that you're not offering elsewhere.

So an investment specialist might have a timeline that assessed the market and predicted what was going to happen next, but he'd keep the names of the top-earning stocks for the subscription-based timeline. A health expert would talk about trends and techniques on her public timeline but the subscription timeline would provide more detailed

Tips

for Success

Do the Marketing

Don't expect TwittExperts to bring you subscribers. You'll have to do that yourself, and the best tool you have for doing that is your open timeline. Tell your followers about your paid timeline and encourage those with personal issues or who want specific advice to contact you there.

Make it clear that you're not doing this for the money but that you're charging as a way of filtering out the masses and being able to focus your advice on those who need it most. Your free timeline should still offer good content and useful information.

Deliver Value

TwittExperts might not demand anything of you, but your subscribers will. Once someone has signed up, you want to keep them on board. You'll only do that if your timeline offers a combination of high value broadcast tweets and personalized answers. Look at your followers' timelines to see the issues that affect them most and make your responses fit their needs.

advice and target it to the subscribers. Because there will be fewer of them, the relationship can be a great deal closer. It's the difference between a lecture and a private class.

But the public timeline would still have to provide good value too. Although some subscribers might come through TwittExperts—especially if the site does actually take off—most will come through the free advice offered in the public timeline. That's how the majority of followers find experts.

The amount of income generate through TwittExperts depends on the number of followers your timeline can build. The best way to build those paying followers then is to create a large and high-quality free timeline. Prove you're an expert and show that your knowledge and advice is valuable and worth paying for.

When you apologize to your followers for not being able to answer every question but point out that you are offering personal suggestion on your other timeline accessible through TwittExperts.com, you should find that some of those followers are prepared to pay.

Getting Started

The first step isn't to sign up at TwittExperts.com. It's to start building a good free timeline of your own. TwittExperts doesn't appear to be too selective about the experts it's accepting—at least not yet—but a good timeline of your own will show that you're serious, knowledgeable, and understand how Twitter works.

Most importantly, it will also give you a foundation for your own marketing.

Once you've got a timeline up and running, invite questions and put the effort into providing solid, useful answers. The information you provide on your free timeline will be a showcase for your paid timeline. You want followers to feel that if they can get this much helpful information for free, they should be able to benefit a great deal more from the private consultations you're offering through TwittExperts.

Then sign up at TwittExperts.com.

A Model to Follow

TwittExperts founder Alex Puig (@alexpuig) has the most popular paid timeline @web_twittexpert. You can access the timeline for five days for free but pay attention to the kinds of tweets he's posting.

In particular though, note why Alex is currently the leading twitterer at TwittExperts. It's not because the site pushes him particularly hard (although he does have top listing in the Experts List). It's because of his status as the site's founder—and therefore an expert in his own right.

To pick up subscribers, you'll need to build up your status too.

READ THE STATS BY TRACKING YOUR CLICKS

What is Click Tracking?

Twitter can help anyone to build a huge audience. You don't have to pay for website hosting, fancy designs (unless you want to) or buy images. You just have to write interesting tweets and be sociable enough to join the conversation.

But while building an audience might be nice, it's only going to be valuable if you can drive at least some of that audience to take the kind of action that's going to deliver revenues.

On websites that's usually done by placing ads in prominent positions. Embed pay-per-click ads into content, recommend affiliate-linked products and a small percentage of your readers will click and earn you revenue.

On Twitter, it is possible to do something similar. Inserting ads into a timeline is difficult and controversial, but links are easy to include and they're an important part of supplementing the information in your timeline.

One of the most important aspects of generating revenue from a website though isn't just ad placement, it's testing strategies and checking the results. Whether you're using Google's AdSense or any other revenue system, you'll be able to see how many people clicked on an ad unit and which ad units are delivering the highest revenues.

Through careful tracking, you can discover the most valuable spots on your Web page and the content that's most likely to deliver ad revenue.

Some URL shortening services can deliver similar statistics.

You'll be able to test different kinds of tweets and see which deliver the highest number of clickthroughs.

Next time you include a link in your tweet—whether it's to an ad-optimized Web page, an affiliate page or a sales page—you'll know how to phrase the tweet to generate the highest number of clicks.

How Twitterers Are Tracking Clicks

There's a whole host of different URL shortening service, but not all of them offer tracking statistics. Three that do are bit.ly, tr.im and Budurl (www.budurl.com), all of which also offer "301 redirects." That allows Google to credit your link when calculating search engine rankings. Because a tweet that contains a link can be retweeted, reposted and appear in all sort of unexpected places, that supplies some very useful extra value.

Both bit.ly and tr.im are free. Budurl also offers a free service but, in addition, provides a "Premium Click Stats Report" that includes timestamp, referrer, IP address and keywords used. Rates range from $4 per month for tracking up to 500 URLs to $49 for 50,000 URLs. It's unlikely you're going to track more than 500 URLs but it's also unlikely you'll need to know IP addresses or timestamps, however interesting that information might be. Knowing the referrers could be interesting but most of the people who click a link in one of your tweets will do it in your timeline. Even if they do it in someone else's timeline after the tweet has been retweeted, there will be little that you can do to encourage a follower to keep retweeting. And both bit.ly and tr.im offer referrer data too.

The most important figure will always be the number of clicks a shortened URL receives and the type of tweet in which the URL appears.

To pick up that information twitterers tend to use either Budurl or bit.ly.

How to Do It

The choice of URL shortener shouldn't be too difficult. More difficult is testing different kinds of tweets to see which is most likely to generate clickthroughs.

for Success

Keep Good Notes

The aim of tracking your Twitter links is to make sure that you get the maximum number of clickthroughs each time you want to send your followers to a Web page. That means taking good notes. You'll need to know exactly what kind of tweet converts what percentage of your followers.

The time you tweet may count too. Twitter is dynamic so you might find that tweeting during work hours delivers more responses than posting at weekends or in the evenings. That data should form part of your records too.

Compare Twitter Clickthroughs with Site Conversions

Driving your followers to a website is only half the story though. You'll also need your followers to do something when they get there, whether that's click an ad, sign up for a service or make a purchase. In addition to tracking the numbers of people who

(continued on next page)

for Success

(continued)

click a link in your tweet then, you should also keep track of the conversion rates when they get there. That will tell you which types of pages you should link to as well as which kinds of tweets to put them in.

There' s no limit to types of tweets that people are writing and which include URLs. Perhaps the most popular are those which offer nothing more than the headline of a blog post. If the reader is interested in the subject of the post, they'll read it. If not, they won't.

Some twitterers though are looking to incentivize their followers a little more. Clyde Boom (@linuxtraining) uses a free offer to motivate his followers to check his Linux course: "Free Linux Commands Training Course with Linux eBook, Linux Audio Podcast (mp3)—7 Lessons!—Click http://budurl.com/FreeLinuxTraining1."

Pepper Assistants (@pepperva), a Philippines-based virtual assistant service makes things a little more interesting with a competition: "Win one year of free personal assistant service http://budurl.com/win1"

And Internet marketer Mark Attwood (@markattwood) simply tries to use curiosity to tempt people to click: "Trailer for DVD of my lecture at Manchester Uni on Internet Marketing http://budurl.com/7d8j."

Which of those three examples would work best for you. Tracking URLs gives you the opportunity test each type and see. You can try a giveaway and count the number of clicks you generate over the following few days. Then try a contest and compare the results. And finally, tweet a post that generates curiosity and see if that update delivers more clickthroughs.

It shouldn't take too long before you know exactly what kind of tweet to post to get your followers clicking your links.

Getting Started

Begin by writing a tweet that will include a link to a Web page. Shorten the URL using one of those three URL shortening services and make a note of both the short URL and the tweet itself.

Wait a few days and post another link using a different kind of tweet. You'll already be starting to see which kinds of tweets are most likely to motivate your followers.

A Model to Follow

There's no one model to follow for tracking tweets. Instead you should look at the models for different kinds of tweets. The larger your library of tweet types and their relative results, the more tools you'll have at your disposal when you want to drive followers to a Web page. @linuxtraining, @pepperva and @markattwood are all good places to start but every time you see a link in a tweet, ask yourself what the twitterer has done to encourage his or her followers to click—and test it on your own followers.

⟨78⟩ ENGAGE YOUR MARKET EFFORTLESSLY WITH AN AUTORESPONDER

DIFFICULTY

SKILLS REQUIRED

INCOME POTENTIAL

What is an Autoresponder?

Create a Twitter timeline and every day, you'll be able to see people signing up to read your tweets. Those people have expressed an interest in your business. If you can engage them, make them feel close to you and build a relationship of trust, they'll buy from you.

They might not buy from you right away, but the next time they need the sort of products you sell, they'll remember you. They'll even recommend you to other people who need your products—whether they've bought from you or not.

Your tweets will do most of that work. Replies to their tweets will do even more. But a direct message should be the most powerful way to connect with a follower.

A direct message is personal and confidential. It's a private message from one friend to another.

But when you've got thousands of followers, and your follower list is growing by the day, you can't possibly send personal, direct messages to everyone of your followers.

What you can do though is send automated direct messages to each of them. As soon as someone hits the "Follow" button, they receive your message in their inbox.

On Twitter, these kinds of auto-responders have become both popular and controversial. Marketers have used them not just to thank new followers but to make offers and bring people to their sales pages. Recipients have been known to find them intrusive and spammy; instead of

274   Ⓖ GEEKPRENEUR

being greeted by someone they're hoping to consider a friend, they're being buttonholed by someone who wants to sell them something.

And with so many people using them, twitterers following new people on a regular basis have become accustomed to ignoring direct messages.

But there's also anecdotal evidence that despite the often commercial nature of automated direct messages, they can work: they can deliver clicks to websites, and those clicks can generate revenue.

How Twitterers Are Using Autoresponders

Automated direct messages tend to consist of the following elements: a note of thanks for the follow; an invitation to get in touch; and often, a link to a website.

Martin Zwilling (@StartupPro), for example, sends out this automated message to each of his followers: "Thanks for following. Tweet if you have business questions, or see daily tips at http://blog.startuppro-fessionals.com".

Scott Monty (@ScottMonty), Head of Social Media at Ford, does something with his automated message: "Thanks for the follow! If you ever want to get my attention, just '@' me."

As greetings, both of these autoresponders are friendly and welcoming, but they're also very easy to ignore.

"Chris" (@RizzoTees) takes a slightly more sophisticated approach. His bio warns new followers that they'll be receiving an automated direct message: "T-shirt seller dude. Follow me and I'll auto-DM you an invitation to join my Facebook fan page, where you'll get a chance to win free tees. Thanks!"

That bio does a number of important things: it helps to allay the impersonal nature of an automated direct message; by telling followers what to expect it shows an understanding of what his followers want; and it also incentivizes them to click by telling them they'll receive an offer if they agree to follow.

In effect, it's turned a direct message-based autoresponder from a greeting into a special offer delivered to every follower.

Tips *for Success*

Warn Your Followers

Twitter's strength is the personal nature of the relationships that twitterers develop. An automated message is very impersonal. A recipient of an automated direct message however feels that they're being treated as part of a crowd rather than as an individual. You might get a click to a website from an automated direct message, but the price you pay could be the loss of the relationship—and that could be very expensive.

Tell your followers exactly what will happen when they hit the follow button and they won't mistake the automated message for a personal one. They'll just consider it an extra piece of information that you want to share with them.

You'll still get to contact each new follower individually, but you won't ruin your relationship with them.

Give Them a Reason to Click
One mistake that many twitterers make is to

(continued on next page)

Tips

for Success

(continued)

include the same link in their automated message as the website placed above the bio. Or they invite their new followers to reply to them.

But their followers know how to reply and don't feel they need an invitation to reply. It's also likely that they've already looked at the website so giving them a second link is unlikely to make too much difference.

The link in the direct message then should be different to the one above the bio. And followers should be incentivized to click it with a special offer or a discount coupon.

Discontinue If It Doesn't Work

Automated direct messages have become very controversial on Twitter, with plenty of users asking for them to be banned. If you're losing followers as a result of sending an automated message, then it's likely that you'll be better off not using one.

How to Do It

Creating an automated direct message couldn't be simpler. Sign up for the free trial at TweetLater (www.tweetlater.com) and you'll be able to send automated direct messages for a week before you have to pay to continue. You'll even be able to write more than one direct message and have TweetLater send each message at random.

The format for multiple messages is: "{Direct message one| Direct message two| Direct message three}". Each message of course, can be no more than 140 characters.

Being able to randomly send a number of direct messages does provide a huge benefit. It means that you can test different kinds of messages. You can create three different landing pages and place three different links in each of your messages. Track the number of clicks you receive through those shortened URLs and you'll be able to see which of your messages gives you the best results.

Getting Started

Begin then by placing a Web page on three different sub-domains. Shorten the URLs of each of those addresses using one of the shortening services that also allow you track clicks. Sign up for TweetLater's free trial and create three different automated direct messages that each lead to one of the pages you've created. Check regularly to see how those messages are converting new followers.

A Model to Follow

Chris from @RizzoTees comes the closest to finding a solution to the impersonal feel of an automated message by telling his followers what to expect. It's a great way to turn an automated notification from something that has the appearance of a personal message into an automated special offer that followers might just appreciate.

BUY AND SELL PREMIUM TWEETS

79

What is Buying and Selling Premium Tweets?

TwittExperts allows specialized twitters to sell their information. TwitPub (www.twitpub) does something similar: twitterers can create closed accounts then use TwitPub sell subscriptions to those accounts. Publisher can set their own prices and TwitPub will take 20 percent of the subscription fees.

And that's about it. While TwittExperts put the emphasis on direct access to an expert who can provide detailed information and advice, TwitPub talks sells timelines and tweets, as though the information posted in the timeline itself has a value.

With prices for monthly subscriptions generally floating around 99 cents, they don't seem to be too valuable though.

But TwitPub is signing up publishers and some of those publishers are landing subscribers. Find the right formula—a valuable topic with tweets that contain valuable, actionable information—and it's just possible that you could see some cash flow from TwitPub.

How Twitterers Are Buying and Selling Premium Tweets

TwitPub offers a surprisingly eclectic range of subscription-based accounts. There' s no shortage of timelines offering information. @lillyfenshui, for example, offers an average of fifteen tweets per week that provide quick tips for good Feng Shui, such as: "Feng Shui tips for

DIFFICULTY

SKILLS REQUIRED

INCOME POTENTIAL

Tips
for Success

Put a Button on Your Website

One of the problems with private timelines is that they lose what is perhaps Twitter's most valuable advantage: the ease with which tweets can generate viral marketing. Because other twitterers won't be able to see your tweets, you'll find it difficult to show them the value of your posts on Twitter and convert them into subscribers.

One solution is to look elsewhere.

Chee Ming places a TwitPub button on his blog www.cheeming. com, advertising his Chinese tutoring timelines. Visitors to a blog already understand the value of the publisher's content so they might be persuaded to pay a small amount extra to read particularly valuable supplementary information. Chee Ming though has placed an ad for his Twitter-based Chinese class on a blog about computers. Expect to do better when the timeline matches the blog.

(continued on next page)

wealth #11 Place pictures of things you wish to buy in the Southeast corner."

Even at a dollar a month it's difficult to see why someone would pay for information that they could just as easily find in a book, for free online or even for free on Twitter from experts such as Perrie Burton (@FengShuiAvatar), an Australian "Feng Shui master." It's perhaps not surprising that after almost 100 tweets, @lillyfenshui has yet to sell a subscription.

Asking people to pay even a small amount for content that they can access for free elsewhere might be one way to use TwitPub, but it's unlikely to be the most effective.

More hopeful are those timelines that provide a service that has real value. A number of TwitPub's timelines are offering language classes, particularly in mandarin. Clearly, timelines like these can only help with writing skills, and again, it's always possible to find native twitterers to converse with on Twitter. But someone paying a subscription fee might feel more comfortable about asking for their responses to be corrected.

These services too are struggling to pick up subscribers.

Perhaps timelines most likely to succeed then are those that offer really valuable information. @darwinstrades provides stock tips and argues that the value of the advice he gives can earn followers large profits. While it's difficult for potential subscribers to assess the accuracy of that claim—and again, there's no shortage of other twitterers offering similar advice for free—the timeline has attracted one or two subscribers.

At 99 cents each though, it's likely that the twitterer would have earned far more writing full-length blog posts.

How to Do It

You can sign up as a publisher by registering your account with TwitPub. Complete your details, set a your price and start tweeting.

That all sounds simple enough but it does appear that TwitPub's publishers do make a couple of mistakes during this process.

They don't include sample tweets that will allow subscribers to see exactly what they're buying; and many of them don't tweet at all until they've got subscribers.

Part of the information that subscribers can see is the number of subscribers the publisher has already picked up, the number of tweets they've already published and the frequency with which they tweet.

All of that information is important. With so much free content available on Twitter, to persuade someone to hand over even a dollar a month will require you to prove that the tweets you're offering are special and can't be obtained any other way.

Getting Started

The first move will be to open an account at TwitPub. The site is free to join and the registration process is very straightforward but do be sure to complete all of the details properly. The idea of followers paying to read tweets is tempting enough to attract all sort of twitterers, even those who have nothing to offer but accounts of their daily lives.

To win subscribers you'll need to show that you're professional and have professional-quality content to offer.

That means displaying a professional appearance, complete with sample tweets that show your wares, a high frequency of tweets that prove subscribers will get their money's worth, and a description that doesn't just explain what you'll be tweeting about but also explains the benefits of reading your tweets.

A Model to Follow

TwitPub's publishers have yet to be successful enough for any of them to have created a model to follow. @darwinstrades' timeline posts information that purports to be genuinely valuable—a useful characteristic when you're asking people to pay—and Chee Ming markets his timeline outside of both Twitter and TwitPub.

If you are going to use TwitPub, both of those should form part of your earning strategy.

for Success

(continued)

Answer Tweets

There are few differences between TwittExperts and TwitPub but one of them is that TwittExperts suggest that their twitterers will be answering questions, not just writing tweets.

That's a small difference ... but it could well be the one that brings in money.

Readers might not be willing to pay for tweets; but they could be willing to pay for special attention. Make it clear in your profile details that you invite questions.

Create Multiple Timelines

TwitPub doesn't restrict you to just one field of expertise. You can create multiple timelines on a range of different subjects and see which ones turn out to be the most popular. If one timeline doesn't take off, you can just shut it down.

80 TWITTER FOR SEARCH ENGINE OPTIMIZATION

DIFFICULTY

SKILLS REQUIRED

INCOME POTENTIAL

What is Search Engine Optimization?

Traffic to a website may come from a number of different sources. It may come from a user typing the URL directly into the browser, something that requires the user to already know about the site—or for the site to have a particularly useful domain name.

It may come through links placed on other websites, something that requires the publisher to produce good enough content for other sites to want to link to it.

Users can also come from advertising, which costs money, or best of all, readers can reach a website by looking for the site's content on a search engine, seeing it listed in a prominent position and clicking through to the site. That's free traffic and it can come in a steady stream.

But it will only come if the site is displayed on the first few pages of the search results—and ideally, the first few places on the very first page. As a result, some publishers spend large sums making sure that their sites have effective search engine optimization (SEO). Fees of $3,000 and more are not unusual for optimization services.

Although no one outside the search engines understand exactly what it takes to reach the top spots, it is clear that SEO requires a combination of links, traffic and keywording.

Twitter can supply at least some of those elements, making it a useful—and cheap—tool for those hoping to improve their sites' search engine rankings.

How Twitterers Are Us ing Twitter for Search Engine Optimization

It could have been very easy to use Twitter to improve your search engine rankings. Because search engines count the number of incoming links to a website (as well as the quality of the site on which those links are placed), a publisher could simply have posted tweets that include a link to a page on his site several times a day. In no time at all, they would have created hundreds of new links, making their site look more popular than it really is.

Google though got wise to that strategy and asked Twitter's founders, former Google employees, to make the links on bios and posted in tweets "nofollow." They'll direct traffic but as far as search engines are concerned, any link placed on Twitter counts for nothing. (The only major exception is Ask.com but with just 2.5 percent of the Web's search engine traffic, it's not going to have a huge effect on a site's traffic flows.)

But even though the links don't count, Twitter can help a site's rankings in a couple of other ways.

First, links do generate more traffic, and the volume of traffic counts too when search engines rank sites. A timeline with several thousand followers should find that it's generating a significant number of extra views every time it posts information about a new article or includes a URL. That's especially true if the timeline's followers retweet it.

And if the result of that retweeting is that someone blogs about the article the link leads to as well, then the link in that blog post would count towards improved search engine rankings.

The second SEO benefit on Twitter is a little more complex. Google might ignore the links placed in a tweet, but it doesn't ignore the tweets themselves. When CNN's tech expert Chris Pirillo (@chrispirillo) was looking for a blog post that he'd written that included the phrase "OEMs suck", he was shocked to find that third place in Google's search engine rankings for that phrase went to one of his tweets. (First and second place went to posts on Jaiku, a rival microblogging site.)

Again, it's unlikely that anyone on Twitter is deliberately using that knowledge to push keyword-rich tweets to the top of search engines. It's not clear why a tweet would receive a higher ranking than a Web page on the same subject, for example, and it's impossible to generate

for Success

Include Links in Your Keyword Tweets

Although Twitter can deliver two separate SEO benefits— rankings from higher traffic; and the ranking of the tweets themselves—it's a good idea to combine the two.

Bringing searchers from Google to your timeline will have a benefit, but ultimately you want them to visit your website. Even when you're posting the occasional keyword-rich tweet then, be sure to include a link and give searchers somewhere to go when they've finished reading the tweet.

Experiment with Different Keywords

It will be difficult to identify keywords to place in tweets that could land high search engine rankings, and once the tweet has been written there's little more that you can do to promote it. The only characteristic you'll be able to play with, in fact, is the keywords themselves. Vary them and see which the search engines like the most.

links to a tweet. But it does show that tweeting on a topic can bring searchers to a timeline—and from the timeline, it's only a short step to the Web page.

How to Do It

Benefitting from the improved search engine rankings caused by the extra traffic from a link in a tweet is a nice bonus. But it's not a benefit that's easy to measure. There are all sorts of reasons that a site's rankings might improve, and it's possible that the extra visitors only played a small role.

On the other hand, the aim of improving your search engine rankings is to win extra traffic, and as linked tweets in a popular timeline will do that anyway, linking to your website from Twitter is always going to be worthwhile.

To win those higher search engine positions then you won't need to do anything more than most publishers are doing anyway: announce updates to your blog; link frequently to you Web pages; and give people a reason to click through.

You'll get the extra traffic from Twitter—and the additional visitors from search engines too.

Winning high rankings for individual tweets is a little more hit-and-miss but may be possible to do with a little simple experimentation. Write a post with a particular keyword phrase, wait a day or two then search for that phrase on Google. It's likely that the number of followers a timeline has affects its rankings (and that even a high ranking tweet will drop rapidly as the same phrase appears on other sites) but beyond posting the tweet on a popular timeline and ensuring that you have a good choice of keyword, there seems to be little more that you can do to optimize the tweet—except enjoy the extra traffic.

Getting Started

There's little more to do to help your SEO efforts through Twitter than writing tweets that contain links, and some that contain keywords too. Just be careful not to overdo it. Although some timelines contain nothing but tweets pointing to Web pages, timelines work best when they're personal and interactive. Talking to your followers is likely to generate more clicks, more traffic and better search engine rankings than serving link after link.

A Model to Follow

It's not clear at the moment that any twitterers are deliberately targeting search engines. That tweets were indexed has come as a surprise to many and the benefits of Twitter to a site's SEO are much smaller than traditional linking and keywording. Chris Pirillo's stumble onto his tweet on Google does provide one model to follow: search regularly for your tweets and track they keywords they contain.

81

GET PAID PER TWITTER CLICK

What is Pay-Per-Click Tweeting?

Many of the moneymaking strategies offered on Twitter have focused on the most obvious way of converting followers: placing ads in timelines. Services like Be-a-Magpie and Twittad insert advertising messages into timelines, paying the twitterer an amount related to the size of his or her following.

For twitterers though, both of these services require a certain amount of lost control. They don't get to write the message that their followers are receiving and there's a risk that many of them will be put off by the advertisers' content.

Similarly, for advertisers, an advertising model that demands payment based on the size of a twitterer's following carries risks too. It's likely that only a fraction of the twitterer's followers would see the tweet and only a small percentage of them would act on it. The return on the investment then is likely to be low—and difficult to trace too.

Advertisers would prefer a model that pays them only when a follower takes action, even if that action is just to click a link. Twitterers would like to retain control over the messages that they're sending to their followers.

That's the solution that Betweeted (www.betweeted.com) aims to offer. The service allows twitterers to choose links to present to their followers but also lets them create the messages that surround those links. Advertisers pay per click—the same advertising model used on Google's AdWords systems—and twitterers have an incentive to write the kinds of tweets that are least likely to be intrusive and most likely generate clicks.

The service only launched at the end of April 2009, but was reported have paid out over $1,000 to twitterers on its first day.

How Twitterers Are Earning on a Pay-Per-Click Basis

Betweeted's novelty means that so far few twitterers are earning with Betweeted. Like Google's AdSense system, advertisers set both a maximum amount that they're prepared to pay for each click and a limit to their advertising budget as a whole. Because clicks pay wherever they're shown—even when they're retweeted—advertisers appear to be burning through their budgets relatively quickly.

And because the service is fairly new, Betweeted quickly found itself with advertisers who had exhausted budgets and no one to replace them.

If that indicates a surprisingly high clickthrough rate, Betweeted's future should be secure. As long as it can find advertisers whose landing pages convert visitors, it shouldn't have any problem attracting twitterers to take the links.

And those high clickthroughs may be happening because Betweeted also offers the easy revenues of pay-per-click advertising with the flexibility of affiliate linking. Jimmy Rogers (@loyaleagle), for example, swapped his Be-a-Magpie account for Betweeted system, and even used an announcement of his change to work in a paid link: "to all those of you who care (:P) I have turned off Magpie for this account and am sticking to @betweeted_com http://tinyurl.com/cuzb88". It's the shortened URL in that tweet generates revenue, this time from Betweeted itself.

It's notable though that few, if any, of Betweeted's publishers are telling their followers that the link they're providing is paid. When Tim Watson (@TimDub), placed a link on his timeline to one of Betweeted's advertisers, he actually addressed it to the advertiser but he didn't mention that the advertiser was paying him: "RT @addresstwo: business contact manager with support for Twitter and LinkedIn http://tinyurl.com/cuk6h6".

Tips

for Success

Spread the Link

The links that Betweeted provide act like affiliate links: they credit the publisher wherever they appear. Place them on your own website or use Facebook's Twitter app to push them to your friends and you'll be able to extend the reach of your ads.

Personalize Get Retweets

And that applies to retweets too. Betweeted's publishers tend to place "RT" at the beginning of their tweets because it's included in the advertiser's suggested tweet. But this only indicates that the tweet has been published elsewhere. Adding "please RT" will help to make sure that your link appears elsewhere too—and personalizing the tweet will help to increase clickthroughs too.

That's a strategy that suggests the tweet is personal rather than commercial, but it does give the advertiser a second, free link in the tweet. When it becomes clear that the link is paid—which will happen when the advertiser's budget empties and the link becomes void—followers may feel that they've been deceived.

The best option then is to choose links carefully, personalize the message and admit that you're being paid. Treat Betweeted like an affiliate system and only select sites that you can genuinely recommend. Instead of regarding the service as a store for paid links, look at it as a directory of sites and services that your followers might be interested in learning about. And when you tell them that you're getting paid for the link, indicate that you'd be recommending it even if you weren't being paid.

If you can't say that honestly, maybe you shouldn't be recommending the link at all.

How to Do It

To earn from Betweeted, you'll need to register at www.betweeted.com. At the moment, the service is only available to US members. The site requires that publishers submit their tax details before they register.

If you qualify, you'll then be able to browse the list of advertiser categories available. These range from "agriculture" to "telecommunications" and take in "computers," "network marketing" and "pharmaceuticals." While the temptation may be to browse the categories for those with the highest paying links, you'll be much better off by choosing links that you can recommend wholeheartedly. You might receive fewer dollars by click, but you'll receive more clicks overall—and you'll irritate your followers less too.

Work the links into your timeline so that they look natural and personal, and mention that while you're being paid for the link, the recommendation is real. (You don't have to do this in the tweet itself. An occasional tweet telling followers that you sometimes post paid links in your timeline to carefully chosen websites would give sufficient notice without affecting your clickthrough rate).

But choosing the links carefully and recommending the sites personally will be the key to success.

Getting Started

To get started, you won't need to do any more than register at Betweeted.com and start browsing the links in the categories that suit the topics you cover in your timeline. Timelines—particularly personal timelines—tend to cover a range of different subjects so that should give you a fairly broad selection of categories to choose from. Pick a link that few followers will be interested in though just because it has a high click price, and you should find that you get few clickthroughs.

You'll then need to go through a process of reviewing each of the links you might want to offer. Check that the site is trustworthy, the products worth buying or the content worth reading. That might take a few minutes but it could preserve the relationship you have with your followers.

A Model to Follow

Betweeted's novelty means that there are still few good models to copy. More importantly, the freedom that publishers have to change the tweets surrounding the link means that the best examples of paid tweets won't be visible at all; they'll be completely integrated in the timeline. Tim Watson's timeline @ TimDub though provides one example of a publisher who has carefully chosen tweets that match his followers.

82 EXERCISE YOUR INFLUENCE AND WORK YOUR CALL TO ACTION

DIFFICULTY

SKILLS REQUIRED

INCOME POTENTIAL

What is Influence on Twitter?

There's no shortage of ways to build up a following on Twitter. Reply to tweets, post frequently, follow other members, and wait, and eventually, you'll find your follower list growing. But when you're looking to earn money with Twitter, it's not enough to have lots of readers. You have to be able to influence those readers, driving them to take a particular course of action.

Usually, that will mean clicking on a link but it could also involve encouraging retweets or winning recommendations from other followers.

In order to improve the amount of influence you have over your followers—and use that influence in a way that beings you the most benefits—you'll also need to be able to measure the level of your timeline's influence.

There's no single metric that will tell you how influential your posts are. Instead, you'll need to look at a number of different factors, including retweets, link clicks and what happens when followers do click through to a landing page.

Combining those figures should reveal the best strategies for leading twitterers to take the actions most valuable to your business.

How Twitterers Are Exercising Their Influence

Twitter is a real-time content stream. Members who are following thousands of other twitterers only ever see a fraction of the posts their followers are writing. Influence then isn't only a matter of being able to move your followers. It's also a question of understanding how many of your followers you're capable of moving at any one time.

Marketer Joel Comm, conducted a very simple test to discover how responsive his then-43,000 followers were to his timeline. He asked them to name their favorite color.

Over two hours, he received 240 replies, a response rate of just under half a percent. About 50 percent of the responses came within just ten minutes of the post being tweeted. It's possible that a more controversial question would have produced a higher response rate and it's possible too that the time when Joel tweeted his question might have affected the number of people who saw it. But the figures do show that responses rates on Twitter can be relatively low and that they fall off quickly.

One strategy then to increase influence might be to use different methods at different times to push people to take the same action. Followers who miss the first tweet might respond to the second or third. One question could ask people which of two products they prefer. The second question could send them to two images on TwitPic, which records automatically the number of views each image receives.

Measuring the response to a question won't take any more than a good query and the patience to count the responses and record when they came in. For other kinds of influence though, twitterers are using a range of different tools to see what effect their tweets are having—and how to make the most of them.

TwitterAnalyzer (www.twitteranalyzer.com), for example, provides a host of different metrics, including tweet frequency, hashtags and even apps and the subject terms that turn up most frequently in tweets. But it also shows who has been mentioning your tweets, how often they did so and the proportion of retweets an original tweet has received.

And TwitterAnalyzer lets you run these stats on any timeline, not just yours. So it's possible to use the service to identify the most powerful influencers in your follower list and tweet to them directly in order to extend your own reach. You can also see which Twitter users are doing the most evangelizing for other twitterers in your field and encourage them to follow you too.

A quick glance at TwitterAnalyzer's "Friends writing about User" metrics, for example, suggests that the 80/20 rule holds true on Twitter, with a minority of a timeline's followers doing most of the retweeting

for Success

and replying. Bring those active people into your timeline and target them with your tweets and you should find that your messages have greater effect.

How to Do It

There are two aspects to exercising the influence a timeline yields: measuring that influence; and making the most of it.

Neither of those things is particularly easy.

It's impossible to come up with completely accurate figures for a timeline's influence. Individual followers come and go, causing changes in the rates at which your followers as a whole will click links, view pictures and retweet posts at your request. It is possible though to try different kinds of tweets at different times of day and measure the responses.

When you post a tweet then that leads directly to sales page, to an ad-supported blog page or which encourages people to take a particular course of action, you'll know when to do it, what kind of tweet to post, and who to target to make sure your message spreads.

Getting Started

Start by measuring your influence with a few simple, innocuous programs. Once you have a reasonably large following (and if the response rate at any one time is lower than 1 percent, then you'll need more than 100 followers to get even one reply) mention your favorite book or movie and ask your followers to submit their own. That will give you an idea of your followers' responsiveness.

Follow that up by asking other questions at different times and track those results. Eventually, you should build up a picture of what it takes to move your followers and when to do it.

A Model to Follow

It might be difficult to measure a timeline's influence—and to exercise that influence in the most effective way—but it's even harder to spot twitterers doing it. While professional AdSense publishers, for example, will spend a great deal of time reading their figures to know what content to produce and where to place their ads, at the moment at least, most twitterers are posting randomly.

That may change though. The tools are available to allow professional twitterers to post intelligently and in a way that optimizes results. Just don't expect to see those twitterers shouting that they've done it.

83 INCREASE THE REACH OF YOUR PRESENTATIONS

DIFFICULTY

SKILLS REQUIRED

INCOME POTENTIAL

What Are Presentations on Twitter?

Twitter's Fail Whale, the image that the site presents whenever the servers are incapable of handling all of the users' requests, has already become a cultural icon. It's at the biggest risk of appearing whenever there's a major conference. Events like MacWorld and SxSW (the event that gave Twitter its initial boost) are always well covered on Twitter, as tech types post about they're seeing, doing and hearing from the stage.

It's a practice that grants benefits all round. Followers get to read the highlights from a presentation that they couldn't attend.

The twitter gets to add some easy extra value to his or her timeline.

And the presenter gets to spread their information beyond the walls of the conference hall to reach those reading at home and in real time.

Usually those tweets happen spontaneously. Conference attendees simply want to share with their followers the major points of the presentations they're listening to.

Occasionally though, presenters have deliberately recruited people to tweet on their behalf while they're giving their talk. That's usually happened when discussions on Twitter before the timeline have generated interest from followers who want to know what the person they're following is going to say.

It's a practice that can be hugely beneficial to twitterers, making them appear to be going out of their way to help followers who can't attend their talks in person. But it can take a little work to organize, and the benefits are likely to consist more of branding and a closer relationship than be directly financial.

GEEKPRENEUR

How Twitterers Are Increasing the Reach of their Presentations

For the most part, twitterers are relying on the goodwill of the people in the audience to pass on what they're saying to their followers.

That's a practice that contains both strengths and weaknesses.

On the one hand, when audience members are tweeting to their own timelines, the presenter's messages are stretching fairly broadly. They're reaching people on Twitter that the speaker wouldn't have been able to reach alone. That's particularly true when more than one person in the audience is exercising their thumbs.

On the other hand, those tweets are going to be of little help to the presenter's own followers who won't get to see them—unless they happen to be following an audience member's timeline.

When Stephen Fry gave a talk at the Apple Store in London though, he wanted his followers to know what he was saying. So rather than rely on audience members to tweet to their followers, he handed control of his timeline to his technical assistant who provided Twitter-based commentary as Stephen was speaking.

As a way of communicating to his followers, the idea was remarkably simple. It was also likely to have been a very effective way to get lots of followers looking at his timeline simultaneously, creating the kind of shared experience that builds community feeling.

But it wasn't a complete success.

Stephen Fry's tech expert might have been good at maintaining his website and delivering audiocasts but he wasn't so good at typing. He soon lost track of the presentation, forcing other people in the audience to step into the gap, and revealing that it takes more than a friend with your username and password to make presentation tweeting work.

How to Do It

In theory, you won't need to do any more than make sure that there's a friend or colleague in the audience with access to your Twitter account. In practice though, you'll want to do a bit more than that.

Whoever is tweeting your presentation won't be able to do more than provide selected highlights of what you're saying. So do the preparation: tell them what to say in advance.

Tips

for Success

Use Multiple Twitterers

Your friend will be able to tweet to your followers but if you have lots of people tweeting to their followers too, then the information that you're providing in your talk will be able to reach even further.

When you begin your talk, ask people to turn their phones on . . . and start tweeting.

Synchronize Hashtags

When you have lots of people posting about your presentation, Twitter users interested in what you're saying will struggle to follow. At the beginning of your talk tell anyone tweeting which hashtag to use. That will allow readers to follow the tag rather than specific timelines.

Tell Your Friend What to Tweet

Give a friend control over your timeline and you're taking a risk. You've got no idea what he'll post or what effect those tweets will have on your followers. Give him a list of the main points

(continued on next page)

Tips

for Success

(continued)

to tweet, and you'll have greater influence, make life easier for your friend and ensure that your followers read the most important bits.

You could do something as simple as give them a copy of your Powerpoint notes and tell your friend to tweet them as the points come up. Or you could go further and write the tweets in advance so that your friend only has to copy and send them as you mention those points in your talk.

While you could also type in the tweets yourself and use a scheduling service like TweetLater to broadcast them while you're talking, there's a good chance that the timing will be off.

Your friend should also be free to add his or her own tweets too. Describing the audience's reactions, tweeting their questions and your answers, and commenting on your presentation skills should keep the timeline personal and lively while still letting people know what you're saying.

Getting Started

The first step then should be to break out the most important points from your presentation that you'd like your followers to know. If you're lucky, you won't have to look any further than the headings and subheadings that you've put in your notes.

The second step will be to find a friend willing to tweet on your behalf!

A Model to Follow

There's no shortage of presentations that are regularly reported on Twitter, especially those on technical subjects. Stephen Fry's address at the London Apple store though is the model to copy, if only because it was a rare and deliberate use of Twitter by the speaker himself.

It wasn't perfect but even where the technique fell down revealed what a presenter needs to do to make the system work.

WORK YOUR MARKET'S INFLUENCE-HOLDERS

84

What Are Influence-Holders on Twitter?

One of the most attractive characteristics of Twitter is the extent to which people on the site are willing to help each other. It doesn't take much more than a question and a request for retweet to receive a bunch of helpful offers.

Sometimes those requests are made to an individual who has the answer the twitterer is looking for. And sometimes, it's just a random tweet to a large timeline that brings in plenty of solutions.

Twitter is now full of stories about arrested journalists sprung from jail in distant countries and travelers finding hotels after being stranded at snowy airports.

Sometimes though, those calls for help can take the form of a request for a recommendation, a message that can influence the opinions of others. When those calls come up, matching those in need with people who can supply that help doesn't just benefit each of those two sides. It also puts both sides in debt to the middleman, shows that you're willing to help—and makes it more likely that other people will provide recommendations to you too.

DIFFICULTY

SKILLS REQUIRED

INCOME POTENTIAL

How Twitterers Are Exercising—and Exchanging—Influence

In December 2008, Curt Moss (@curtmoss), Director of Communications for WebLink, a software company that services business associations, was searching Twitter for references to "chamber of commerce." He saw a tweet from a woman asking whether joining a chamber of commerce was worthwhile.

for Success

Focus Your Help

Search around for people needing help on Twitter and you won't have to look too far. The site is filled with people looking for places to eat, books to read, movie recommendations and advice on changing their hard drive.

While it might be possible to act as a kind of advisory center for as many people as you want, sending them to places where they can find the answers they're looking for, you'll always be better off making recommendations that everyone can trust.

Know who you want your recommendation to benefit, and look for people who could use that person's help.

Don't Look for the Rewards

The biggest drawback of this strategy is that you can't rely on the rewards.

You can't measure the value of gratitude, even when it's felt by both the person you're recommending and the

(continued on next page)

Curt checked her profile and found that her business was located near one of his company's clients. He sent the client a link to the woman's tweet, together with the contact details that he was able to pick up from her timeline. His client then forwarded those details to a chamber of commerce closer to the woman . . . who joined the chamber.

In that example, two businesses were brought together. But Curt's own company got nothing tangible out of the relationship directly, and neither did his client. Giving referrals is simple enough and costs nothing. Winning the rewards in return is much less straightforward.

But he did get something less tangible but perhaps no less valuable.

He showed his client that he was looking out for him, and that he was on their side.

Twitter's strongest point is its ability for businesses to build relationships with each other. Keeping an eye out for ways in which you can help your clients—or anyone else you'd like to maintain a close relationship with—provides a golden opportunity to cement your connections with them and build a platform that can hold sale.

How to Do It

Most of these recommendations will come naturally. Twitterers generally spot an opportunity to lend a hand and are happy to take it.

Curt Moss, for example, was looking to help his own business when he spotted a chance to help his clients. But it is possible to take a more pro-active approach and look for people to help. You'll need to mash a keyword phrase that's related to your business with the kind of phrases used by people looking for assistance, such "does anyone know" or "has anyone tried".

Even with this method though, it's unlikely that you'll come across too many opportunities to offer referrals and recommendations.

It will be important then to make the most of any opportunities you do find and be quick with your help.

And if actively finding people to help is going to be difficult, then cashing in on the goodwill your offer generates will be even harder. You can't remind someone that you gave them a referral and ask them for one in return. The most you can do is send out the help as often as you can and to as many people as you can, and rely on their own generosity—and the viral power of the thanks they express in their own timeline—to bring you solid benefits.

Getting Started

This isn't a strategy that you can easily use systematically so there's no obvious starting point. What you will need before you can start offering help though is an idea of where you want to send people.

So if you were an artist and you were hoping to build a relationship with a gallery owner, for example, you would search first for a suitable exhibition space.

The next step would be to look for someone that gallery owner could help and make the recommendation. Include the gallery's username in your tweet to make sure that they see it, and you'll make sure that they can see you too.

That should give you the beginnings of a useful relationship.

A Model to Follow

The best model to follow is the one used by Curt Moss—and just about everyone else on Twitter. It's a model that's completely effort-free.

Use the site, enjoy using it, and when you see someone you can help, lend a hand and wait for the rewards.

for Success

(continued)

person you're helping. Nor you can you measure the strengthening of the relationship that that gratitude brings.

The best you can do is build up as much of that goodwill as possible and assume that it will all lead naturally to return referrals and extra business.

And, of course, you can enjoy the pleasure that comes from helping people.

85

PROMOTE YOUR BUSINESS WITH A TWITTER VIDEO

DIFFICULTY

■■➡

SKILLS REQUIRED

■■■■➡

INCOME POTENTIAL

■■■➡

What is Video on Twitter?

As a communication tool, Twitter is about as slimline as it gets. No pictures, no sound and nothing bigger than 140 characters.

So that certainly means no video either.

But just as developers have created services like TwitPic to allow twitterers to attach images to their tweets so other sites offer methods that let twitterers link tweets to video messages.

Twiddeo (www.twiddeo.com), for example, is a dedicated Twitter service. Users can upload video from the Web, cameraphone or webcam and link the video automatically to their timeline. You have to already own a Twitter account to use it.

12Seconds (http://12seconds.tv) operates independently of Twitter but uses the same idea of strict limits to keep content short and interesting. Videos are limited to just twelve seconds, making it a perfect partner to the short posts of microbloggers.

As a promotional tool—and even as a social tool—video messaging is much less popular than attaching images, probably because it's far harder to produce a usable video than snap a quick shot.

But that doesn't mean it's less powerful. In fact, with the right video—and a solid base of followers—a video can make for a very effective form of Twitter-based marketing.

How Twitterers are Using Video

It should come as little surprise that most of the videos on Twiddeo and 12Seconds are posted as entertainment. Like YouTube, both services have plenty of cats doing silly things and vloggers talking directly to the camera.

But among those uploads are videos that are more commercial and have been created to help a company put across a message to its followers.

One of the simplest—but no less effective for being simple—is to link to video testimonials. Rina Hoffer (@pizzarina), for example, wrote a tweet that said nothing more than "pizza testimonials!!!!!" and included a link to Twiddeo.

The video was a simple as the tweet. Shot apparently at a party, it consisted of people munching on pizza and saying nice things about the toppings. The production values might have been low but as a way of demonstrating that the product was worth buying—and creating a sense of fun around the product too—the clip could be very effective.

DJ Steve Reed (@SteveReedShow) uses Twiddeo in a way that's slightly less commercial. Because he needs his listeners to feel that they have a connection with him and enjoy his company, his clips tend to be excerpts from his life.

With accompanying tweets as mundane as "Just got back from early morning shopping," they're unlikely to be blockbusters or win many retweets. But they may well satisfy his current fans and keep them tuning in.

Television personality and comedian Dave Coulier (@dcooler) uses 12Seconds in a similar way, creating short, pithy clips that show off his comedy skills. One clip even marketed his t-shirt store. 12Seconds has spotted the commercial nature of videos attached to tweets and called them "12omercials".

There is a third way of combining video with Twitter, but it's even rarer than uploaded video clips. Marketer Joel Comm (@joelcomm) uses a UStream app to stream directly from his iPhone. He uses Twitter to let his followers know when he's doing it.

As well as telling followers what you're doing right now—the traditional way of using Twitter—live streaming lets you show your followers what you're doing right now. It's not the sort of thing you'd want to do all the time but for occasional special events such as product launches or announcements, it could be a very effective of bringing your community closer.

for Success

Pay Attention to the Tweets

Videos only have value if your followers actually watch them. Persuading them to do so is a two-step process. The first step is to make sure that the tweet that comes with the link is exciting enough to generate clicks. Fortunately, followers are loyal enough to want to watch any video a twitterer they're following posts but do make sure that your video tweet is clear, interesting and targeted to your followers.

Make the Still Memorable

The second step is to persuade the viewer to click the ad itself. Clips from 12Seconds need the viewer to take action to start the video and while Twiddeo links start the clip automatically, the clips that appear in the site's public timeline have to be started manually. That me ans making starting image enticing. YouTube is a good place to look for ideas here.

(continued on next page)

And you could then upload part of the stream to Twiddeo for future viewing.

How to Do It

To upload videos with Twiddeo, you won't need to do any more than log into the site using your Twitter username and password. You'll then be able to select your video clip from your hard drive and write your tweet from Twiddeo's own site.

Bear in mind though that Twiddeo's own link will be included in your tweet, leaving you with just 113 characters to invite followers to click.

You can also email the videos in from your mobile phone, making it possible to upload on the move. If you're using a video to promote a product or a company though, you'll usually be better off editing to give the clip a professional look.

12Seconds is a little more demanding. You'll need to create an account first, then enter personal details to create a profile. Include your Twitter username and password, and whenever you upload a video to 12Seconds, you'll a tweet will be sent automatically to your timeline.

Getting Started

Creating effective videos is often a learning process. While Rina Hoffer's video appears to have been her first (and her timeline is new too), it could have been improved with some steadier camera-handling, some forethought about backlighting when recording the testimonials and some post-production too.

Good videos take experience.

The best way to start then will be to produce an idea for a short video clip to promote your business or your timeline, and only upload it through Twiddeo or 12Seconds once you've edited it to give it a professional look.

Once you've created one good video, regular additions should flow fairly easily.

A Model to Follow

Dave Coulier's timeline contains a number of different types of tweets. They all show off his comedy skills but they're also very simple, and the clip for his store in particular, demonstrates one very easy way to place a quick commercial video on Twitter.

Tips
for Success

(continued)

Don't Forget the Ad!

While any video will help to create a closer relationship between twitterer and his or her followers, when you're creating a Twitter-based commercial, you want that relationship to bring sales. During the post-production, try running a call-to-action at the bottom of the screen or end by telling viewers how to place orders.

86 WIN A TWITTER COMPETITION

DIFFICULTY

SKILLS REQUIRED

INCOME POTENTIAL

What Are Competitions on Twitter?

We've seen how some companies are using Twitter-based competitions to build their followings and raise their profiles. Because the announcement of a competition is almost guaranteed to deliver plenty of retweets, even the award of something as simple as a $25 Amazon gift card may be enough deliver plenty of new followers.

It's then up to the owner of the timeline to make sure that those followers keep following and act on what they're reading.

That means that Twitter represents a bonanza—if only a small and occasional one—for people hoping to pick up freebies.

While you can never rely on winning a competition as a source of income, it's generally true that the more contests you enter, the more you're likely to win.

When many of the competitions on Twitter rely on little more than retweeting someone else's competition announcement, searching, finding and entering contests on the site should be a simple way to pick up an occasional prize.

How Twitterers Are Winning Contests

Competition organizers are giving away prizes in return for doing all sorts of things on Twitter. Ben Behrouzi (@BenBehrouzi) enters anyone who retweets an announcement of his contests into a free draw.

CLFDX.com (@clfdx), a snowboard and skateboard design site, referred followers to a page on their site advertising a competition run by a resort. Participants had to send in a picture or a video demonstrating how much they wanted a free session. The contest itself cost nothing to run but CLFDX benefitted by telling people about it—and twitterers benefitted by hearing about it on Twitter.

"House in Spain" (@WinHouseinSpain) sells a 49 Euro lottery ticket to enter a chance to win a house in Andalucia, and Colin Phillips of Prize4 (@prize4) has an equally commercial competition timeline that charges 12 Euros to enter a spot-the-ball contest whose prizes include cars, mobile homes and even a tea house in the English county of Cornwall.

So challenges to win the prizes range from the incredibly simple to the slightly skilled.

The biggest challenge though will be finding the competitions.

How to Do It

And that's not much of a challenge at all.

It shouldn't require more than some careful searching on Twitter to dig up places where prizes are being offered. Looking for the phrase "win a" will yield a number of announcements, "prize" should generate a few more results, and "contest" some more places to enter.

Those competitions will be time-limited though. "Hunkydory home" (@hunkydoryhome), for example, entered new followers into a draw but only up to a certain date: "Let your friends know—only 1 week left to win a @hunkydoryhome bag of lovelies. New followers until the 15th May are entered into draw." Other competitions reward followers who enter at a certain landmark such as the 3,000th follower. (Although competitions like these encourage people to follow, they also reward them for not following earlier and for putting off following until the last minute—not a great strategy for the advertiser.

New competitions though will be cropping up all the time, so you'll need to repeat the search fairly frequently to make sure that you don't miss any you want to enter.

You might also find that it's a good idea to create a separate timeline just for entering competitons. If some twitterers are demanding that you retweet a message to your followers in order to enter a draw, then creating a timeline separate from your personal one will allow you to enter without bothering your friends.

for Success

Don't Step in the Spam

If the biggest challenge in using Twitter to win prizes is finding the right competitions that's not just because there's no accepted hashtag for online contests.

It's also because there's so much spam on the site hoping to tempt twitterers with offers of grandprizes.

WINFreeStuff (@WINFreeStuff) was a timeline with almost no followers, no bio, no link, no unique background, no profile picture and no broadcast tweets either. It sent tweets about competitions directly to individual twitterers in the hope that enough people will click the link in the tweet. If they did, they were taken to a "free lotto" site.

In general, a timeline that displays those characteristics and tweets nothing but posts about similar competition is best avoided. @WINFreeStuff was suspended.

Think Before You Pay

Other competitions though appear to be legitimate but *(continued on next page)*

for Success

(continued)

do cost money to enter. It's possible that those contests do offer good chances to win grand prizes but make sure you do some careful research before paying anything to an online contest. Use WhoIs (www. networksolutions.com/ whois/), an index of domain registrations, to discover who stands behind the site, and ask the timeline's followers if anyone knows anything about the contest.

Twitter isn't just a good place to learn about competitions. It's a good place to find out if they're worth entering.

Don't Expect to Win!

While it might be nice to be able to pick up a prize a week, especially when those prizes include houses, cars and iPhones, the best you can say is that the more competitions you enter, the greater the chances that you'll win something at some time.

You wouldn't want to rely on this strategy but you might have some fun— and pick up a few valuable prizes—using it.

And when some timelines offer prizes for following (as @hunky doryhome) does, you might want their tweets to appear on a page you rarely read.

Getting Started

The first thing to do then will be to create a unique timeline for entering competitions. You don't have to do that, of course, but when you're following people you wouldn't otherwise be following and re-tweeting tweets you know your followers wouldn't want to read, it is a good idea to keep your own timeline clean.

Then it's a matter of doing a few quick searches.

There are no set hashtags for Twitter-based contests, so you'll need to search for different phrases. Favorite the competitions you want to enter so that you can find them easily then unfavorite them once the competition has ended.

A Model to Follow

There's little evidence that twitterers are systematically entering Twitter-based contests but there are several timelines that are worth following to keep track of them. Ben Behrouzi's timeline seems to offering fairly regular prizes in return for retweets while Colin Phillips' Prize4 timeline does at least make for some interesting reading for those interested in entering contests and lotteries.

SCALE YOUR BUSINESS BY FINDING PAID HELP

87

What is Business Scaling on Twitter?

New businesses tend to go through a familiar curve. Initially, there's more time than clients. Every new customer gets endless attention and much of the day is spent pitching for new business.

As word spreads and clients stick around, the business develops a firm base. The time spent marketing falls and the entrepreneur can devote much of his or her day to fulfilling orders rather than looking for new ones.

But the clients keep coming in anyway. Low-paying clients give way to those with bigger budgets but eventually there comes a time in every successful business when it's necessary to scale up. That might mean looking for someone who can do the same thing as you so that can take on more work, but it might also mean outsourcing some of the less valuable tasks to some who can do them better than you allowing you to focus on the higher value stuff.

None of this means employing someone full time. Twitter is a great place to look for the kind of freelance help that's perfectly suited to virtual working. You'll be able to advertise to tech-savvy people, anyone who follows you and applies for your position will be familiar with your work, and reading their timelines will give you good idea of who you're hiring.

Twitter might not be the best communication tool for describing job specs and explaining what needs to be done—it's too public and the posts too short for that—but it is a good place to look for and judge freelancers.

DIFFICULTY

SKILLS REQUIRED

INCOME POTENTIAL

for Success

Don't Rely on Your Own Ad Unless You have Lots of Followers

Posting an ad in your own timeline will always be the easiest way to try to find likely candidates. You won't have to do any more than post a quick tweet. But it's not the most efficient or the most effective.

Actively searching for freelancers on Twitter will take a little time. You'll need to play around with keyword phrases to find the best candidates. But it can be fun and approaching someone directly will always yield the best results.

Read the Tweets

The tweets that a candidate posts in their own timeline can be incredibly revealing. If you're looking for someone to work with you for the long term rather than just to complete a one-off freelance job then you'll want to find someone who's not just reliable and capable but someone you can click with as the business grows.

A timeline gives you a glimpse into their life and their interests.

How Twitterers are Looking for Paid Help

People are looking for help on Twitter in a number of different ways.

The most basic method is simply to post an ad on your own timeline. Web developer Al Winter (@alwinter) posted this tweet on his timeline: "I need a Zen Cart expert to do some freelance work. Get at me asap!"

With several hundred followers though, that tweet was not apparently strong enough, and Al followed it up two days later by tweeting directly to a website manager who had indicated in his bio that he was available for hire. In general, twitterers are very amenable to being approached this way, and while searching for suitable candidates might take a little time, being able both to read their tweets and view their websites will make the review process much easier. It will lower the chances of picking the kind of flaky candidate who might let you down in the future.

One alternative to posting in your own timeline is to place an ad on one of Twitter's freelance jobs timelines. Place a job ad at hotfreelancejobs.com (www.freelancejobs.com), for example, and the post will also appear in the site's timeline @hotfreelance.

While that will get your posting seen by more people than follow your timeline alone, responses have to be made through the freelance site. You can expect to receive plenty of unsuitable applications, each of which will have to check and assessed.

If you're looking for help with the kind of administrative tasks that take up your time but deliver little value though, then Twitter can also be a good place to find a virtual assistant. VADirectory (@vadirectory) provides broadcast tweets about virtual assistance and Korryn Campbell (@AustralianVA) is just one of many virtual assistants marketing themselves on Twitter. To find a virtual assistant, pick one assistant and review their follower lists to discover others on Twitter. And as you review them, place less attention to the location than to the time they have available and their willingness to do tasks that go beyond the day-to-day.

Every client's needs are different so you'll want an assistant who is willing to be as flexible as you need them to be.

How to Do It

Scaling your business with Twitter has two stages: first, you'll need to find suitable candidates; then you'll have to assess each one in turn to choose the best person for the job.

After that, it will be a matter of negotiating, continuing to work with them, keeping your virtual team member motivated and informed, and ensuring that they deliver on time.

And you'll have to pay them, of course.

Placing an ad in your own timeline is simple, but unless you have thousands of followers, many of whom are likely candidates, it will limit your field. A more pro-active approach is always likely to yield better results. Searching Twitter for a keyword related to the task will give you a good list of candidates.

While you won't be able to interview those candidates on Twitter, you will be able to see the portfolio on their websites and get a feel for their personalities, interest and attitude through their tweets.

There is a list stage to scaling your business though, and that's moving the relationship off Twitter—and checking your assistant's timeline occasionally to see if he or she is tweeting about working with you.

Getting Started

The very first step though isn't to place a request in your timeline start searching for a freelance designer, a virtual assistant or a writer to outsource your SEO copywriting overflow to.

It's to understand exactly what you need done and—no less importantly—understand how much you should be paying for it. Browse other freelance sites such as Elance (www.elance.com) and Guru (www.guru.com) to get a feel for market rates and calculate how much you can afford to pay for help.

Understand too that while there are plenty of bargains to be had from workers in far-flung places, when it comes to freelancers, you almost always get what you pay for!

A Model to Follow

Al Winter might only have been looking for temporary help with a one-off project but he did create a good example of how to go about finding help. First, he published a request in his own timeline then, when he discovered that that didn't work, he approached other twitterers directly.

Usually, that's all you'll need to do.

ATTRACT TWITTER BRAND SPONSORS

What Are Brand Sponsors on Twitter?

Timelines have value. That's why companies create them. Their tweets help them to build their brand, communicate their corporate message and engage with customers. They form one part of a marketing and branding strategy that has been shown to increase sales both in the short-term through the use of discounts and bargains, and in the long term through better customer service and a strong image.

But timelines are limited. The tweets they contain are only visible to people on Twitter who follow them or who stumble upon the timelines. While replies and tweets directed to a company's timeline can extend that reach to other twitterers, all of the marketing power remains on Twitter.

One option then is to extend the reach of a timeline even further and deliver tweets beyond Twitter to other websites.

There are a number of widgets available that allow website publishers to place their tweets on their pages. (Twitter itself offers a bunch of them at twitter.com/widgets). That's always a useful strategy to turn your website users into followers and keep them informed. But widgets—and therefore your tweets—can only be placed on your own website.

Corporate twitterers have shown that they're willing to pay to be allowed to show their tweets on other publishers' websites too.

Clearly, you'll need a website to do this, one with plenty of users and ideally one that also offers content that matches companies actively using Twitter. You'll need to approach them and persuade them of the

for Success

**Make the
Sidebar Visible**

Different areas of your
Web page will have
different effects on
your users and produce
different numbers of
clickthrough. Mashable
puts its Twitter module
next to the comments at
the end of the post. While
that fits with Twitter's
own conversational
characteristics, it's possible
that not everyone will see
it down there.

In general, the most
valuable place for an ad unit
is embedded in the text.
You might prefer to keep
that slot for your pay-per-
click ads but the module
should ideally be above the
fold so that even users who
only glance at your site can
see it.

(continued on next page)

benefits of working with you. With few companies currently advertising on this way, that might be something of a challenge. If you can pull it off though, you'll be adding dynamic content to your website and delivering potential customers to companies in your field.

How Businesses Are Attracting Twitter Brand Sponsors

The site best-known for using brand sponsors on its pages is Mashable (www.mashable.com). The site, which calls itself "The Social Media Guide", places a module with two tabs on the side of its pages. One tab is marked "What's this?" and explains that ""Mashable features brands that want to engage with the social media community." The other tab is marked "Twitter Brand Sponsors" and shows the avatar and the latest tweets from the site's corporate sponsors. These have included JetBlue (@JetBlue), Etsy (@Etsy), Mail Chimp (@mailchimp) and 6S Marketing (@6s_marketing). Mashable also feeds the tweets from one non-profit as well.

Mashable hasn't revealed how much those companies are paying, and the companies themselves haven't discussed they've received the benefits that they've generated from their exposure on Mashable.

Nor has Mashable described how it approached the companies to persuade them to advertise on their site. The publication though is well known and highly respected in the social media community, so any contact would have been treated seriously.

How to Do It

Bringing corporate sponsors from Twitter to your website won't be straightforward. Companies aren't looking for sites on which to place their tweets so you'll have to identify likely businesses, approach them, persuade them of them benefits of appearing on your Web pages, and charge a fee that makes their presence worthwhile both to you and to them.

GEEKPRENEUR

And, of course, you'll also have to code an RSS stream from your sponsors' timelines into your module. That will require a little coding knowledge but nothing too strenuous for a capable developer.

It's the selling that will require most of the effort.

A pitch will need to persuade potential advertisers that your site has a large enough user base to justify the expense. It will need to show that many of your users are interested in the company's products or services. And it will need to prove that the sponsors' tweets will be displayed in a prominent enough position to be seen by users.

Although you could charge for each new follower that your sponsor receives from your site—which is likely to be the sponsor's preference—or even for every click on a tweet, you're likely to find that a sponsor receives a burst of new followers when they start advertising but those sign-ups fall off quickly. Many of your users after all, will be loyal readers who return regularly.

It's a better idea then to charge on a pay per impression basis. Your readers will, after all, be reading the company's content and see the firm's name each time they reach your page.

Look for companies that match the content of your website, and contact their marketing department to make your pitch.

Getting Started

The first step will be to place a widget on your site that contains your tweets. That's very simple to do but it will show potential sponsors how—and where—their tweets will appear on your site.

By monitoring the numbers clicks on the tweets and new followers you receive in the weeks after placing the widget, you'll also be able to give sponsors an idea of the sorts of results that they can expect from appearing on your page.

Those figures will form a crucial part of your pitch.

You'll then need to know how much you're currently receiving for ads that appear on your Web page, identify potential sponsors on Twitter, and either give them a call or drop them an exploratory email.

Tips

for Success

(continued)

Reveal the Figures in the Pitch

Because this is a relatively new strategy, you might struggle to persuade corporate twitterers of the value of putting their tweets on your page. Figures speak though so place the module on your site first and tell advertisers about the results you've already seen. You could even experiment with the timelines of friends and other businesses

A Model to Follow

Mashable's module is clearly the model to copy for this strategy. Note though that while Mashable is strong enough to land paying sponsors, its module is not in the prime position on the page.

Nor are all the ads targeted to suit Mashable's audience: 6S Marketing is a social media firm but other sponsors are just companies known for using social media.

And Mashable also sweetens the pill of offering ads to its readers by giving space to one charity. That's something worth bearing in mind too.

BUY AND SELL WITH A TWITTER AUCTION

89

What is a Twitter Auction?

eBay made its name by acting as a venue where buyers and sellers could meet. It also provided a structure through which sellers could show off their goods for a limited time and buyers could place their bids.

With the addition of seller reviews, the site soon developed into a free marketplace at which sellers can—with perhaps just a little smart promotional work—find buyers, and buyers can always be certain that they're paying the right market price (while still hoping that they'll find a bargain.)

Tweba (www.tweba.com), which was originally called Tweebay, tries to emulate eBay's system but on Twitter's platform. The site looks like Twitter with a central vertical timeline, followers, and short posts but there are some important differences.

The home page is dominated by functions allowing you to add a new listing; import a lot of new listings; complete your profile; and customize your profile. And while Twitter's sidebar links to mentions, direct messages and favorites, as well as saved searches and trending topics, Tweba has a big "Add New Listing" button, followed by various links to feeds marked @selling, @buying and @wanting. You can also see direct messages, "communicate" messages, "watches" and "feed-back".

It's all far more complex than Twitter's simplicity, a difference reflected too in the permitted size of the posts.

Tweba's tweets can be up to 240 characters in length.

DIFFICULTY

SKILLS REQUIRED

INCOME POTENTIAL

Tips
for Success

Create a Profile

Tweba uses OAuth to log in users but it doesn't take all of a Twitterer's details when users sign in for the first time. Tweba's users have to create unique profiles, which they can do by clicking the Settings link at the top of the page.

While you'll keep your Twitter username, the description will initially read "Just another Tweba User." If you're serious about selling through Tweba, change this for text that explains what you sell and suggests that you're serious and reliable.

Include a Picture with Your Listing

When it comes to selling online, no strategy is ever more effective than including a picture so that users can see what they're buying.

Twitterers are accustomed to keeping everything textual. On Tweba, a picture can say far more than you can fit even into 240 characters.

Altogether, Tweba, while similar to Twitter and built on Twitter's platform offers a completely different set of features and uses. For retailers, sellers of antiques and used goods, the site can be a powerful way to reach a new site of possible customers.

How Twitterers Are Buying and Selling at Auctions

Although Tweba was designed to be a kind of Twitter-based eBay, in practice twitterers aren't quite using it that way. That might be because for an auction site to work well, it needs enough bidders to push the price up to the correct level and it's not entirely clear that Tweba has enough of an audience yet.

Instead, Tweba's users are mostly using the site as an adjunct to their eBay auctions, a way of bringing more people in to bid on their sales.

Pete Crebbin (@TheUrbanRooster), for example, is a seller of vintage and retro items. His timeline on Twitter consists largely of his postings to Tweba, and those postings tend to link to the sales page on eBay rather than accept bids on the site itself.

Most of Tweba's users are doing the same thing. They benefit from the appearance of their ad in their own timeline, in Tweba's timeline (@tweba), and in Tweba's searchable marketplace to promote their eBay auction.

A few companies though are using Tweba not to sell the kinds of used products that generally turn on sites like Ebay, but to market their own services. Santosh Kumar Kori (@santoshkori) of CBO Technologies (www.cbotechnologies.com), a computer security firm, used Tweba to list his company's services.

It's unlikely that he would have picked up too many extra sales with his ad for "network data archival software" but it's equally unlikely that as Tweba grows we won't see more companies using the site to market their services too.

How to Do It

Although joining Tweba requires nothing more than logging in with Twitter, the site isn't intuitive. Click the "Add New Listing" button on the home page, and you'll be taken to a form where you can post the details for four different kinds of listing.

You can start an auction; list an item for a fixed price; link to a listing on another site such as eBay; or place a request for an item you'd like to buy.

At the moment, most listings appear to be linked to eBay pages.

You'll then need to write a title for the item. This is the text that will appear in the tweet, so make sure it's accurate and inviting. Placing the listing in a category and sub-category will make it easy for user to find while browsing the site, and tags will help active searchers to find you.

There's then a long list of figures to include in the tweets, including the duration of the listing, the currency, the reserve price, the "have it now" price, national and international postage rates, and the rate at which an auctioned item rises with each bid.

Finally, you can include a photo and a 240-character description.

It's easiest to do all of this from the new listing page but Tweba does allow users to use syntactical shorthand to include all of the data in the text field. To offer an item for sale, for example, the syntax is: Sell title price postage length description. So tweeting "Sell 'Antique porcelain tea set' $75 $10 7 "Beautiful Wedgwood 8-piece tea set in mint condition. Tea bags extra" would automatically create a week-long listing for an antique porcelain tea set on offer for $75 plus $10 shopping.

For occasional sales, it's probably best to use the new listings page but if you're going to be using Tweba regularly, then learning the syntax could save you some time.

Getting Started

Tweba might have been built using Twitter's API and shares its looks but it feels very different to use. Begin then by browsing the site to see the kinds of items that are on offer, how sellers are advertising them and how they appear to on Twitter.

Remember that listings placed on Tweba also appear in your timeline and at @tweba, giving you extra views.

Once you've got a feel for the way the site works, place an ad, even if it's just a link to your eBay page, and see if you pick up more bids than usual.

A Model to Follow

Pete Crebbin's timeline can certainly be one model to follow for Tweba sellers but another is SadieBellsBooks (@sadiebellsbooks). Her Tweba timeline contains a carefully written profile, a list of the books she's offering, and pictures of the covers of each of the books. The timeline ends up looking something like a simple online catalog.

Clicking through to the complete listing on Tweba reveals a complete description of the product, and clicking from there to the listing on sales site Blujay (www.blujay.com), makes it easy for buyers to make their purchase.

OFFER
FREE PROMOS

90

What Are Free Promos?

DIFFICULTY

SKILLS REQUIRED

INCOME POTENTIAL

Twitter is fun. You'll get to interact with all sorts of interesting people, read thought-provoking content and share your views, thoughts and ideas.

And you can make money too.

But building your followers—and keeping them—takes time. You have to find the right people to follow, engage them in conversation, write the kind of tweets that generate replies, produce content that keeps them coming back for more . . . and if you want to earn money, convert your followers too.

One method that a number of marketers have been using on Twitter to build followers quickly, reward them for reading their tweets, and promote their own products and services has been to launch giveaways.

In return for retweeting a message that drives other twitterers to their timeline or a landing page, followers are given a free download.

Or twitterers may offer an occasional but larger prize such as an iPod or a camera as part of a free lottery.

But organizing these kinds of freebies takes effort too. Marketers have to be able to keep track of everyone eligible to receive their prize, tell them how to receive it, and track the results too to make sure that it was worthwhile.

TwiveAway (www.twiveaway.com) aims to make promotional giveaways easier by automating the process. Marketers can register through their Twitter accounts, then create two different kinds of campaigns.

Tips
for Success

Make the Retweet Exciting

The most important factor in determining the number of retweets and new followers you receive will be the prize. But the nature of the retweet is important too. Make it informal, fun and personal rather than promotional and spammy.

Track the Value

An effective giveaway campaign will cost you money, even if it's only lost sales of a product you're now offering for free. Track your follower rates with TwiveAway so that you can see how much of an increase your campaign is buying.

"Everyone wins" campaigns search for a retweeted message and automatically send a direct message to the twitterer telling them where they can download their reward.

"1 Person wins" campaigns keep track of everyone who qualifies for a prize and at the end of the promotion picks a winner at random.

The result should be an effortless way to deliver ebooks that promote your services and your brand while rapidly building your follower list and rewarding the followers you already have.

How Twitterers Are Offering Free Promos

Marketers on Twitter are using TwiveAway to launch both "everyone wins" and "1 person wins" campaigns.

"Lisa" of @prepaidlegals, for example, posted this tweet in her timeline: "I Have Completely LOST It! Giving Away a $97 eBook! http://budurl.com/694b."

The link led to a landing page that offered an ebook about Internet marketing to anyone who followed a two-step process that involved retweeting a message and following the timeline. TwiveAway's system then issued the sender a message telling them where to download the ebook.

Rob Demaio (@FitnessDiet) took a slightly different approach. He told his followers that he was "giving away a new Ipod Touch to 1 lucky winner every week. Go to http://www.fitnessdiet.info . . . to learn how to win."

Clicking that link took followers to a landing page similar to that used by @prepaidlegals. Viewers were encouraged to retweet a message and follow Rob's timeline. TwiveAway picks a winner at random every Saturday.

Although both campaigns are equally simple to create using TwiveAway, the costs and benefits are very different. A new iPod Touch costs around $200. Giving one away each week then means that Rob's campaign is costing him around $800 a month. His ad-supported website needs to generate a large number of additional clicks to make the campaign worthwhile.

But with no cost to enter, it's likely that the campaign would create a rapid rise in the number of his followers, and in website views too.

"Lisa'''s campaign costs much less. An ebook "valued at $97" rarely sells for $97. Even if it sells for $20, the only cost would be lost sales from people who might bought if it wasn't available for free. In practice, the costs would be fairly negligible and the extra followers would be almost free too.

But because the ebook has a comparatively low perceived value and a specific market, it would also generate a relatively low number of new followers.

The most important decision to make then will be whether to make the giveaway high value and rare, or low value and available to everyone.

How to Do It

TwiveAway is free to use. You'll need to register and send a tweet announcing that you're using the service. Brad Callen (@bradcallen), the service's creator, gives away the service in order to promote his own timeline and Internet marketing business.

Once you've decided whether to reward all of your retweeters or only a few of them, creating the campaign won't take more than few minutes. TwiveAways even provides a PDF user manual to talk you through the process.

You'll need to create a message to be retweeted and write a thank you note that will be used in the direct message. Most importantly though, you'll also need to tell people about your giveaway.

This is not part of TwiveAway, which only monitors participants in the promotion and tells them where to find their prize. Once you've created your campaign, you'll still have to tell people what you're doing by announcing it in your timeline and by telling people offline too.

Getting Started

Many of TwiveAway's users drive retweeters to a landing page to be eligible for their prize. That's not strictly necessary. TwiveAway works by regularly scanning Twitter for the retweeted message. It would be possible simply to tell followers what message to retweet. But sending them to a landing page allows you to give more complete instructions and also makes it likely that users will surf around the site to learn more.

The first step then will be to create a simple landing page that tells users what to do. Both @prepaidlegals and @FitnessDiet based their landing pages on Brad Callen's instructions. They make for easy models.

A Model to Follow

The campaign use to promote @prepaidlegals makes for a standard promotional model. Giving away an ebook costs very little—and TwiveAways even makes a number available to its users to give away—so any additional followers will be almost free. The tweet itself says nothing about the book, creating the kind of curiosity that generates clicks, and the landing page follows Brad Callen's advice completely.

It's a simple model to copy and can make a good start to your use of TwiveAway.

LAND
BARTER DEALS

91

What is Bartering?

DIFFICULTY

Back in the days before money—and even before the Internet—goods and services were exchanged not with a swipe of a credit card or even a bag of cowry shells, but for other goods and services. Beans were swapped for chickens, labor for corn and so on. These things still happen. Internet users might regard the Web as a place where everything is free—unless it's on Amazon—but there's no shortage of barter sites on which cash-strapped users attempt to swap things they no longer want for other things that they now need.

SKILLS REQUIRED

INCOME POTENTIAL

Those calls are appearing on Twitter too. Twitterers are putting out appeals to the Twitterverse and offering items of value that they can supply in return.

And they're getting replies and making deals.

You'll need to be able to get your appeal to a wide number of people, you'll have to know the value of what you're offering and what you want to receive, and it's likely that you'll also need to be a mean negotiator. But Twitter has proven that it can function as a useful forum for barters and enable the exchanges.

How Twitterers Are Bartering

When Gary Vaynerchuck (@garyvee), a wine expert and host of Wine Library TV, was putting on an exhibit at a wine fair in Boston in January 2009, he found himself in need of a large screen television.

Tips
for Success

Make Your Offer Valuable

If you're looking for something specific, you'll need to offer something that looks valuable to the recipient. The Web Laureate's offer of a poem was easy for her to make but it's hard to see how it would compensate a designer for the value of creating a website. She might have done better offering other wordsmith services such as Web copy in return for a design.

That would have been an exchange of roughly equal value—and equal usefulness too.

Negotiate

Just as it's difficult to estimate what to offer someone in return for something you want, so it's hard for others to respond to your appeal. Look for ways to add value to their offers and negotiate the price.

(continued on next page)

He posted a tweet on Twitter stating that he needed help and asking if anyone was involved with a television renting company.

Real estate blogger James Shiner (@JamesShiner) saw the tweet, replied to Gary and told him that he had a 40 inch flat screen television that he uses at trade shows. The two communicated by direct message and in return for use of the television—which would have cost about $1,500 to rent from a hire company—Gary Vaynerchuk provided two tickets to the wine expo which were worth about $350.

That's fairly typical of the way in which most barter deals are conducted on Twitter. They're started by twitterers trying to offload something they don't want or looking for a low-cost way to pick up something they do.

The Web Laureate (@weblaureate), for example, offered a poem in return for site design for her blog. Benjammin509 (@benjammin509) used Twitter to try to offload a $10 gift voucher to Ted's Montana Grill.

These are very simple requests and they tend to be one-offs. It's possible to think of these kinds of Twitter-based offers as alternatives to eBay for unwanted gifts or to Craigslist to sell low-cost services.

But there are also a number of twitterers who specialize in barter. SwapCove (@swapcove), ValhallaTrade (@valhallatrade) and NuBarter (@NuBarter) are just three barter companies that use Twitter to offer tips about bartering, help their clients find trades and announce deals that link back to their websites.

How to Do It

For one-off deals, you won't need to do any more than post a tweet describing what you're offering or what you're looking for. Include "#barter" to make it easy for barterers to find you and also ask that your followers retweet. You want your request to spread as widely as possible so that you can drum up competition and choose the best offer.

If you're looking to barter regularly though, you might want to set up a special timeline only for bartering. Most of those currently available focus on providing information about barter but a timeline made up of barter offers—even a timeline made up of offers for particular kinds of barter—could well become popular too.

You'd need either a steady stream of items to swap to benefit from this kind of timeline or access to plenty of people who wanted to barter.

Once you've built up a long list of followers, you might then be able to charge people a small fee to advertise in your timeline.

More likely though is that if you wanted to make more than one barter deal, you'd need to post your offer occasionally and negotiate each deal separately.

Getting Started

The challenge with bartering isn't just finding someone with something you want; it's making sure that what you want is worth what you're offering.

Before you post a tweet inviting a barter deal then, it's a good idea to make sure that you know the rough values on both sides of the deal. You'll need to know what the product or service you're offering is worth and you'll need to be able to value the offers that come in.

Be prepared to receive lots of low-ball offers and look for ways to negotiate upwards.

You should also know how far you're prepared to move from those cash values. Because you can never tell what sort of offers you're going to receive, in addition to measuring the cash value of the products and services you're offered, you'll need to be able to measure how useful they'd be to you. The wine expo tickets that James Shiner received were only worth a fraction of the price that Gary Vaynerchuck would have paid had he rented a television. But they were still valuable enough for James to be willing to lend Gary his screen.

for Success

(continued)

Get the Retweets

The more responses you can generate, the greater the range of choices you'll have in return for your own offer. You won't need to do any more than ask your followers to "please retweet."

Many will do it because they want to lend a hand.

A Model to Follow

Roger Galligan (@rogergalligan), a publisher of Irish blogs, provides a good example of how a barter procedure can—and should—take place on Twitter. He posted this tweet in his timeline describing what he wanted and what he was offering in return: "#ie #barter Looking for pest control for ants!! Will offer 3 month box ad on BrowseIreland.com and premium link in 2 categories."

(continued on next page)

A Model to Follow *(continued)*

The service that Roger was looking for was valuable—it's the sort of service that pays a pest control company's bills. So in return, Roger offered something that cost him little but whose value equaled the service he wanted. Being specific both about what he wanted and what he was prepared to provide made it very easy for people to respond.

He also included a couple of relevant hashtags to make sure that the barter opportunity turned up in search results. Roger was eventually able to choose between two companies interested in his offer and he conducted the final negotiations by telephone.

MAKE A PROFIT ON TWITTER'S CLASSIFIEDS

92

What Are Twitter Classifieds?

Twitter's short posts and non-commercial nature tend not to make it a very good platform for direct advertising. But there is one type of advertising that fits the format completely. Classified ads have always been short and to the point. Advertisers, usually individuals paying by the word, have grown accustomed to squeezing as much information as possible into a small amount of space in order to attract attention and generate offers.

It's an approach that's well suited to Twitter . . . provided buyers and sellers can find each other easily among the millions of other tweets on the site.

That's the solution that iList Micro (@ilistmicro) aims to provide. The service trawls Twitter looking for specific hashtags related to buying and selling, and allows those tweets to be found easily on its website, micro.ilist.com. Buyers and sellers can then contact each other by hitting the Reply link.

Even more interestingly, iListMicro also provides trending data from both buyers and sellers, allowing each side to gaps in supply and demand, and set their prices accordingly.

The result is a valuable Twitter-based classifieds service which works in real time, allows sellers to reach new buyers, shoppers to find rare items and helps each side to negotiate intelligently too.

DIFFICULTY

SKILLS REQUIRED

INCOME POTENTIAL

Tips

for Success

Use #ihave

iList Micro filters a number of different hashtags when delivering search results but the most popular for sellers—and the one most recommended by the site itself—is #ihave. Use that hashtag and your item should be indexed in minutes and easily found.

Add Pictures

Pictures are always vital when selling items. iList Micro's ability to display images posted to Twitpic and even pages on Craigslist provides a very valuable extension to Twitter's ability to persuade buyers. Even if all you have is a camera phone, it's worth making the effort to shoot a quick picture and upload it with your tweet.

(continued on next page)

How Twitterers Are Using Classifieds

While classifieds might have been intended to allow individuals to offload items they no longer need and for buyers to find low-cost used goods, they've always attracted businesses too. You can find plenty of people offering concert tickets and laptops through iList Micro, but there's also no shortage of firms trying to sell their services and products.

Juan Valdovinos (@theaircoguy), for example, doesn't use his timeline to interact with other prospects, offer advice on his topic and brand his business—always the most effective ways for a business to use Twitter. But he does use the iList Micro's #ihave hashtag so that anyone looking for an air conditioner on the site will find his offers: "Latest: Free estimates on your central heating and air conditioning: http://www.theaircoguy.com/ Pasadena or Los Angleles #ihave"

Hilda Hernandez, a real estate agent in Maryland, uses iList Micro to list properties, linking back to the listing's full page on her website: "#IHave #foreclosures in Silver Spring, Germantown, Kensington, Takoma Park, Gaithersburg, Laurel, Hyattsville http://bit.ly/10f2uB (expand)" Although not a replacement for traditional property listings, iList Micro does provide an easy way for Hilda to extend her reach and show her properties to additional prospects.

Employers and jobseekers are using the service too. Miranda Crawford (@crawf1me) posted a tweet using the #iwant hashtag to pitch for a job as a booking agent, and "viv" (@VivatSALE) has used Twitter for no other purpose than to advertise for a graphic designer and interns on iList Micro.

Often, the ads posted through the site contain links to pages where interested parties can learn more about the product on offer or images. Links to a picture of the product on Twitpic or even to the posting on Craigslist are shown as previews on iList Micro, but some sellers have gone even further and included links to videos of their products. Amy Ressa (@aressa1), for example, uses the #ihave hashtag to tell potential buyers about the work she has available and point out where they can see it: "Check this video out—Rose Wine Glasses for Wedding Reception http://tinyurl.com/dk8z93 (expand) #ihave"

For the most part then, iList Micro is being used by individual sellers with items such as iPods and laptops looking for a second-hand market. It's also being used by businesses to sell products and even find employees.

That still leaves some of the iList Micro's potential untapped. There are people who are earn their livings buying and selling on eBay. The potential for that sort of activity exists on iList Micro too. It should be possible to review selling prices for products on eBay, then offer lower prices for those products to sellers on iList Micro. The service could well serve as another source of underpriced items for professional sellers to pass on to their customers.

How to Do It

One of iList Micro's advantages is its simplicity. For buyers, the site works as little more than a typical Twitter search engine, filtering the hashtags to return the appropriate search results. So a buyer looking for a Macbook Air, for example, would have to do nothing more than type "#ihave macbook air" into iList Micro receive a list of options. The same search on Twitter's own search engine however might well return nothing.

For sellers, the system is just as simple. It's possible to place a listing on the site with nothing more than the briefest of descriptions and one of the hashtags that iList Micro filters. Postings are likely to be much more effective though if they also link to a page—and especially a picture—that allows the potential buyer to learn more. Demanding that anyone interested hits the reply button to ask more is likely to put off some buyers and will generate questions from buyers who are less than serious.

Getting Started

Before posting an ad, spend some time browsing the site to see how other sellers have placed ads for similar products. You could even contact some of them to ask for more information and come up with a correct price for your own items.

When you come to place your ad, make sure that you include all of the most important details. You won't have space to produce gripping copy, so you'll need to rely on the specifications to do the selling.

for Success

(continued)

Use the Trending Data

iList Micro supplies a small amount of trending data that shows the name of the product, the level of supply and the level of demand. For resellers, that can be a vital map to bargains. You'd be free to make low bids on items with little demand, then offer them for sale at sites where the demand— and therefore the price—is higher.

If you're looking to buy an item, make sure that you get as much information as possible. Unlike eBay, you won't be able to rely on feedback reviews to assess the seller's reliability, but you can read their previous tweets and search Twitter for tweets about them. If someone had been left with a bad deal, there's a good chance that the Twittersphere would know.

A Model to Follow

On a site where listings tend to consist of little more than "I'm selling my . . . Anyone interested?", an ad which provides enough information for a buyer to feel interested will always stand out. Irene Cecilia Lee's (@dearren) ad for her Macbook Pro was packed with specs and even included a flexible price. If it had come with a picture, it would have been both simple and perfect: "For Sale: My Macbook Pro months old; .4GHz; 2GB MHz DDR2 SD-RAM; 200GB HD; Warranty; Photoshop, Illustrator, Office, etc: 1450 OBO! #ihave"

CREATE A SPONSORED TWITTER FEED

93

What is a Sponsored Twitter Feed?

Twitter attracts readers because it acts as a platform for interesting content. Users are free to browse the site, read tweets posted by entrepreneurs, businesses, industry insiders, celebrities and anyone else they find appealing.

That content is valuable. It's also free to readers, and it might just be free to publishers too.

One major publisher has been able to generate cash by feeding Twitter's posts onto its website, displaying them in a special module and attracting sponsorship money.

It's a unique way of adding valuable extra content to its Web page and monetizing that content. It made the page sticky—at least for the duration of the event that the twitterers were posting about—and it gives the twitterers some welcome added exposure too.

But streaming other people's tweets into a module that appears on your Web page has sparked some controversy. While some of the twitterers have signed up to the system and are being rewarded financially for the syndication of their tweets, others are unaware that their posts are appearing on a site other than Twitter.

Although Twitter's terms "encourage users to contribute their creations to the public domain or consider progressive licensing terms", they also make clear that "materials uploaded remain yours." So far, no one appears to have complained that their posts are being published elsewhere but there is the possibility that reposting other twitterers' content on your own site could lead to copyright complaints.

DIFFICULTY

SKILLS REQUIRED

INCOME POTENTIAL

Check the Legal Stuff

When GlamMedia launched Tinker, it said that it had over 25,000 offering more than 100,000 tweets on subjects ranging from fashion to festivals. Only a small fraction of them would have been the kind of professional writers included in GlamMedia's network. While it appears that there may be a copyright issue with the remaining contributors, it's not something that's come up yet. Use GlamMedia's Tinker widget though, and there's a good chance that in the unlikely event that a group of twitterers do ever complain, they'd make the complaint to GlamMedia, not to you.

One safe alternative would be to use Tinker's filters to post tweets that only come from twitterers you've selected. You could approach them first and secure their agreement in return for the extra publicity, and if you land a big sponsor perhaps even a share of the ad revenue.

(continued on next page)

How Publishers are Creating Sponsored Twitter Feeds

Glam Media, publishers of Glam.com (www.glam.com), a fashion site, first popularized this strategy when it used a widget containing streamed tweets to cover New York Fashion Week. Within just three days, top bloggers and fashion reporters were signing up to make sure that their microposts were appearing on Glam's widget and on its website.

The company then used the feature again to feed tweets from Twitter that included the #oscars hashtag during the Academy Awards ceremony. The tweets appeared on the side of the page in a widget that also included an audio and visual element. That widget carried the name of the skin care product that was sponsoring the feed.

Glam then was able to add dynamic and free content to its website, covering the Oscars in real time, and earn extra revenue too.

How to Do It

GlamMedia might have worked hard to create its widget but the company has made it easier for everyone else to use the same system. It's created Tinker (www.tinker.com), a service that allows users to view filtered tweets. Unlike Monitter though, filters can be viewed by other users and they can also be published on other websites.

So a publisher that wanted to see tweets about the Superbowl, for example, could create an "event" stream that displayed tweets containing a particular set of related keywords. It's even possible to limit the stream to certain twitterers, exclude some twitterers, and censor the tweets by not showing those that contain profanity. Having created the stream, it's just a matter of pasting the widget's code onto your own Web page to show those tweets to your followers. Users will be able to add tweets directly from the module by signing in with their Twitter username and password.

That will deliver an active feed of relevant tweets to your page, an addition of new, free content that could be valuable at keeping your users interested in your site.

To earn money directly from that stream though, you'll have to work a little harder. The easiest option is to apply to be a GlamMedia publisher. You can make your application at www.glammedia.com but the network is really looking for sites related to fashion and entertainment. Websites covering other topic will need to approach sponsors themselves, offering deals in return for temporary name placement near an active feed related to their brand.

So just as Glam.com itself placed a Twitter feed about the Oscars on its site and took sponsorship from a skin care company, so the publisher of a sports site could place an active Twitter feed about a game and approach a sportswear company to sponsor it.

You'd have to offer prominent name placement, a competitive rate and, of course, high viewer numbers.

Getting Started

There are three stages to earning with a sponsored Twitter feed. While it's possible to create your own widget, the easiest way to begin is to sign up at Tinker.com.

The second step will be to decide on an event that you'd like to feature on your site and create a widget.

And the third—and hardest—step will be to find a sponsor. Unless you're accepted into GlamMedia's network that won't be easy. But if you can target the right companies and show that you'll be offering exactly the sort of customers they need, you should make it possible to land a deal.

A Model to Follow

While GlamMedia's own coverage of the Oscars at Glam.com was certainly one model to follow, a permanent example can also be found at TwitterMoms (www.twittermoms.com). This site places a Tinker widget right in the center of the page so that it looks like the most important element on the site. The tweets in the widget related to a sponsored topic (so tweets about swimming are sponsored by a swimwear firm) and the site shares revenue with Tinker.

Tips

for Success

(continued)

Add Extra Content

The widget that GlamMedia's sites use also includes an audio-visual element that makes the event look much more exciting and the sponsorship deal much more attractive. If you can't pick up GlamMedia's own widget then try combining your widget with a UStream (www.ustream.tv) broadcast from the event itself to offer more to sponsors.

Do the Marketing

The toughest part of this strategy will be finding a sponsor. If you're going to make that effort then make sure that you get the most out of it. Tell your readers what you're going to do, and get the benefit of viral marketing by asking likely contributors to share the news too.

94

CREATE TREND SPAM... OR NOT

What is Trend Spam?

DIFFICULTY

SKILLS REQUIRED

INCOME POTENTIAL

Just as it didn't take long for entrepreneurs to spot the benefits of being able to build valuable networks on Twitter, so it didn't take long for spammers to see the same advantages, and try to pick them up the easy way. Instead of taking the time to forge relationships and build communities with interesting conversations and valuable content, they tried to drive as many people as possible to their timelines or to their websites.

Usually, that involves sending automated direct messages or posting cut-and-paste tweets containing a link to other twitterers.

Some spammers have also taken over the identities of popular twitterers and tried to cash in on their trust by using a similar username.

Both of those methods though take some effort. The tweets have to be posted individually and even the direct messages are only sent when someone agrees to follow the spammer in return for their own follow. Creating a fake timeline requires no less work than forming a real one.

And the people at Twitter are pretty good at squishing spammers. Send too many direct tweets that contain the same message or pick up complaints for using someone else's name and they'll shut down the timeline in a jiffy. @spam, the timeline used to report spammers, is both busy and fast.

Spammers though have found a new way of putting their message across to many people at the same time. The sidebar on the right side of a Twitter page shows a list of trending topics. Clicking one of those topics or following it in a real-time monitoring service like Monitter lets them follow that topic as the conversation on Twitter develops. By placing the trending hashtags together with their spam link, spammers are able to put the messages in front of thousands of people with just one tweet.

Clearly, this is not a strategy to be recommended. It is a strategy though that some people are using, even at the risk of losing a timeline—something that can be replaced very easily.

And there are ways to make better use of trending topics without spamming twitterers, breaking into the conversation with an inappropriate marketing message, or seeing your timeline shut down.

How Spammers Are Creating Trend Spam

It's no surprise that spammers aren't taking a particularly sophisticated approach to spamming trends. They create a Web page that pitches a product—usually not their own but one taken from a wholesale service such as ClickBank (www.clickbank.com)—then write a tweet that contains a link to the page. The link is shortened so that viewers can't see where it leads them and they insert their own message into the tweet with a popular hashtag.

This tweet from @Fordq222q, for example, turned up with a hashtag for a discussion of Beatles trivia: "Need part time job?I made over $4000 last month just for filling surveys .More info @ http://tinyurl.com/ouxt5o #beatlesfacts"

The link itself led to a page that offered money for completing online surveys. The spammer would have received a commission for anyone who signed up. He would also have annoyed everyone who was following the topic and found that the timeline that he created to do the spamming had been shut down pretty quickly.

It's unlikely though that many people would have clicked through to the landing page. The tweet itself had no relevance at all to the topic being discussed so it was easy to ignore. But it would also have cost nothing to produce so even a tiny conversion rate would have been enough to allow the spammer to make some money, especially if he did the same thing on a range of different topics using a number of different hashtags in the same tweet. That same tweet, for example, was sent from a number of different timelines, with each tweet sent two minutes apart and carrying a different hashtag.

for Success

Don't Do the Spamming

Trend spamming requires very little effort. Once you've created the landing page, you won't need to do any more than post the occasional hashtagged tweet—and create new timelines as Twitter shuts down your old ones. But the returns you get are unlikely to be worth the effort, and they certainly won't be worth bothering the community for.

Some people might be trend spamming. But you shouldn't join them.

Make the Content Good

Instead, offer genuinely valuable content. Once you've spotted a rising trend, you should be able to post a page that sums up the issue in less than an hour. That page could then generate some revenue for a day or two.

It's work, but it pays and it provides a service to the community too.

How to Do It

The best approach is not to do it. Spamming trends is not a good way to use Twitter. It's an abuse of Twitter, annoys other users, disrupts conversations and results in timeline closure. There are plenty of legitimate ways of using Twitter—and earning from Twitter—without trying to use black hat methods.

If you want to make the most of trending topics, for example, you'll need to quickly create good, optimized content that you can then promote easily as the trend develops.

You'll need to be fast. Twist (twist.flaptor.com) will be a good tool to show you how a trend is developing and growing. If you can get a page of good, related content on the Web just as the trend is starting to rise, surround the content with ads, and tweet a link to it, you'll be offering other twitterers solid information while giving yourself a chance to earn with a popular subject.

It will take a little effort. But you won't be spamming anyone and you might just make a little extra income.

Getting Started

Spammers can start work by sourcing a product that will give them affiliate payments and launching a landing page. They'll also need an anti-social manner and a thick skin to deal with the criticism that will fly their way from the Twitter community.

Those who want to earn from trending topics though will need a website that allows them to add new pages quickly and easily. They'll also need membership of an ad system such as Google's AdSense that can serve targeted ads as soon as the page is launched.

Then it will be a matter of keeping an eye on trends as they rise, shooting out some quick content and referring trend followers to your page.

A Model to Follow

There are no good models for spammers to follow. Timelines are shut down within hours of the first spam tweet hitting a trending topic. To see how it's done though, just type a currently trending topic into Monitter and wait. It won't be long before a tweet floats past that has nothing to do with a topic but which carries a shortened link.

95

BUILD YOUR OWN CLASSIFIED TIMELINE!

DIFFICULTY

■■➡

SKILLS REQUIRED

■■■➡

INCOME POTENTIAL

■■➡

What is a Classified Timeline?

Twitter's short posts lend themselves well to classified ads. Publishers are used to keeping them short and to the point; readers know how to decipher the abbreviations and decide whether the ad is worth following up.

iList Micro has made it very easy to buy and sell used items on Twitter but there is another way to earn with classifieds and microblogging.

At least one website offers targeted classifieds and uses Twitter as one way to reach potential customers. The postings themselves are free—in fact, they can be drawn automatically from other listings services such as Craigslist (www.craigslist.com) and FriendFeed (www.friendfeed. com). Viewing the abbreviated posts on Twitter is free too, of course and to see the entire ad, followers can simply click the link and be taken to the original posting.

To browse more ads though, they'll need to click the link above the bio which leads to a Web page which, in addition to the classified ads, also contain news, targeted content . . . and optimized AdSense units.

How Twitterers a re Creating Classified TImelines

The easiest way in which twitterers are creating classified timelines is by automating the process as much as possible. They leave it to established classified sites to bring in the advertisers, using their freely available content to attract users—and Twitter to bring thos users in.

Dallas Listings (@Dallas_Listings), for example, describes itself as "Dallas and Fort Worth Real Estate, Classifieds, Events and Job listings, DFW metroplex listings…We are a civic social service." The timeline is not interactive. There are no tweets directed at followers, who nonetheless vastly outnumber the twitterers that the timeline is following. Instead all of the tweets consist only of a headline indicating the offer and the location, and a shortened link: "Drummer Looking for band! (Dallas/Fort Worth) http://ff.im/2S5KF."

It's also notable that all of the posts reach the timeline through FriendFeed, a Twitter rival that allows for longer posts as well as uploaded pictures. The creator of Dallas Listings has created a timeline on FriendFeed at friendfeed.com/dallaslistings, used FriendFeed's feed features to bring in ads from Craigslist, and then sent them to Twitter to attract a larger audience and generate exposure for the optimized Web page.

Although only a small percentage of the Twitter timeline's followers will click through to the website rather than the link to the ad on FriendFeed, once the timeline has been set up, Dallas Listing's creator has to do nothing more than enjoy the traffic. The content will arrive automatically.

How to Do It

Setting up an automated classified timeline on Twitter can take a little skill. To follow the method used by Dallas Listing, you'll need first to create a timeline on FriendFeed. Click the Settings link, followed by Services, and you'll be offered a range of different sources from which you can feed content into your FriendFeed timeline. These include Facebook and Digg, as well as Amazon and YouTube. It also includes an option to add any RSS feed.

Browse to the Craigslist page whose ads you want to promote. At the bottom of the page, you'll find an RSS button. Paste the URL from that page into RSS feed option on FriendFeed, and your FriendFeed page will be updated automatically with ads from CraigsList.

You'll then need to move those ads from FriendFeed to Twitter. Click the Tools and API link at the bottom of a FriendFeed, and in the "Share your Feed" section, you'll find an option to post your feeds automatically to your Twitter timeline.

So far though, all you'll have done is share Craigslist ads with friends on FriendFeed and followers on Twitter. To monetize the con-

for Success

Make the Listings Targeted

Dallas Listings works by providing a very select service: it only serves ads in a particular area, and most of them are related to real estate.

That's important. While it's possible to feed multiple pages from Craigslist into Twitter, followers are likely to be interested in only one small area and one kind of ad. You'll be better off creating multiple timelines so that followers can choose which kinds of ads they want to see.

And by creating multiple Web pages, you'll be better able to target the ads that surround those listings too.

Choose Your Feed Source

Despite the ads on its Web page, Dallas Listings sees itself as a "civic service" which may be why it chooses to send Craigslist's listings on a convuted route through FriendFeed before they reach Twitter.

That approach increases the exposure but it does mean the links lead to

(continued on next page)

for Success

(continued)

FriendFeed rather than the ad-supported Web page. Sending the classifieds from Craigslist to your Web page and from the Web page through TwitterFeed to Twitter might bring you better financial results.

Do the Marketing

The advantage of this approach is that the content is automated. Once all the feeds are in place, you won't need to any more than wait for the checks from AdSense. Except marketing the timeline.

Twitter provides an easy way to market the Web page, but you'll need to tell people your timeline is there, build up the followers and make sure the numbers don't fall off. That may mean engaging in the odd conversation.

tent, you'll also need to create a Web page. Place the RSS feed from Craigslist on the Web page and surround it with ads from AdSense, Amazon or any other ad system, and make sure you include the link to the page in your Twitter bio.

Of course, there are other ways of transferring the content of a Craigslist page to Twitter. You could send the RSS feed directly to your Web page, then use TwitterFeed to direct the content to Twitter. That would lose you the exposure on FriendFeed but it would mean that link in the tweet itself—which are likely to generate more clicks than the bio link—would lead directly to the Web page.

Getting Started

While your first step could be to play around with FriendFeed, the best place to begin is by creating the Web page that will display Craigslist's ads. It's this page, after all, that will be bringing in the money.

The feeds will act as the bait that delivers users to a page where they can see more content. Your hope is that some of them will also click on the ads, and because the entire system is automated, any ad revenues you pick up will be profit.

Take a little time then before you start feeding the ads to Twitter to make sure that the page looks good, the classifieds are in a prominent position—and that the ads are highly visible too.

A Model to Follow

Dallas Listings is clearly the model to follow but pay attention to the service's inefficiencies as well as its use of free content. The links in the ads lead to FriendFeed rather than to the Web page or even to the original source.

It's possible to create a classified timeline that works more efficiently—and is more productive—than that.

PRODUCE A NICHED TWITTER DIRECTORY

Why Should You Create a Niched Twitter Directory?

Listing your timeline on one of the directory services can clearly bring benefits. It helps other Twitterers find you, makes your marketing easier, allows you to offer promotions and it helps with your branding too.

But the companies that are creating Twitter directories are often doing it for a reason. While some simply want to help the Twitter community, others are hoping to benefit from the exposure a good, targeted directory can bring.

Even though a number of directories have now sprung up, each of them has its own flavor and its own appeal. Although they generally aim to be comprehensive, in practice, they each aim at different markets.

Twellow, for example, is business-oriented. Twibs primarily serves artists and retailers. WeFollow is particularly strong at identifying celebrities.

There are also a number of other lists, vicariously updated, that target specific professions or industries.

Each list though, if genuinely useful, delivers a service to users, and therefore brings traffic and branding power to the directory's creator.

DIFFICULTY

SKILLS REQUIRED

INCOME POTENTIAL

for Success

Make the Listing Easy—and Viral

The popularity of directories tends to grow very quickly when the directories make use of Twitter's viral power. So joining WeFollow simply means tweeting hashtags. The directory automatically categorizes and lists the timeline but it also tells followers what you've done, sending the directory's name spreading quickly across Twitter. Twellow too sends out a tweet informing followers that someone has registered.

Whatever niche you choose to create a directory for then, make sure that your directory includes either a tweet sent automatically after registering. Alternatively, allow twitterers to join simply by tweeting a hashtag.

(continued on next page)

How Publishers Are Creating Niched Twitter Directories

Publishers are creating different kinds of directories in a number of different ways—and picking up a range of different kinds of benefits.

WeFollow, for example, aims to be a comprehensive service that lists as many followers as possible across a number of different categories. The only benefit to Kevin Rose and Digg though, the creators of the service, is the branding and goodwill that comes from making the service available.

Understanding that Digg is offering a valuable resource to twitterers makes the site look like good guys in tune with the needs of the online community.

Twellow offers a similarly comprehensive service but publishers WebProNews are a little more proactive in pushing for the benefits. At the top of the page, a toolbar leads to pages that include "Self-Service Marketing." There's a large graphic ad on the right of the page and the company's name appears in several places, making it clear who created it, and that the company has its fingers on the social media pulse.

ExecTweets (www.exectweets.com) takes a slightly different approach. The site does not intend to be inclusive. Instead, it targets one particular group of twitterers: business leaders. Created by Federated Media (www.federatedmedia.com), a social media publishing company, the site is sponsored by Microsoft.

In return for giving Federated Media money then, Microsoft is able to put itself in the same company as executive twitterers like Zappo's Tony Hsieh or O'Reilly Media's Tim O'Reilly. Its sponsorship of a niched Twitter directory enables it to associate itself with at least a little of Twitter's coolness, while also maintaining its professional and business-like character.

Other directories also offer targeted list of twitterers. CelebrityTweet (www.celebritytweet.com) provides a list of celebrities on Twitter, together with their latest tweets. It attempts to monetize the site by placing an ad above the fold and beneath the celebrity's bio. LocalTweeps (www.localtweeps.com) sorts twitterers by location but hasn't yet started monetizing, while Elizabeth Davis's teacher list was created solely to benefit other teacher without apparently any consideration for monetization.

It should be clear then that while a comprehensive directory would face stiff competition from established lists, there's still room for targeted directories, whether sorted by category or by location. Those directories can then be supported by ads (like CelebrityTweet), by sponsorship (like ExecTweets) or just used for self-promotion and branding (like WeFollow).

How to Do It

Creating the directory though will be a little tricky. While some directories make use of Twitter's API to display tweets and list timelines, others appear to have been coded from scratch—or even listed on a spreadsheet manually and made available for download.

In general, you'll find it easier to attract sponsors and advertisers to a targeted directory that also looks attractive and professional. CelebrityTweet does that and was built on Twitter's API, so with a little bit of smart API developing it shouldn't be too difficult to create a similarly effective site. You'll just need to know a friendly developer.

Getting Started

The first step to creating a Twitter directory then might be to find a developer. But it's more likely to be finding the right niche.

That's harder than it sounds. A successful—and profitable—directory will need to meet two vital criteria: the category will need to contain enough contributors to make a directory worthwhile; and it will need to be valuable enough to attract ads or a corporate sponsor willing to pay to show it name to readers.

Then you'll need to buy the domain name, create the directory, list contributors—and bring in the ads.

for Success

(continued)

Choose Your Niche Carefully

The most important decision you make will be what kind of directory you want to build. Look not just at the number of twitterers the directory might contain but also at the kinds of businesses that might want to advertise on or sponsor the directory. There's little point in building a directory that only lists three people or which can't attract advertising.

A directory of lawyers, doctors or computer specialists though should be both large and easy to monetize.

List the Tweets

While some directories are happy to settle for justing names and bios, others also show the latest tweets—like a timeline. That doesn't just give more to users, it keeps users on your site. And with the Twitter API, it's not too difficult to do either.

A Model to Follow

The directory model that you should follow will depend on the kind of directory you want to create. CelebrityTweet though does offer a good example for anyone thinking of creating a niched directory. The site offers timelines from a long list of popular twitterers. It looks professional and well-designed, offers a spot above the fold for advertisers and includes tweets from the people it lists, allowing followers to find all of their favorite contributors in one place.

It offers a genuinely valuable service—and that's always the key to success with Twitter.

GEEKPRENEUR

CREATE RESPONSE BOTS FOR PASSIVE REVENUE

What Are Response Bots?

DIFFICULTY

SKILLS REQUIRED

INCOME POTENTIAL

Twitter's CEO Evan Williams (@ev), once mentioned that Twitter can be thought of as a command line. It sits above a user base which can be used to both receive commands and issue automated responses.

That creates the potential to create an effort-free referral system, sending affiliate links on demand to people actively searching for a particular class of product.

It's an opportunity that currently only a few people are taking advantage of—but what even those who aren't monetizing their bots are still demonstrating the potential of passive revenue generation.

How Twitterers Are Selling Hard-to-Find Items

If you're looking for event tickets in the UK— and don't want to try TicketMaster, the venue, or anywhere else—you can send a tweet to @ ticketbot followed by the name of the band or show you'd like to see. Ticketbot will pick up the tweet and send you a link telling you where to buy the ticket.

Click the link in the tweet and make your purchase, and the timeline's creator, Paul Clarke (@pauly), will receive a commission for the sale. That's not going to be huge—Paul reported earning about £20 for locating a couple of sold out Leonard Cohen tickets—but it's automated, scalable and useful extra income.

Tips

for Success

Make the Affiliate Page Persuasive

The automated tweets should contain enough information to pique the questioner's interest but it's unlikely to contain enough detail to choose to purchase. Insert a link to your own Web page that offers more data and which includes the affiliate links.

But do make sure that that page looks professional and inviting. If the looks look recommended as well as suggested—and recommended by a trusted source—there's more chance you'll win the conversion. Pay attention to the page's layout and to the design.

Make It Known

You'll also need to do the marketing. If no one knows they can ask your bot where to find Chinese herbs or rare comics, you won't be making many sales. Create separate timeline then and use to follow people who are discussing the products you'll be promoting. Join

(continued on next page)

It's also repeatable. In addition to @ticketbot, Paul Clarke is also working on @holidaybot, a timeline that will source travel tickets in the same effortless way that @ticketbot finds concert tickets.

Other bots work in similar ways. TasteKid (@tastekid), for example, returns recommendations to similar films, books or music based on titles mentioned in tweets sent to it. The tweets take the form of a short list and a link to a longer list on the service's website TasteKid. com (www.tastekid.com): "M Is For Magic, No Country For Old Men, Time Enough For Love, I Will Fear No Evil . . . http://tastekid. com/t/01bk".

Although those recommendations aren't monetized, turning them into text-based Amazon links could generate commissions.

How to Do It

You can earn commission on sales of items like concert tickets, hotel reservations or collectibles in one of two ways.

A low-tech method would be simply to invite twitterers to tell you what they're looking for. You could also monitor Twitter for mentions of band names, venues or references to tickets and tweet them back with affiliate links to places they can make purchases.

That would be very simple. Monitter would let you keep track of the references in real time while TweetBeep (www.tweetbeep.com) would fill your mailbox with leads to follow up.

You might expect a low response rate though from twitterers who didn't tweet to you directly. (Some of Paul Clarke's offers have been met with a less than polite response.)

Sourcing the tickets and writing the tweets will also take effort and time. You'll be earning your commissions.

Paul Clarke though has automated the process as much as possible. He has created a bot that checks Twitter for tweets directed to the @ticketbot usernam, and tweets back a response containing the details and a link: "30 events, next best Sandweaver, Run Don't Walk 23/05 6.00 http://bit.ly/DeGP5".

Paul though is a professional developer and creating a bot like this will take a little technical skill. But if you're not a developer yourself, Twitter's wiki will help you to find someone who can create the system for you.

Alternatively, you can also use "t411"'s (@t411) bot platform to create your own bot. The system allows you to define the format of the question sent you by direct message and create an automated response. So a twitterer could send you a direct message with the name of a disc, and your bot would respond automatically with an affiliate link to a website that sells it.

While using "t411"'s script might make the programming relatively simple, because it uses direct message, you would miss the viral benefits of a public tweet.

Getting Started

It may seem then that your first step—if you're better at spotting opportunities than coding—will be turn to apiwiki.twitter.com/Developers and start looking for a developer to help you create the bot.

But before you can explain to a developer what you want done, you'll first need a source for the items you're hoping to sell.

Paul Clarke uses his own website, FolkestoneGerald.com (www.folkestonegerald.com) but anywhere that has a suitably large inventory, a way of paying commissions and access for your bot would do.

Once you've located that source, you'll just need to create the bot, launch the timeline and let people know it's there.

Finally, you can start scaling by using your bot to offer the same service for different kinds of items.

Tips

for Success

(continued)

the conversation and tell them where they can go to find the products they want.

List t the Tweets

One of the easiest ways to promote your timeline will be to keep the tweets public. While it's possible to build a bot that works with direct messages, using tweets will make sure that other people see the questions you're being asked, spreading news of your service quickly across Twitter.

A Model to Follow

Paul Clarke's Ticketbot and Holidaybot might be set up to earn money—and at least one is doing so—but it's not optimized. The landing page is unattractive and hard to follow, and the tweets themselves confusing.

TasteKid's service though looks much more attractive. The tweets supply immediate answers to the question being asked, they're enticing enough to persuade recipients to click and the landing page is well-designed.

Adding affiliate links to those suggestions would be just one small—but valuable—enhancement.

---

98 BUILD YOUR FUTURE REPUTATION

DIFFICULTY

SKILLS REQUIRED

INCOME POTENTIAL

What is Your Reputation on Twitter?

One of the biggest challenges for anyone using Twitter is to decide who to follow. Toss a keyword into Twitter's search engine to see who's discussing your topic, and you'll see a list of people have mentioned it recently.

But that list won't tell whether those people discuss your topic regularly, how they're viewed by other members of the community and whether their tweets on the subject are regular and valuable or occasional and worthless.

One indication is the number of followers but those figures might be the result of prodigious following rather than careful tweeting.

While following the wrong people won't cost you any more than the time it takes to unfollow, it does mean that you might be missing out on a valuable connection with a leader in your field.

Equally, it makes it difficult for other twitterers to find you.

It appears that Twitter is working on a solution. Taking inspiration from Google, where Twitter's founders cut their teeth, the service's VP of Operations, Santosh Jayaram, has stated that Twitter will be crawling and indexing links placed in tweets.

Entrepreneurial twitterers do this anyway, tracking their clicks to test the effectiveness of their posts and the extent to which they can drive followers to take action. But when Twitter is crawling tweets, it will have enough data to rank its members according to reputation. A member with a large following, for example, could rank lower—and turn up lower in search results—than someone with fewer followers but whose readers are more likely to click their links or read their tweets.

GEEKPRENEUR

The branding power of a high Twitter reputation though would be tremendous. Just as a high listing on Google suggests authority, reliability and trustworthiness, so a high reputation on Twitter would look like a recommendation from the site itself.

For companies looking to use Twitter to build a community and forge loyalty around a brand, it would be a huge and valuable boost.

How Twitterers Are Building Their Reputations

But it doesn't appear to be happening yet. At the moment, Twitter's search results are returned chronologically. The most recent posts are shown first and, when using search.twitter.com, updates to indicate the number of new tweets added since the page was loaded.

In practice then, twitterers are currently relying primarily on quantity to build and display their reputations. They're looking to build up their follower lists as quickly and as largely as possible, often by following other people. The numbers alone, despite their limitations, are functioning as a sort of reputation counter.

And there are benefits to that too. While search results might appear chronologically, directories such as WeFollow and Twellow tend to return timelines according to the number of followers—even if those followers are constantly changing and rarely return to the twitterer's timeline.

Savvy twitterers though, especially marketers, are measuring their own performance by looking at the number of clicks their links receive, the number of retweets they generate and the number of replies and mentions they pick up in other people's timelines.

Although those aren't the sort of figures that Twitter's users are sharing—and therefore they don't measure reputation so much as effectiveness and influence—if Twitter does start to rank timelines and skew search results, those figures will quickly become the measures of influence.

Twitterers then who are paying attention to what their tweets are actually doing, and not just the numbers of people who are reading them, will be well-placed as brand leaders. They'll find it even easier still to persuade followers to take action such as reading sales pitches,

for Success

Track Anyway

At the moment, Twitter has only indicated that it will be tracking clicks on links. It hasn't said what it plans to do with that information. The founders' associations with Google and the obvious benefits of being able to rank timelines has got many Twitter users wondering but it's not clear what form, if any, reputation will take on Twitter.

In the meantime, track your clicks anyway. Tweet regularly. Try to win replies and retweets. The more effective your timeline, the greater the benefits you'll get out of using it anyway.

Use Your Reputation

If—or when—Twitter does start ranking timelines by reputation, you should also be ready to cash in. A high ranking on Twitter will also mean a high ranking for your website so make sure that your tweets include plenty of links—and your site lots of ads.

taking subscriptions or retweeting messages, and they'll be seen as the leading experts in their field.

How to Do It

It's possible that Twitter will primarily be using data from bit.ly although it's also likely they'll be counting clicks across other link shortening services too. But bit.ly's stats do make it a valuable resource for measuring effectiveness.

Although we know that link clicks will be counted by Twitter, it is unlikely that the site will stop there. Google, after all, looks at several metrics in addition to incoming links to determine page rank. Twitter is also likely to consider other figures such as follower numbers, tweet frequency, retweets and mentions.

To build up your reputation on Twitter then—or to build up your influence ready for when Twitter announces reputation rankings—you'll need to consider a number of different factors.

You'll need to track your clicks.

You'll need to build up your follower list.

You'll need to pick up retweets and post the sort of tweets that generate replies and mentions.

And you'll need to post frequently too.

Getting Started

Start by using a URL shortening service that delivers a good range of tracking information. Twitter seems to like bit.ly so maybe you should too. But just get in the habit of collecting metrics about your timeline.

Look at how quickly your follower list grows, how often you tweet and how many retweets you receive. As you're looking to build reputation, those figures are all likely to be important.

A Model to Follow

As reputation-counting hasn't been put into practice yet, there aren't yet any models to follow twitterers trying to improve their figures.

There's no shortage though of twitterers using contests, giveaways and other methods to increase their readership—one factor that's likely to contribute towards reputation.

99 HIRE A GHOST TWITTERER THE RIGHT WAY!

DIFFICULTY

SKILLS REQUIRED

INCOME POTENTIAL

What is a Ghost Twitterer?

Just as some writers are marketing themselves as professional twitterers—and other social media creators—so businesses, brands and individuals are turning to professionals to do their tweeting for them.

The benefits should be clear. Twitter offers a business all sorts of advantages—brand awareness, customer service, loyalty, community, direct sales, etc.—but the cost is the amount of time and effort that has to be put into creating and maintaining a timeline.

Tweets have to be written, posts read and answered, and followers discovered and added.

Most twitterers—even corporate twitterers—find it all enjoyable. The posts aren't long enough to cause any serious head-scratching, twitterers understand that not all replies can be answered and it's pleasant to be able to respond immediately to a satisfied customer.

But it does take time, and even if that time brings rewards, it's time that might be better spent by someone else, while you focus in giving talks or doing the things that bring greater value to your firm.

Some twitterers are choosing to hire ghost-twitterers, and sometimes they're even getting to enjoy the benefits without facing too many repercussions.

How Businesses Are Hiring—and Using—Ghost Twitterers

Because Twitter is such a personal networking tool, few businesses choose to hire ghost twitterers. Either the personalities find the time to write and post their own tweets or they have employees create accounts and have them tweet in their own names on behalf of the company.

One brand that does use ghost twitterers is blogger and evangelist, Guy Kawasaki (@guykawasaki), who uses his timeline primarily to promote his RSS aggregator Alltop (www.alltop.com).

The bio on Guy Kawasaki's timeline indicates that his tweets are written by "RSSurai with Annie Colbert, Gina Ruiz, and Bill Meade." Each writer is expected to leave his or her initials after each tweet to indicate who wrote it, a practice also used on Britney Spears' timeline.

The benefit for Guy Kawasaki is that he gets to run just one timeline instead of having multiple timelines for different aspects of his brand and operated by different contractors or employers. But he doesn't have to write all the tweets himself, ensuring that the timeline stays active and his followers stay close, even when he's too busy to post. He gets to use Twitter for the purpose that he wants to use it for: not as a way to get personally close to his followers but as a marketing tool for his business.

There is a cost to that approach though. While Guy Kawasaki's followers are able to get some information each time a new post is placed on his timeline, there's no question that they'd prefer to read tweets written by the man himself. In using ghostwriters, he weakens the link between himself and his audience.

That's less true when politicians hire people to tweet on their behalf. Readers understand that a politician in the middle of a compaign will have little time to spend in front of a computer or to answer questions sent to the timeline. They'll be grateful and impressed when it happens, but they won't expect it.

Interestingly though, that's only true of politicians. Twitterers are less forgiving of business leaders like Guy Kawasaki who use professionals than they are of public servants. Maybe they expect politicians to use spin anyway.

Tips
for Success

Consider the Costs

Readers generally expect their timelines they're following to be written by one person, and that person will be the name at the top of the page. If you're not going to do that, you'll be giving up one of Twitter's biggest advantages: the personal connection with audiences. Only if the benefits of reach and branding outweigh those costs and the risk that readers will see you as out of touch should you hire a ghost-twitterer.

Assign Tasks

If more than one person will be contributing to your timeline make sure that everyone knows what kind of tweets they should be submitting and how often. A good timeline has a balance of broadcasts and replies, links and original content. Keep control over your writers so that you can keep control over your timeline.

(continued on next page)

for Success

(continued)

**Make the
Author Clear**

One way to avoid some of
the bad feeling associated
with using ghostwriters
is to take away their
ghostliness. Name them in
the bio and in your timeline
and followers won't feel
like they're being deceived.

How to Do It

Finding ghost twitterers isn't too difficult. Companies like Twit4Hire are offering their services directly. PR firms may be able to offer social networking as part of a complete publicity package. And you can always advertise for a writer either on Twitter itself or on a freelance site like eLance (www.elance.com).

You'll need to be clear though about what you want your ghost twitterer to tweet. Having them answer replies for you should be useful: most popular timelines receive far more directed tweets than they can possibly answer.

You could also instruct your ghost twitterers to add occasional links to interesting topics unrelated to your timeline. Guy Kawasaki's timeline, for example, includes links to interesting scientific news on the Web, features that suit his subject and will interest his followers but which don't have to come from him directly. Those tweets are generally added by his writers (and come from Alltop's own network of sites) while he adds the personal tweets about his own lifestyle that his contractors wouldn't be able to write themselves.

To allow a team of writers access to your account you can either share your username and password or, more safely, use one of the many services such as HootSuite (www.hootsuite.com) that lets a number of people log in and use the same Twitter account.

Getting Started

The first step will be to advertise for a ghostwriter. Although that could be done on Twitter, it's a better idea to do it off the site. Ghost-twittering is controversial so announcing that you're looking for someone to help you to do it is likely to draw some criticism.

Either get your PR company to do it for you, or advertise through a freelance writing service.

A Model to Follow

Guy Kawasaki is one of the few people who has managed to create a personal timeline that isn't written by him and without putting off too many followers. It works because he does contribute to it occasionally but most importantly, it works because he's very upfront about what he's doing and why.

He's stated very clearly that he uses Twitter for marketing. With a following well into six figures, it's an approach that seems to be working.

CONCLUSION

There are lots of different ways to earn money with Twitter. Some are easier than others. Some earn more than others. Some will suit you more than others. In this book we've looked at 99 different methods that twitterers are using right now on the microblogging service.

We don't expect that you'll use all of these ways. We do expect though that you'll be inspired by all of them.

Whether you've been using Twitter for pleasure until now or are already generating some income through your tweets, you should find plenty in this book to expand your strategies and employ new methods to earn extra money.

Twitter is fun. It's also free and there's no penalty on the site for trying a strategy and finding that it doesn't match your business or your product.

The second most important strategy to use on Twitter then is to experiment. Try different methods, see which work best for you and expand it to increase your income.

The most important strategy though is to start!

INDEX

Index

TWITTERERS CITED